TASTING AND TESTING BOOKS

A Volume in the Series

STUDIES IN PRINT CULTURE AND THE HISTORY OF THE BOOK

Edited by

Greg Barnhisel, Joan Shelley Rubin, and Michael Winship

Tasting and Testing Books

Good Housekeeping, Popular Modernism,
and Middlebrow Reading

Amy L. Blair

University of Massachusetts Press
Amherst and Boston

Copyright © 2024 by University of Massachusetts Press
All rights reserved
Printed in the United States of America

ISBN 978-1-62534-820-3 (paper); 821-0 (hardcover)

Designed by Sally Nichols
Set in Adobe Jenson Pro
Printed and bound by Books International, Inc.

Cover design by adam b. bohannon
Cover art by James Montgomery Flagg, *Emily Newell Blair.*
Courtesy *Good Housekeeping*, Hearst Media, Inc.

Library of Congress Cataloging-in-Publication Data

Names: Blair, Amy L., 1972- author.
Title: Tasting and testing books : Good housekeeping, popular modernism,
and middlebrow reading / Amy L. Blair.
Description: Amherst : University of Massachusetts Press, [2024] | Series:
Studies in print culture and the history of the book | Includes
bibliographical references and index. |
Identifiers: LCCN 2024016788 (print) | LCCN 2024016789 (ebook) | ISBN
9781625348210 (hardcover) | ISBN 9781625348203 (paperback) | ISBN
9781685750916 (ebook) | ISBN 9781685750923 (ebook)
Subjects: LCSH: Books and reading—United States—History—20th century. |
Middle class women—Books and reading—United States—History—20th
century. | Blair, Emily Newell, 1877-1951. | Good housekeeping (New
York, N.Y.) | BISAC: LITERARY CRITICISM / Books & Reading | LITERARY
CRITICISM / Subjects & Themes / Women
Classification: LCC Z1003.2 .B58 2024 (print) | LCC Z1003.2 (ebook) | DDC
302.23/2097309042—dc23/eng/20240828
LC record available at https://lccn.loc.gov/2024016788
LC ebook record available at https://lccn.loc.gov/2024016789

British Library Cataloguing-in-Publication Data
A catalog record for this book is available from the British Library.

for my girls

Contents

Illustrations ix
Preface: A Tale of Two Blairs xi
Acknowledgments xvii

INTRODUCTION
Choose for Yourself
1

CHAPTER ONE
This Is Your Guaranty
24

CHAPTER TWO
Your Taster and Tester
69

CHAPTER THREE
The Arcadia of the Ozarks
110

CHAPTER FOUR
The Modernist Racket
143

CHAPTER FIVE
The Contagion of Reading
173

EPILOGUE
Trouble, Antidotes
198

Notes 215
Index 239

Illustrations

FIGURE 1. Launch page, Emily Newell Blair's January 1928 column (*Good Housekeeping*, January 1928, 51).   3

FIGURE 2. The 1926 version of the *Good Housekeeping* guaranty (*Good Housekeeping*, February 1926, 6).   33

FIGURE 3. Emily Newell Blair at her desk in the "Department of Tasting and Testing Books" (*Good Housekeeping*, April 1926, 51).   80

FIGURE 4. Many products, like the Battle Creek Health Builder, echoed Dr. Eliot's Five Foot Shelf of Books by promising results in only fifteen minutes a day (*Good Housekeeping*, January 1929, 184).   127

FIGURE 5. Frances Parkinson Keyes, boarding a boat; this illustration accompanied Blair's May 1929 column, "A Hamper of Books" (*Good Housekeeping*, May 1929, 98).   153

FIGURE 6. The first two pages of the seventh-grade list, *What Children Like to Read: The Winnetka Graded Book List* (New York: Rand McNally, 1926), 130–31.   179

Preface
A Tale of Two Blairs

Over the twelve years that I have been writing—or, perhaps more accurately, accreting—this book, I have continuously imagined Emily Newell Blair in her home office, or on a train, or in a hotel, working through the nights to meet her deadlines. Despite our shared surname, Blair and I are not related in any way, a fact that I have often lamented (particularly in the wee hours of the morning), because if we were I might have inherited some of her stamina and enterprise. Between February 1926 and November 1933, then again in August 1934 (a swan song? A "make-up" column to fulfill remaining contractual obligations?), Blair authored ninety-one lengthy book review columns for *Good Housekeeping* magazine, discussing on average fifteen books in each column. That comes to roughly 1,365 books reviewed over a span of six years, all of which she insists she read before reviewing. And I want to believe her; her reviews only rarely include the boilerplate language I have found in many contemporaneous reviews of the same titles, so I infer that, at the very least, she relied only occasionally on any publicity materials that may have been sent along with her advance reader copies. Column titles like "Housecleaning Time in the Library" (May 1927); "From a Flood of Books . . . Emily Newell Blair Selects a Desirable Dozen" (August 1928); "Books for a Tired Woman" (October 1929); "Books for a Busy Month" (September 1930); or "When Do You Read?" (January 1931) also hint at her heavy reading schedule. Directly answering unconvinced *Good Housekeeping* readers, she publishes "Books—*and* Books: Reviewed Just as They Came" in February 1931, writing about the first eleven books she read that month, in order, without any winnowing. She offers lengthy plot summaries on the regular, unconcerned about "spoiling" the endings of novels, and my experiments with completist readings of the titles in selected columns unearthed no glaring inaccuracies (although, as I will discuss below, she does offer a number of idiosyncratic interpretations). Fine, I was persuaded—presumably some measure of Blair's contemporaneous audience was too, after her periodic columns "proving" her authenticity. And, again presumably, like the *Good*

xi

xii   PREFACE

Housekeeping readers who prompted Blair's self-defense with their skeptical letters, I was also chastened. If indeed she really did read all those books, well, then, I now looked at Blair's *Good Housekeeping* oeuvre with an equal mixture of awe and envy.

This led me to think a little more about envy, identification, and emulation in general—more about that in the introduction—but also about where my identifications (if such they were) truly lay. Was I identifying with Blair, or with her readers? As I hope the pages that follow attest, Blair's columns are terrific fun to read, frequently more entertaining than the books about which she writes. When I set myself the double tasks of, first, reading the whole of the issue in which her inaugural column appeared, and, then, reading all the books she mentioned in that first column, I did not fully anticipate the tedium that would follow. As a writer, yes, I have aspirationally identified with my name twin (not namesake, not doppelgänger, no relation), but not as a reader; Blair was an omnivorous and speedy reader with an impressive attention span and capacity for returning quickly to a book after shifting focus. "I was fortunate, I think, to have chosen [*Pearls, Arms and Hashish* by Henri de Monfreid] for that day. For few books could have been finished as that was, by train time at six o'clock. But it roused just enough curiosity to make me pick it up whenever fifteen minutes to myself offered opportunity, and yet not enough to make me annoyed with the interruptions."[1] She was also, apparently, unbothered by motion sickness, reading on trains, in cars, aboard ships: "A trip to me is not only a journey from place to place and lecture to lecture, but also a passage from book to book; in other words, an opportunity for reading."[2] In all these respects, we are dissimilar.

I am, on the other hand, irresistibly attracted to magazines of all sorts. As a child of the 1970s, I read *Reader's Digest* cover-to-cover monthly, gravitating first to the regular humor columns (Laughter Is the Best Medicine and Humor in Uniform) and then reading each feature in increasing order of interest until finishing with the highlight of each issue, Drama in Real Life (months without it were bleak). Speaking of *Highlights*, I read that one cover-to-cover too, and *Ranger Rick*, and *Jack and Jill*, but I also claimed priority over the family copies of *Time, Newsweek,* and *National Geographic* (only one version in the 1970s, text-and-image dense, highly satisfying uniform yellow spines on a bookshelf and perfect for show-and-tell). We did not subscribe to *Life* and *People*, so I had to sneak peeks at those while visiting my friends or in line at the grocery store. My grandmother, alas, subscribed only to the

PREFACE   xiii

religious magazine *Guideposts*—visits to her house were challenging, but I
did manage to find enough to sustain me between the most recent issues and
her extensive archive. My mother was not a *Ms* woman, and *Cosmopolitan*
was far too racy for our family (although my best friend and I, fascinated by
the forbidden, constructed our own, comparatively tame, versions in secret).
My father did not have a stash of *Playboys* in his closet. When I finally convinced my parents to invest in a subscription to *Mad* magazine, I felt like
I had really gotten away with something; *Young Miss*, later *YM*, was sanc-
tioned, but *Seventeen* was too mature, and I was too embarrassed to confess
my longing for the *Beat* magazines (*Tiger* and *Teen*) and their pullout heart-
throb posters. I eventually rounded out my serials diet with *Games* magazine
and, just after it launched, the US *Elle* magazine, with its glorious squarish
dimensions and European aesthetic sensibilities. I was emphatically not the
latter's "target market," described by Marybeth Russell in 1985 as "the kind
of woman who will toss over $100 for this month's In bracelet (rhinestone-
studded, polka-dotted, charm-bedecked, fur-lined, whatever), knowing full
well that by next month it will be Out. But that's not all she is. She's between
25 and 49 years old. She's not a yuppie. She's not a preppie. She's 'fashion forward.' She's 'experimental.' She is, one editor says, 'the first one to try a new
drink.'"[3] I was thirteen, with braces and what I believed to be an egregiously
tiny allowance (I was wrong) that I spent on *Elle* magazine.

   I do not know that I was a typical child—my best friend was as serials
fixated as me, but then, she was my best friend—but I know that these magazines had a profound impact on me. *They* were the things I could pick up
and put down when I had fifteen spare minutes, and their variety suited my
peripatetic mind. Their arrival in our mailbox was occasion for celebration;
each issue was a gift, or multiple gifts, full of surprises (mostly positive—but
sometimes, the absence of a Drama in Real Life). They were also predictable.
Their arrival was regular, for the most part, and, for the most part, I knew
what types of things I could expect in each issue. They marked the passage
of time, anticipated seasons just on their way. When a magazine with a
"springy" March cover arrived, it made February's monochromatic northern
hemisphere bleakness a little easier to endure. We were a bookish household
too, in our middling way, frequenting the library and receiving a Book of the
Month, but the periodicity of magazines exerted a palpably different pull.

   No, my family did not subscribe to *Good Housekeeping*. We were a *Better Homes and Gardens* household—my parents preferred that magazine's

recipes and garden designs. But any appliance or tool that came into our home bore the Good Housekeeping Seal of Approval. I could never understand why anyone would buy anything that did *not* have that imprimatur. Its significance was so naturalized in my child world that I still feel a little odd if I see the seal on something that seems beneath its dignity. This, at least, is an experience borne out by data; a 1975 study "found that the Good Housekeeping Seal had a consumer recognition rate of 98 percent, higher than any other seal or certification mark, including 'U.S.D.A. Choice' and 'Underwriter's Laboratory,'" and in 1980 another study "found 60.4 percent of high school graduates and 48.2 percent of college graduates reported looking for seals before buying a product."[4] The internet has changed things, of course. The proliferation of easily accessed, and easily posted, peer-to-peer advice, and the general decline in print magazine subscribership across the board, prompted Hearst to work on revivifying the *Good Housekeeping* brand. In 2006 they doubled down on the seal, setting up the Good Housekeeping Research Institute in the "glassy new Hearst tower in Midtown Manhattan."[5] If it can reliably offer more scoops like the Pirate's Booty Exposé of 2002, it will have been a wise investment.

When I tell people I am writing about a reading advice column that ran in *Good Housekeeping* during the 1920s and 1930s, responses range from intrigued to quizzical, with the latter sometimes surprised that the magazine is that old, sometimes surprised that it ever had anything to do with books. Unwinding that surprised response has been one of my key motivations in this study. There is book advice to be found on the *Good Housekeeping* website in 2024, if one is looking for it; a general Google search will take the curious to *Good Housekeeping* UK, but by searching specifically on the *Good Housekeeping* US launch page, one can find multiple articles: "The Most Anticipated Books of 2024 (So Far!)"; "How to Read the Percy Jackson Books in Order" (pitched to an audience that is purchasing for younger readers but also for the adult who is curious about the popular YA series); "The Best Relationship Books."[6] There is also a book club, the "GH Book Club—your destination for ☀ one feel-good book a month! ☀,"[7] which has been running since 2021. The full archive of their previous picks is available for perusal, and it is a list that would greatly repay scholarly attention.

I will not be the one to attempt that study, certainly not in the pages that follow. True to form, I only thought to look for a twenty-first-century version of Blair just before my own book goes to press, but such behavior is perhaps

PREFACE

a defining characteristic, and certainly an occupational hazard, of being a periodicals scholar-junkie, particularly when studying a franchise that is still extant. There is more content forthcoming from *Good Housekeeping* magazine, but even without reaching into 2024, I have piled around my desk ample material to fuel at least twelve more years of study. There are still hundreds of book recommendations in Blair's columns that I have not mentioned here, and that could reinforce, nuance, or probably contradict many of the claims that I make in the chapters that follow. I choose, therefore, to identify with Blair's readers—idiosyncratic, sporadic, almost certainly less conscientious and with shorter memories than Blair might have preferred (more on this in the epilogue). But as I am, in this moment, a writer, looking forward to hearing what one (or more!) of my own readers might make of their reading, I shift to identification with Blair to echo the request she made of her audiences nearly a century ago: "Please, some of you, write and tell me."[8]

Acknowledgments

Without the generous invitation of Günter Leypoldt and Philipp Löffler to speak at the Heidelberg Center for American Studies in the summer of 2013, I might never have returned to my decade-old work on Emily Newell Blair's columns. I could not have imagined this as a book without Nancy Glazener's vision, encouragement, and astute commentary in Heidelberg and after.

I am grateful to the amazing communities of reception, middlebrow literature, and periodical studies scholars—too many for me to thank them all individually—who have read and listened to countless essays, conference papers, and effusive emails and texts about Blair, her columns, the books I have read when following her advice, and the side quests that have frequently lured me astray. Ellen Gruber Garvey, Philip Goldstein, Jamie Harker, Barbara Hochman, Charles Johanningsmeier, Cecilia Konchar-Farr, Allison Layfield, Jim Machor, the late Patsy Schweickart, Gillian Silverman, Erin Smith, Kelsey Squire, and Ildi Olasz, in particular, have my deepest gratitude. In myriad ways, Donna Campbell, Mary Chapman, Jackielee Derks, Melissa Homestead, Cynthia Patterson, Debbie Rosenthal, and Shirley Samuels rendered writing a communal rather than a solitary experience, and without them I could not have persisted. Kristin Matthews has been my constant interlocutor, hype woman, and sister from another mother. Yung-Hsing Wu is the Frances Parkinson Keyes to my Emily Newell Blair.

The English Department at Marquette University has been a supportive home and a resource. Special thanks to Cedric Burrows, Gerry Canavan, John Curran, Jason Farr, Leah Flack, Paul Gagaliardi, Jenna Green, Rebecca Nowacek, Ben Pladek, Al Rivero, Angela Sorby, and Sarah Wadsworth, for your collegiality, friendship, scholarly wisdom, and faith in the bookness of this book. Eons ago, Brian Kenna was an able and patient research assistant.

Marquette University supported this project with a Summer Faculty Fellowship, a yearlong sabbatical leave, and a postpandemic Research Recovery Grant. I am also grateful to the Marquette University Women's and Gender

xviii ACKNOWLEDGMENTS

Studies program for funding a collaborative research project that enabled my student Ruby Thompson and me to travel to the Western Reserve Historical Society in Cleveland to work with the Emily Newell Blair Family Papers. Thank you to Vicki Catozza, in particular, at the WRHS for welcoming us, and to the rest of the staff for answering queries over the years. Many thanks to Betty Carbol of the Winnetka Public Schools, who took a whole day away from her other obligations to search through the school archives with me, sharing stories of her elementary school teacher Mabel Vogel and looking around, in vain, for any *Winnetka Graded Book List* ballots that might have avoided the dustbin of history. I must similarly thank the staff at the David M. Rubenstein Rare Book and Manuscript Library at Duke University for their assistance with the J. Walter Thompson Company archives, both recently and decades ago when, as an undergraduate, I conducted a rhetorical analysis of the Ponds Cold Cream campaigns throughout the decades. That was the project that made me love archives, and I have always been grateful that they welcomed me into that space. During the pandemic lockdown, the librarians at the Silver Special Collections Library at the University of Vermont generously worked with me from afar, tracking down letters and sending scans from the Frances Parkinson Keyes Papers without which I could never have understood the extent of Keyes's and Blair's connection. In the final years of writing, Maxwell Gray at the Raynor Library of Marquette University Library (and the Marquette ILL team) accomplished heroic feats, and I thank them.

I would never have found Blair, would never have thought about or been able to look at *Good Housekeeping*, were it not for the Home Economics Archive: Research, Tradition, History (HEARTH) Collection, housed at Cornell University's Mann Library, which holds a nearly full run of the magazine. As a graduate student, I was fortunate to work with the physical copies of the magazine; when I looked into revisiting the work, I was far away from Ithaca, but the HEARTH collection had been digitized and was available without a paywall. During the pandemic summer of 2020, as I was about to begin a yearlong sabbatical to try to complete the manuscript, HEARTH was integrated with the rest of the Cornell University Library Digital Collections; while the image quality was undeniably superior, the new interface made *Good Housekeeping* difficult to navigate. Michael Cook, head of collections for the Mann Library, answered my frantic emails with unmatched grace and generosity. He quite literally saved both this project and my sanity, and I can never thank him enough.

ACKNOWLEDGMENTS

Although none of this book has appeared in precisely this form elsewhere, I have published some pieces that have been remixed and repurposed here. Fragments of "American Readers and Their Novels," originally published in *The Oxford History of the Novel in English Volume 6: The American Novel 1870–1940* (Oxford University Press, 2014), 34–53, can be found in chapter 5. Scattered throughout the book (and of course in the title) are portions of "Tasting and Testing Books: *Good Housekeeping*'s Literary Canon for the 1920s and 1930s," *R. E. A. L.—Yearbook of Research in English and American Literature* 31 (2015), 167–83; and portions of the introduction and chapters 2 and 4 appeared first in "The Book Advice Column as Evidence of Reception," *Reception: Texts, Readers, Audiences, History* 9 (2017), 87–91. Portions of the epilogue appeared in "The Middle Class," *American Literature in Transition, 1930–1940* (Cambridge University Press, 2018), 27–41.

I am beyond honored that this book will be a part of the Studies in Print Culture and History of the Book series at the University of Massachusetts Press. I am profoundly grateful to Greg Barnhisel, Joan Shelley Rubin, and Michael Winship for supporting the project and to Brian Halley for his editorial guidance and for swapping publishing war stories; I apologize that I have sometimes been That Author. Two generous anonymous readers for the press offered suggestions that have absolutely made this a better book, and Sharon Brinkman was an extraordinary copyeditor. All of the remaining errors and shortcomings are my own. Sally Nichols, Ben Kimball, and the whole of the editorial, design, and production department has created a beautiful book, which I would be proud to have judged by its cover, and for which many thanks are due to the Hearst Publishing Company's permission to use the glorious James Montgomery Flagg illustration. It graced Blair's columns on several occasions, and it captures their ethos perfectly.

Claire Polizzi Briggs will be surprised to find our childhood hobbies discussed in the preface—I hope pleasantly. Maggie O'Dell, thank you for reminding me why I do all this. To Bethany Bradd, Maya Hughes, Cindy Petrites, and Jenny Smadi: without you, this book simply would not be. To my parents, thank you for filling our home with books and magazines and for never suggesting that it would not be perfectly grand to keep centering my life around reading. To Bob, for being patient with me. And finally, and forever, to my daughters, who amaze, inspire, and sustain me every day with their strength, their wisdom, and their love.

TASTING AND TESTING BOOKS

INTRODUCTION

Choose for Yourself

> But what, you may ask, is a middlebrow? And that, to tell the truth, is no easy question to answer. They are neither one thing nor the other.
>
> —Virginia Woolf, "Middlebrow," 1932[1]

The January 1928 issue of *Good Housekeeping* magazine is a substantial 192-page volume. Its cover is a quintessential Jessie Willcox Smith image, soft in muted pastels, depicting a mother and baby gazing intently at each other.[2] Below this image is listed an impressive roster of contributors whose work appears inside: Jessica Cosgrave, founder of the Finch School in Manhattan, will be beginning a series on "Problems of Youth." She will be accompanied by Fanny Heaslip Lea, Faith Baldwin, Temple Bailey, Bruce Barton, Frances Parkinson Keyes, and Frederick L. Collins—fiction writers, journalists, religious writers, and motivational speakers sure to appeal to a middlebrow reader. On the spine of the magazine, one is reminded of its particular promise to the consumer: "Every Advertisement Guaranteed." This is the magazine's distinguishing feature—the "Good Housekeeping Seal of Approval," which the magazine had since 1909 been giving to products that passed the tests in the Good Housekeeping Research Institute. *Good Housekeeping* offered quality fiction, editorial features, and regular departments in cooking, homemaking, and parenting, but its key distinction from the other "Big Six" women's magazines[3] was its "Money-Back Guaranty," offered for every product advertised in its pages.[4]

This issue opens rather easily to page 51 because it immediately follows a slightly thicker page, printed in full color, featuring an installment of James Swinnerton's "Near-to-Nature Babies" comic.[5] The recto of this page contains a full-color reproduction, suitable for framing, of a Dean Cornwell painting of the biblical story of "The Woman at the Well."[6] After registering or avoiding these eye-catching distractions, a 1928 reader would find,

2 INTRODUCTION

bracketing an image of a serious young woman with bobbed hair, the large-font exhortation: "Choose for Yourself."[7] The message is striking, centered in a margin of whiteness just under the woman's picture; the eye is drawn to it immediately, only noticing later that it is the end of a longer title that begins in the usual place for a page of English text on the upper left corner of the page. The tone is initially not easy to parse; it might be inviting, but it also might be challenging, even admonitory, or even exasperated? Does the young woman's ambiguous expression intimate impatience with the reader? After opening *Good Housekeeping* in the expectation of guidance from experts and testers, was one now being repudiated and commanded to choose "for yourself"? Flipping back to the issue's contents page, one finds that Blair's article is given the short title "Choose Your Own Books."[8] Perhaps, then, this *is* farewell—Blair, who has been the *Good Housekeeping* books columnist for two years now, is going to vacate the role of reading adviser and leave her readers in the wilderness.

Regrouping, turning back to page 51, and beginning with deliberation at the upper right corner of the page, one encounters a much more reassuring situation. In fact, this article's lengthy title reads: *Few People Agree About Books:* EMILY NEWELL BLAIR *Gives You a Clever Summary of the Newest Ones so That You May With Confidence* CHOOSE FOR YOURSELF.

This article, it seems, will not be judgmental after all. It won't even be particularly opinionated! Beginning from the principle that "few people agree about books," this reading adviser will not pass judgement on the "newest" books, telling which ones to read and why, but will present "summaries," enough information for the reader (who might be lacking "confidence" if presented with only a bestseller list or a bookstore or library display) to decide which books are for her. And, as the title's typography suggests, Emily Newell Blair's imprimatur promises accuracy. Her method, or the summary itself, is "clever." To proceed this way, rather than to deem some titles worthy and other titles trash: perhaps *this* is modern, this is a strategy of which the bob-haired young woman in the upper right corner of the page unblinkingly approves. One could *only* imagine *her* choosing for herself, particularly after noting that the small block of text under her image is not part of the article itself but is a caption suggesting that she is "that talented young writer, Martha Ostenso" whose novel, *The Mad Carews*, presumably summarized below, represents "a long step forward in her career."

Few People Agree
About Books

EMILY NEWELL
BLAIR

Gives You a Clever
Summary of the Newest
Ones so That
You May With Confidence

CHOOSE
For
YOURSELF

Photograph by
Campbell Studio

In "The Mad
Carews" that
talented
young writer,
Martha Os-
tenso, takes
a long step
forward in
her career

ABOUT the same time that the Mississippi and the Missouri and perhaps the Ohio rivers go on a rampage and let loose their waters over the rich but long-suffering valleys that line them, a certain group of men in New York and Boston let loose a similar flood upon the mind of the public. This flood is called "The New Spring Books" or "The New Fall Books." For a time thereafter that flood bursts open my front door, and upon my floor appear billows and waves of packages. It sweeps back into the book-room. Finally it reaches the couch, covers it, reaches the table, covers it. Sometimes its high mark even finds the upper floor. Each morning, as postman and expressman arrive, my sister-housekeeper groans, my secretary rushes for scissors and index, my house man works valiantly at cord and wrapping paper. Every day, husband, housekeeper, secretary, and maid beg me, each in his or her own way, "Won't it go down today?" Won't you get through with some of them? Won't you get rid of some of them? That is what they mean.

And to some extent, I suspect, the reading public feels the same way about these spring and fall lists as they see them published in the newspapers, watch the advertisements in the front of many magazines, or tarry about the tables in the big department stores, or try ever so diligently to follow them in the reviewing columns. Keeping up with this increasing stream of new reading is a little like surf bathing. One just finishes one list of books that have been "the talk of the tea tables," to find another waiting, just as one jumps through one wave only to meet another coming.

The same question I strove to answer last January, "What shall we read to keep up?" meets us once again this January. And the answer is a totally different one. Of course, to inveterate readers—and my correspondence convinces me their name is legion—this is a happy thought. But I am not unmindful of the fact that to others it is discouraging.

For this first group I have my little list, a short one but, I hope, a good one, for it is the fruitage of much reading of many volumes, much selection, and much elimination. And for this second group I have a bit of advice: "Don't. Don't keep up." Pick out just one or two of these books as they appeal to you. Read them as slowly as you will or lay them down unfinished. For as one who loves reading I simply can not bear that, even in order to "keep up," it shall become a burden, that, even in order to take part in tea-table conversation, one should be wearied in the endeavor.

And in picking out these two, or perhaps three books, please remember what some of my correspondents seem not always to do, to pick the book that would seem to "belong" to you. For what I am trying to do—and this month more than ever—is to introduce the book to you in such a way that you can determine whether you want to know it for yourself.

When my daughter moved to Pittsburgh, for instance, where I have many friends, I did not merely name those friends to her, leaving her to determine for herself through a process of inspection whether she would like them or not. Nor did I pick out the friends that I most valued and extol them to her. No, for well I knew that her tastes were not my tastes, nor her needs mine. I mentioned these friends by name and then described them as well as I could, saying, in effect: "If you want amusement and diversion, this is the kind you'll get from Mary and John Smith and the crowd to which they will introduce you. If you want to go highbrow, then at the Jones's you'll meet this kind of talk and people who do so and so. If you want good neighbors with the same background as yours, the Browns are this kind of neighbors. They do thus and thus."

It is the same with books. No matter how much I may like a book, it may not be *your* book. But if I tell you why I like it, you, knowing whether you like books for that kind of thing, will know whether you want to meet that book.

For instance, that book which has taken the book reviewers by storm, "Dusty Answer" (Holt, $2.50) by that most beautiful of writers, if we can believe her pictures, Rosamond Lehmann. If I were to say that it is a perfectly exquisite work of English composition, revealing an innocent girl's heart in all its beauty and the yearning of youth in all its pathos, as well as the frustration of love's and youth's desires in all its poignancy, well might my reader say to me:

"But perhaps I do not see the beauty, or at least the same beauty, in a girl's innocence as you. I do not see the normal end of youth's fancies as poignant."

Or, reading the book, accuse me of having led her to a most unpleasant tale.

But what I say is this: Here is a story of a young girl told through the mind and reactions of that young girl, a lonely girl living in the English country, who had known for a few years in her childhood a family of young (*Continued on page 138*)

FIGURE I. Launch page, Emily Newell Blair's January 1928 column (*Good Housekeeping*, January 1928, 51). Credit: *Good Housekeeping.* Hearst Magazine Media, Inc.

INTRODUCTION

A habitual *Good Housekeeping* reader in 1928—a subscriber; or a subscriber's neighbor who read the magazine midmonth in exchange for her own *Delineator* subscription; or someone who regularly flipped through the magazine on the newsstand or in a waiting room—might not have needed to perform such interpretive gymnastics on opening to page 51. For one thing, such scare copy, both in titles and in advertisements, was by this point commonplace, a result of the professionalization of advertising and a feature of the blurring between advertising copy and editorial copy that attended advertising's ubiquity in the "iconography of everyday life."[9] In other words, a reader well-versed in the magazine culture of the period would know precisely what to expect from *Good Housekeeping*.

It is also likely that a 1928 reader would be able to intimate how Blair's column, initially published under a standard title, Tasting and Testing Books, related to the larger reading advice culture of the period. The January 1928 issue marked the end of Blair's second full year as the regular *Good Housekeeping* books columnist, and by this point the repeat reader would have been nearly as familiar with Blair as she was with Dr. Harvey W. Wiley, the Director of the Good Housekeeping Bureau of Foods, Sanitation, and Health, or Katharine A. Fisher, the Director of the Good Housekeeping Institute Department of Cookery. Blair was not technically named the "director" of an "institute" in the magazine like these others, but she was a regular, contributing a monthly column whose launch page ran in the front of the book alongside the features.[10] There was, moreover, a continuity to Blair's recommendations and an annual rhythm to the kinds of readerly concerns she would address: prizewinners in January, "vacation" reading in June, children's books in November. The charismatic young woman pictured at the top of this page, whoever she was, was not unlike the many other images of women in the advertisements and editorial content of the magazine. She was someone with whom a reader could identify, or to whose mien she might aspire, and the repeat Blair reader would quickly assume she was either one of the authors discussed in the column or one of the friends Blair will mention as a "type" to receive this month's recommendations.

While Blair has thus far eluded the notice of most scholars of American periodicals and American middlebrow culture, her personal history and her column's presence in *Good Housekeeping* magazine make her a significant figure for understanding magazine culture, book culture, and literary-critical culture in the period. She was the only regular book columnist in any of the

"Big Six" US women's magazines in the mid-1920s through the early 1930s, thus informally taking over the mantle of Hamilton Wright Mabie, whose columns appeared in the *Ladies' Home Journal* during the first decades of the century.[11] Women's magazines were, of course, full of substantial articles on a range of subjects that extended far beyond homemaking concerns, and all of the Big Six published fiction and poetry by popular and/or critically celebrated contemporaneous authors. But most reading *advice* and book *reviewing* at the time was located outside women's periodicals, in the "little magazines" of the literati, the "small magazines" targeting an educated and aspiring bourgeois audience, or the other "big magazines" who appealed to the broadest audiences. Newspaper book reviewing columns were particularly influential. Book subscription services and branded publisher "libraries" likewise exerted a considerable influence on US book publication and consumption, and their editors and judges became known critical figures. Blair's columns, which in many ways existed on the perimeter of this activity, functioned largely to synthesize and translate mainstream book and reviewing culture for her readers. Through constant reference to "the critics," "the reviewers," and "the judges" in her columns, primarily but not exclusively without naming names, Blair helps her readers navigate critical and cultural expectations as much as or more than she advises them on how or why to read specific titles. Her guidance is not absent, but neither is it explicit or dictatorial. And as I will show throughout this study, Blair's columns end up more frequently offering a range of possible receptions than demonstrating the likelihood or prevalence, or "typicality," or superiority, of any one reception of a given text. She is able to produce, and thus to demonstrate the possibility of, multiple potential receptions of the texts she "tastes." By playing with the concept of tasting and taste she relativizes and individuates it: "Everyone to his taste. The taste's the thing!"[12] Blair's own apparent popularity and the longevity of her employment by *Good Housekeeping* suggest that this kind of ecumenical, reader-driven approach was embraced by the same audiences that responded positively (through letters, perhaps, but also through subscriptions and newsstand purchases) to the rest of *Good Housekeeping*'s editorial and advertising content. By looking at her columns through the lens of the whole of *Good Housekeeping* and its particular promises to its readers, and by investigating her own career and location in the literary and political culture of the interwar period, we can see that she is both representative of and iconoclastic within the formation scholars have called "middlebrow modernism."

Middlebrows, Magazines, and Modernism

Virginia Woolf's scathing unsent letter to the *New Statesman* in response to J. B. Priestley's review of *The Second Common Reader* succinctly eviscerates the undefinable "middlebrow" as the common enemy of both highbrows and lowbrows because, ultimately, it is "neither one thing nor the other."[13] Indeed, it is not easy to positively define what the "middlebrow" is, even if we seem to think we know it when we see it. Some of the trouble in defining the term comes from determining what in fact it describes—is it an aesthetic that can be identified by certain stylistic or thematic choices in a given work of art? Is it a term for classifying audiences that gravitate toward certain artistic forms or particular themes or narrative arcs? Or does it describe a mode of reception—the way in which a reader, observer, or listener approaches a given text and the way they perceive their relationship to it as audience? From the "Battle of the Brows," which Woolf references in this 1932 essay, through Russell Lynes's "Highbrow, Lowbrow, Middlebrow" (1949),[14] the first half of the twentieth century was a period, as Melissa Sullivan and Sophie Blanch put it, of "great anxiety over taste, aesthetic production, audience, race, class and gender.... But the borderlands between high and middlebrow cultures and consumption practices were not as easily discernable as the reigning interwar critics, media or publishers often successfully suggested to the public."[15] The middlebrow seems, indeed, to be in the eye of the beholder—and more often than not the term is derogatory. This was presumably so for Woolf, who closes her letter: "If any human being, man, woman, dog, cat or half-crushed worm dares call me 'middlebrow' I will take my pen and stab him, dead."[16]

In the latter half of the twentieth century, into the twenty-first, cultural critics have worked to moderate this view of the middlebrow—perhaps, as Nicola Humble points out, because so many in that profession initially got there by virtue of a middlebrow upbringing's reverence for the aesthetic output of the "highbrow."[17] Joan Shelley Rubin's *The Making of Middlebrow Culture* (1992) and Janice Radway's *A Feeling for Books* (1997) told the history of some of the most significant middlebrow cultural arbiters of the beginning of the century, and histories of magazines like *Ladies' Home Journal, Saturday Evening Post,* and *The New Yorker* continued to document mass market periodicals' importance to a middlebrow culture that largely appealed to a striving interwar middle class. Lisa Botshon and Meredith Goldsmith's collection

Middlebrow Moderns (2003), Jaime Harker's *America the Middlebrow* (2007), Gordon Hutner's *What America Read* (2009), and Lise Jaillant's *Modernism, Middlebrow, and the Literary Canon* (2014) are just a few studies that have focused on the middlebrow as a cultural formation that, while significant, is also hybrid, multifaceted, and resistant to definition.

"Modernism" was for some time considerably easier to define positively, although frequently it too has been described as a cultural mode that was rebelling against, or critical of, the middlebrow. As Aaron Jaffe argues, by "demanding rigor and high seriousness, the casting off of amateurish reading habits, the institution of disciplined canons of literary studies, modernism, in a sense, professionalized its readers."[18] Modernist studies has tended to focus *less* on the first part of this construction—the notion that modernism stipulates a particular mode of reading—than on the particular texts that modernism's promoters championed. So, some texts simply *are* modernist— art novels, for example, which, as Mark McGurl explains in *The Novel Art*, "emerged in a series of transformations of the genre's analogical relation, as a generic institution, to other social-institutional, architectural, and geographical spaces, and how these spaces were themselves imagined to construct persons of a certain kind and class."[19] McGurl goes on to demonstrate how proponents of the art novel worked to differentiate "their" novels from the mass cultural works those novels superficially resembled and primarily disdained. In "When Was Modernism?" (1987), Raymond Williams explains that before the 1950s, when "the announcement in New York that what had been significant in the arts and culture of the previous fifty years was properly understood as modernism" was made, it was a retrospective and artificial designation that really did not reflect any organized project of any of the artists so classified. "The people who were making innovations in these different arts were very conscious that they were making something new, and they might occasionally use the word modern in relation to their work, but they did not see themselves as modernists or part of modernism."[20] In the newly transcribed (2002) version of Williams's lecture, we can see how he historicizes what Andreas Huyssen in 1986 iconically termed the "great divide." Huyssen argues that the "categorical distinction between high art and mass culture" was cultivated through "modernism's insistence on the autonomy of the art work, its obsessive hostility to mass culture, its radical separation from the culture of everyday life, and its programmatic distance from political, economic and social concerns."[21] Williams's historicizing of the term attributes the bulk of that work of categorical distinction to latter-day critics, noting that "the questions of value between [a diverse set of artistic projects retrospectively grouped together in the 1950s] are endlessly open and diverse, the appropriation of 'modern' for a selection of what have in fact been the modern processes is an act of pure ideology."[22] In Williams's articulation, the innovative artists of the early twentieth century were not elitists, were not exclusionary, but were themselves the excluded, and their sudden canonization was (or would have been, had they witnessed it) a baffling reversal.

Beginning in the 1990s or thereabouts, scholars of modernism (the term having by this point been naturalized) began to balk at the notion that this literature, and these artists, were elitist or snobbish.[23] Insisting on the extensive, and constitutive, engagement of modernism with mass culture, Lawrence Rainey (2018) points to multiple moments of dialogue between *Ulysses* and *The Waste Land* and mass cultural productions like pulp fiction, films about wayward secretaries, and drinking songs as evidence that Huyssen's thesis is "very *vieux jeu*."[24] In the same volume, Scott McCracken cites such mass culture influences on high modernism, and the presence of modernism "explainers" in magazines like *Vogue* and *Vanity Fair*, by way of arguing that "modernist aesthetics became the cultural dominant not in the sense that most culture was modernist, but in the sense that modernism became the measure against which earlier and newer forms were judged," allowing that "in mass culture this dominant could act as a signifier for elitism, as it does in the hard-boiled novels of Raymond Chandler, whose style was admired by leading modernists such as T. S. Eliot, or as a mark of distinction, as it did in magazines of high fashion."[25] Modernism, McCracken concludes, is not contemptuous of the everyday but recognizes "both . . . the power of the commodity form in capitalism and . . . that what it represents is a concentration of power relations and desires which needs to be slowly unpicked using new artistic techniques appropriate to a new age. That these techniques produce an art that often seems remote from ordinary life should not fool us into thinking that the everyday is not at the heart of modernism's concerns."[26] Be that as it may, there is implicit in this construction a hierarchy of the modernist artist who is able to recognize and critique, through aesthetic reorganization, the commodity's "power"—and, while contempt for the "everyday" might not follow, this orientation certainly facilitates some disdain for those who cannot escape the commodity's thrall.

The problem, truly, with this angle of attack is that it does not think about the text *as it is read* but instead insists on whether the artist him- or herself is valuing or not valuing mass cultural forms. It makes assumptions about those attitudes from the mere presence of such forms or references in the text. There are, indeed, many other excellent studies that illustrate the myriad ways that key works of high modernism, as well as works that have been newly welcomed under the umbrella of modernism through the twenty-first-century expansion of the field, engage with, are beholden to, influence, or otherwise remix mass and popular culture.[27] But that hardly matters if these texts of high modernism were considered contemporaneously as *other* than popular or mass culture. While authors may have been in dialogue with mass culture, critics and readers saw it as something different, something less accessible, and determinedly so. What Joyce was doing with mass culture was different from what mass culture was doing on its own, and what he was doing was "art," while mass culture was . . . not. Even the fact that many publishers tried to market modernism like they marketed Zane Grey, as Catherine Turner adeptly demonstrates, did not mean an embrace of modernism by the general public.[28]

John Guillory echoes and expands on Jaffe's earlier argument by showing that modernist literature precipitates the professionalization of criticism into the academy, not just by presenting textual difficulty but by rendering difficulty (and therefore high modernist literature) something illegible to the "lay reader." Guillory locates the moment of this shift in the 1940s and 1950s, as "criticism was reoriented . . . from the *judgment* of literature to the interpretation of literature. The necessity of interpretation was occasioned initially by the difficulty of the modernists, but interpretation proved to be too interesting and generative to be restricted to new writing. It very quickly came to be the means of recovering the intelligibility of older literature that was rendered 'difficult' as a result of cultural and linguistic changes wrought by the passage of time. Eventually all literature was conceived as *inherently* difficult."[29] This is the very move we will see Blair identifying as the hallmark of the highbrow critical "racket" in her columns in the late 1920s (see chapter 4 in this volume). Blair was not the sole voice of resistance to the progressive marginalization of lay readers in the face of modernist difficulty, but her presence in *Good Housekeeping* lends an intriguing consumer-advocate flavor to her objections. For her it's not just that modernist difficulty is unnecessary—it's an attempt to defraud the reader.

Good Housekeeping in the Middle

What was it like to open this magazine in 1926 to find a "new department" about books in the midst of homemaking advice and serial fiction? How did Blair's column fit in with the rest of the editorial and advertising content in the magazine? Or—crucially—are these questions predicated on a mid-twentieth-century notion of the market for interwar periodicals that sees more distinction between publications and audiences than really existed? Scholarship about "modernist periodicals" was for some time largely focused on the so-called little magazines, smaller-circulation publications that were sometimes hailed by critics as profit-agnostic vehicles for innovative high modernist literature. More recently, however, "modern" as opposed to "modern*ist*" periodical studies has begun to recognize the continuity of the periodical field, or, as Mark Morrisson puts it, to "[challenge] narratives of a decline of modernism into American middlebrow culture" by approaching the "big" magazine as well as the "small" magazines as similarly "making distinct contributions to modernism in America."[30] While this is a relatively recent development from the perspective of scholars whose primary focus has been "modernism"—the history of which is more thoroughly traced by Morrisson than I could rehearse here—general American periodical studies and middlebrow studies have long noted the presence of modernist authors, and even modernist aesthetic inclinations, in the larger-circulation magazines.[31] So while Andrew Thacker so aptly characterizes the "cross-fertilization" of the "periodical field of American magazines in 1920 . . . shown in the multiple networks of connection between and across supposedly distinct categories of publication"[32] to make a claim for situating the little magazines within a larger world of periodicals that includes *Good Housekeeping*, we could also say that it situates *Good Housekeeping* in the same periodical cultural milieu as the little magazines. Put another way: I argue that Blair's reading advice columns in *Good Housekeeping* during the 1920s and early 1930s suggest the inverse of Robert Scholes's influential provocation that "we cannot adequately understand [the little magazines] without an understanding of the mass magazines and . . . 'the elder magazines.'"[33] We cannot understand *Good Housekeeping* in this period without an understanding of the world of literary modernism, which worked so hard to situate itself against, or even outside, *Good Housekeeping*'s purview. But this also requires denaturalizing the idea that particular texts required particular modes of reading.

Like the *Saturday Evening Post, McClure's, Time, Life, Esquire,* and other general-interest "Big magazines," *Good Housekeeping* included content that assumed its audience was completely aware of the presence of contemporary modernist aesthetic discourse.[34] But unlike its "Big Six" rival the *Ladies' Home Journal* or its British sister publication, the US *Good Housekeeping* has not been widely studied by scholars of the interwar period, perhaps because of the absence or unavailability of editorial archives.[35] In chapter 1, I offer a limited history of the magazine, tracing its leadership in consumer advocacy, describing the editorial structure, and offering an overview of the magazine's literary and homemaking content during the 1920s and early 1930s. Working with interwar audience research reports from the J. Walter Thompson Company, I construct a snapshot of *Good Housekeeping* magazine's target audience. I then perform an in-depth reading of the February 1926 issue of *Good Housekeeping,* which was the first issue in which Blair's column ran. By looking very closely at the literary, homemaking, and advertising content of this issue of the magazine, chapter 1 establishes the editorial context of Blair's columns. After identifying the readerly expectations into which Blair was writing, it is possible to extrapolate the various motivations with which readers might have approached her column for the first time. This chapter also underscores the ways that other content in the magazine—advertisements, travel narratives, fashion editorials, parenting advice—was aware of, conversant with, and, yes, imbricated with a modernist cultural discourse.

As we will see in chapter 2, the persona that Blair performs in her columns works to establish her suitability as an adviser in this particular periodical at this particular moment. She does *not* present herself as a "highbrow," telling her audience that they must read particular books in particular ways for the sake of status. She is also not an intercessory translator of modern, or modernist, culture, in the service of cultural aspirations that have sometimes been termed characteristic of a middlebrow sensibility.[36] She is, rather, a denizen and a product of the Midwest and a decided, if well-informed, outsider to the book publishing and reviewing industries. Her January 1928 column, for example, opens with Blair likening the release of new books to the waterways near her Joplin, Missouri, home. "About the same time that the Mississippi and the Missouri and perhaps the Ohio rivers go on a rampage and let loose their waters over the rich but long-suffering valleys that line them, a certain group of men in Boston and New York let loose a similar flood upon the mind of the public." Blair frequently writes about working from her home (although this is not entirely accurate, as we shall see), so this "flood" imperils her domestic space; reviewer copies come in "billows and waves of packages.... Sometimes its high mark even finds the upper floor." Her description of her husband, her "sister-housekeeper," and her secretary all lamenting the influx of books identifies the rooms being overrun by packages, thus ushering readers into her home and family life. Blair's midwesternness (in other words, her "not-eliteness"), her femininity, and her domesticity all differentiate her from the publishing men who have released these books while making her relatable to her *Good Housekeeping* readers. She empathizes with her overwhelmed audience, who "see [the spring and fall lists] published in the newspapers, watch the advertisements in the front of many magazines, or tarry about the tables in the big department stores, or try ever so diligently to follow them in the reviewing columns. Keeping up with this increasing stream of new reading is a little like surf bathing. One just finishes one list of books that have been 'the talk of the tea tables,' to find another waiting, just as one jumps through one wave only to meet another coming."[37] The surf bathing metaphor does not quite match the metaphor of Blair's flooded home, but it captures nicely the idea that something initially undertaken for pleasure can eventually become exhausting. And, again, it shows that Blair, perhaps despite her employ of a secretary, is just another overextended modern woman: in some ways exceptional, but finally, conventional.

The year prior, Blair explains, she had thought her January column should tell her audience how to "keep up." Indeed, the January 1927 column's title promised unequivocal answers: "Which Books Shall Live? Emily Newell Blair Tries the New Books of the Winter and Passes Sentence."[38] The column itself sets out to answer a slightly different question than the one in the title, however, a question that Blair says is the most frequent one she hears: "What shall we read?" Noting that this is often asked with an "emphasis" that "suggested to [her] a similar question, 'What shall we do to be saved?'" Blair finally parses the question as "What shall we read to be saved socially, to be 'in the know,' to be able to hold our own in conversation, to appear well-read and 'up' in current fiction?"[39] The language of "salvation" might sound hyperbolic, but it is precisely the register in which other contemporaneous book advertisements and popular critics were working. In *The Making of Middlebrow Culture*—one of the first, and still the most comprehensive, portraits of the world of reading advice and book reviewing in the United States in the early decades of the twentieth century—Joan Shelley Rubin demonstrates the way culture came to be seen as a commodity that would confer prestige and facilitate social and economic mobility. Such was, indeed, tantamount to "salvation" in a world that worshiped success, or at least the appearance thereof. Even if the reader was not transformed intellectually, the consumption of the right books would enable the public, social "exercise of taste," which would "create favorable impressions in variable circumstances."[40] Crucially, Rubin's work, like Janice Radway's on romance readers and subscribers to the Book-of-the-Month-Club, refuses to malign the readers she studies or to be cynical about their pursuit of culture. She notes that "one must recognize that many Americans . . . not only . . . wanted thereby to gratify their desire for prestige or to differentiate themselves from the working class, but also . . . sought stability, insight, and pleasure in the books to which they were directed." Rubin insists that these desires are "legitimate . . . poignant, and . . . human."[41]

Many popular reviewers and advisers certainly operated from the assumption that "keeping up" was their audience's goal. Some did not explicitly discuss it for fear of sounding gauche or déclassé. The Book-of-the-Month Club's advertising tagline, "Why is it you disappoint yourself?," might be read as inferring the social imperative, implying the target audience's likely inadequacy, and turning their fear of failure into a motive to subscribe to the club.[42] The advertisements for Dr. Eliot's Five Foot Shelf of Books have been a favorite of scholars of middlebrow culture—myself included—because of their willingness to portray and their promise to transactionally alleviate social and class anxiety if you will simply buy their product and devote "fifteen minutes a day" to applying it.[43] Even if such approaches are acknowledging the desire to "keep up," though, they too seem to rely on the cultivation of anxiety and the shame involved in being considered inadequate to make their pitch. As Jaime Harker has demonstrated, however, there was another, frankly utopian, strain arising in the 1920s specifically within the culture of women's magazines that she terms the "progressive middlebrow." Through an analysis of Dorothy Canfield's writings as an editor for the Book-of-the-Month Club and her novel *The Brimming Cup* (1920–21), Harker argues that "middlebrow institutions and aesthetics provided a forum for literary liberalism and pragmatist aesthetics in the twenties and thirties." Rather than looking at such ideals through a cynical lens (such as that trained on much middlebrow culture by the "smart set" and their postmodern successors), and reading "humanistic rhetoric [as] nothing more than a hypocritical mask for bigotry," Harker insists we try to take these writers at their word: "Encouraging identification with cultural others, progressive middlebrow writers like Dorothy Canfield worked to persuade all Americans to question gender roles, abhor race prejudice, accept cultural others, and condemn class hierarchies—and they did so within the ostensibly reactionary confines of middle-class literary institutions."[44]

Returning to the Book-of-the-Month Club's question—"Why is it you disappoint yourself?"—perhaps this is not an attempt to inspire shame but an invitation to reflection and a call to action. Stop disappointing yourself, stop underestimating your capacity to learn, stop undervaluing your opinions about literature, art, society, start having faith in *your* critical acumen. A desire to "keep up" need not be underwritten by material striving; it could be motivated by the democratic urge to fully participate in a liberal society. This is the "keeping up" that Blair ultimately encourages; when she takes issue the Book-of-the-Month Club's "critics," it is not because she disagrees with the club's principles so construed. Her platform makes all the difference. As a reading advisor, a taster and tester, she is a consumer advocate and a facilitator who is not attempting to sell anything to her readers. She does not simply avoid the *perception* that she is weaponizing her middlebrow readers' anxieties against them—she is, instead, *one of* them, struggling with the same expectations and demands. Her January 1927 column offers not just a defense, but a *celebration* of "keeping up," deploying liquid metaphors in this instance to describe not a "flood of new books" but the overwhelming obligations that might be keeping her audience from reading what, or as, they might prefer. Blair's meditation on the matter is worth citing at length; since this is the first January column of her tenure at *Good Housekeeping*, and as it marks the end of her first fiscal year as the magazine's books columnist, it takes on the tenor of a mission statement, or a manifesto:

> Nor do I intend my interpretation of their question in any but a complimentary sense. For to keep up, to be "in the know," to appear well-read, is not an unlaudable ambition. It is the intellectual salvation of many a man and woman hard pushed for time for thought and meditation. Curiosity is a keen driver. Pride is another. Often these will serve to make us read when mere enjoyment would not. And we might just as well face the fact that there is no one thing so easy to forego as reading. Whether this is because it makes demand on qualities so different from those used for housekeeping or money-making, or whether reading can not become a

habit, I do not know. But this I do know—that a person who may seem to be, who may think herself to be, devoted to books, an erstwhile inveterate reader, may easily find herself so "busy," so submerged in details of a home or a business, that for months she will not open a book. Such a thing has happened not only once, but several times in my life. And so I say, all hail the desire of busy housewives to "keep up"! If it tides them over a period when it is difficult to find time or their minds are overwhelmed with professional demands, it has much virtue. Even if it is done as a substitute for a real love for reading, it has some value. At least it saves from vacuity, from mental destitution. And it may lead to a real love of books. It may add a literary flavor to an otherwise stupid conversation. It may put a polish on an otherwise dull personality. It may widen a narrow one. It may do many things to many people, and none of them harmful. So let us rejoice at the question, "What must we read to be saved?"[45]

"Submerged" not by books, this time, but by domestic and business demands, these "busy housewives" might read because they want to "keep up," but the effects go far beyond any superficial performance of culture. This reading practice is time they take for themselves, when they are able to commune with themselves, to have opinions, to escape boredom. In 2024, this will translate as "self-care"; just as one can hear the long echoes of nineteenth-century literary domesticity and "loving literature" in Blair's 1927 manifesto, one can hear the long echoes of her words in the rhetorics of twenty-first-century celebrity book influencers.[46]

A busy woman requires a list, though, and Blair is ready to offer one as she reassures her readers that asking the "salvation" question is an act of strength, not desperation. Her list is specific. Fiction by H. G. Wells, Frank Swinnerton, Arnold Bennett, Hugh Walpole, Lord Dunsany, Rafael Sabatini, Dorothy Canfield, A. Hamilton Gibbs, and Du Bose Heyward all make the cut. Blair mentions May Sinclair's *Far End* but dismisses it as having "the thickness of a piece of paper"[47] and thus does not recommend. She likens Ethel Harriman's *Romantic, I Call It* to Anita Loos's *Gentleman Prefer Blondes*, about which she writes, "Candor compels me to confess I simply could not read."[48] As for nonfiction, Blair notes that "no one who 'keeps up' can evade Will Durant's *The Story of Philosophy* . . . one of those get-educated quick prescriptions of our day,"[49] and offers a number of popular histories in the "if you liked *this one* last year, you will like *this one* this year" mode.

Notably absent from this list, notably, at least, to the twenty-first-century scholar of interwar literature, are other authors who published work in 1926: Ernest Hemingway (*The Sun Also Rises*), Ford Madox Ford (*A Man*

16 INTRODUCTION

Could Stand Up), Wyndham Lewis (*The Art of Being Ruled*), or even Carl Van Vechten (*Nigger Heaven*). Blair never addresses any of these titles in her columns. But as Gordon Hutner demonstrates in *What America Read: Taste, Class, and the Novel, 1920–1960*, those absences should not be at all surprising: "The mainstream were not so happily aware of the achievement of . . . modernist exemplars as later generations might suppose."[50] The thumbnail history of American literature that Hutner rehearses—which I can attest was still circulating through the mid-1990s—chronicles how Anderson and Lewis's "revolt against the village school" transitioned seamlessly into Dos Passos, Hemingway, and Fitzgerald's Lost Generation discussions of postwar malaise. Then, influenced by the fragmentations of Eliot and Joyce (and sometimes Woolf), Stein and Faulkner (and sometimes Toomer) rounded out the decade with their formal and linguistic experiments. Cather and Wharton were occasionally seen popping in here and there to contribute residual realism with a Roaring Twenties flavor and to balance out the gender distribution of undergraduate syllabi. But Hutner shows that this narrative is a post hoc critical reconstruction of the decades that followed and that contemporaneously, even prominently platformed "canonical" critical voices like Sinclair Lewis, Henry Canby, Granville Hicks, and Ludwig Lewisohn are not telling this story in precisely this way. Hutner describes instead critical engagement with a broad field of middlebrow American fiction from the 1920s through the 1960s, ultimately concluding that "the books that fall out of favor inevitably treat the middle class, while revenge narratives against the middle class manage to survive."[51] Booth Tarkington, Louis Bromfield, and Margaret Leech were celebrated in their day and were even considered "the best" literature by many critics. Their books were offered by the Book-of-the-Month Club in lieu of literary modernism, whose progressive middlebrow judges "were much more comfortable with books that attempted to combat despair with sympathy and affiliation" than with "cold indifference, disdain, and cynicism."[52]

There were, of course, hundreds of other contemporaneous authors, and many whose work occupied even more liminal spaces or fluctuated into and out of favor and suitability. As befits an advisor focused not on judgment but on service to her audience, Blair eschewed reviewing texts just to recommend *against* reading them. Her disapproval of a given work or author is more frequently registered in sidelong fashion, by using the title as a synonym for "bad

Choose for Yourself

book" or the author's name as a shorthand for a particular "type" of literature against which she is advising at any given moment. We will see several such instances in the chapters to follow, as when Anita Loos's *Gentlemen Prefer Blondes*, Sherwood Anderson's *Dark Laughter*, and F. Scott Fitzgerald's *The Great Gatsby* figure as antiexamples in sometimes unexpected places. But when it comes to an extended takedown, what would be the point? It would be a waste of her reader's time.

She occasionally *will* wax negative when she thinks her audience expects her to talk about a particular title, or when using the opportunity to demonstrate her awareness of, and ability to converse with, the professional critical class. Such is the case of Julia Peterkin, whose best-selling *Scarlet Sister Mary* was awarded the 1928 Pulitzer Prize for fiction amid scandal and library bans. A protégé of H. L. Mencken, at least to the extent that he found her less boring than most Southerners,[53] Peterkin eventually published a short story, "The Diamond Ring," in the June 1930 issue of *Good Housekeeping*.[54] Both Peterkin's "smartness" and the whiff of scandal surrounding her work mitigate against Blair discussing her in any extended fashion, even as her widespread popularity and her publication in *Good Housekeeping* might otherwise seem to make her a good review candidate.[55] Blair never recommends any of Peterkin's work (although she *does* recommend a book that "echoes" her *Black April* [1927]—more about that in my epilogue), nor does she mention Viña Delmar, whose 1928 bestseller *Bad Girl* was also a succès de scandale, something of a proto-pulp fiction, anticipating the exuberant excesses of pulp in the latter half of the 1930s. Blair's time at *Good Housekeeping* ends before the ascendence of the paperback,[56] but as we will see, some of the fiction published in the magazine seems, like *Bad Girl*, more pulpy than not, and the mix of stories in some issues would facilitate, even require, the "demotic, even democratic" reading that Paula Rabinowitz describes as a feature of the paperback marketplace: "One reads above or below one's 'level,' grabbing whatever is at hand."[57] Delmar and Peterkin seem to delineate a boundary that persists in Blair's columns, one that the magazine occasionally straddles, if only through Hearst's cross promotion of its sister publication *Hearst's International/Cosmopolitan* in ads that function as a soft introduction of edgier artists to the *Good Housekeeping* audience. Viña Delmar, for example, is featured in *Hearst's International/Cosmopolitan* ads beginning in 1937; in January 1942 her work begins appearing regularly in *Good Housekeeping* proper.

John Erskine, "who told us all we should know about Helen of Troy,"[58] contributed a series of "Private Lives" to *Hearst's International/Cosmopolitan* that were likewise widely advertised in *Good Housekeeping* from November 1927 through 1928, even as Blair was vetoing his *Adam and Eve* as a graduation present.

Chapters 2 and 3, which focus almost exclusively on the titles Blair reviewed in her inaugural February 1926 column, explore in greater detail her rhetorics of active inclusion and silent exclusion. They also characterize this column as an opening salvo in Blair's ongoing strategic self-positioning vis á vis the book-reviewing culture of the interwar period. Taking into account the proliferation of book review features in a variety of periodicals, I note that Blair's book *recommendations*, in which she (ostensibly) eschews offering her own opinions in favor of suggesting which types of readers might like a given book, also *synthesize* the prevailing responses of other reviewers in local and national newspapers, in national magazines that specialized in book reviews (like *The Bookman*), and the "small magazines" (as opposed to the "little magazines") or "smart magazines" that explicitly mediated between highbrow critics and middlebrow readers.[59] While Blair is to some degree a kindred spirit of May Lamberton Becker, whose "Reader's Guide" columns in the *New York Evening Post* and the *Saturday Review of Literature* answered reader queries in the spirit of "lack of judgement and subservience to her clientele,"[60] she differs both in writing to a more explicitly feminine audience and in situating herself as a mediator between her audience and "the critics" and "the judges." Becker cites and responds to specific queries, often from writers who telegraph their university affiliations and masculinity, and frequently errs on the side of offering an objective and comprehensive answer to a question instead of advancing her own opinion. She doesn't usually hypothesize the ways her advisees might end up reading and evaluating the books she discusses, and as she confesses on at least one occasion, she never has "space enough to say all [she has] to say about a book."[61] Blair's extended discussions of her principles of selection, by contrast, are all about reading practices; they ultimately delineate not a particular middlebrow "aesthetic," but a middlebrow reading *mode*. While this is relatively consistent throughout Blair's tenure at *Good Housekeeping*, her disagreements with "the critics" become more prominent to the last years of the 1920s and early 1930s, as do her warnings that her readers *not* read a given book just because they feel like they "should."

Choose for Yourself

We can see this shift if we compare Blair's January columns from 1927 and 1928. In 1927, Blair narrates having been asked for help in "keeping up," and as we have seen she answers that request by both providing an annotated list of titles and validating the desire to keep up. She also suggests that readers have an obligation to pay attention to contemporaneous literature, even if "we have to skim through much trash" to do so. "We are the judges who, by accepting or rejecting, make a book live or die,"[62] she explains. All of the writers considered "great" in 1927—and here Blair offers Shakespeare, Dante, Cervantes, and Hugo as examples—wrote "for their contemporaries," and Blair insists that it was contemporaneous appreciation that "kept them alive" for later generations. Being a contemporaneous tastemaker is a heavy responsibility, and Blair embraces her own role as a preliminary taster enthusiastically. Why then would Blair seem to balk at offering a list of explicit recommendations again in 1928? Blair writes that she *does* actually have such a list ready to go, and that she will share it with "inveterate readers," people who find the prospect of a list of new books a "happy thought." But for those who feel instead trepidation, who approach the prospect of still more books with "discouragement," Blair breaks with tradition. This year, her answer to the perennial question is "Don't. Don't keep up." Instead, she is going to summarize some of the books that would be on her list, but she does not want anyone to take her list as a prescription. "Pick out just one or two of these books as they appeal to you. Read them as slowly as you will or lay them down unfinished." Departing from her 1927 assertion that any reading to keep up is worthwhile as an exercise to keep the mind from atrophying, Blair now tells her readers that "as one who loves reading, I simply can not bear that, even in order to 'keep up,' it shall become a burden" or that "one should be wearied in the endeavor."[63] This seems less a prescription against keeping up, however, than a caution that keeping up is not important enough to trump enjoyment or to cause one to read against type. It's an embrace of a particular attitude toward reading, rather than a concern about the things being read—and it leads Blair to increasingly demystify the work of contemporaneous critics who pass judgment on particular texts.

Her January 1928 column spends a good deal of time, for example, summarizing Rosamond Lehmann's *Dusty Answer*. Blair acknowledges that Lehmann's book, which has not been retained in any canon of 1920s literature that I have yet seen, was considered a book that one needed to read to keep up in late 1927 into 1928. But Blair does not want her readers to feel beholden to those judgements:

Now, having heard what the story is about and what it means, the question is up to the reader, "Is it your book?" Do you want to know what Judith wanted from the world and see her disillusionment? Do you enjoy the companionship of young and innocent and slightly stupid girls? Will the pleasure of viewing her child world through rose-colored glasses make up to you for the pain of seeing her break them and throw them away? Will you endure the murkiness produced by these implications for the sake of the beauty unobscured? If you can not answer these questions in the affirmative, then the book is not for you. If you can, it will probably give you, as it did to the critics, extraordinary pleasure. But I beg of you, do not answer these questions "No," then read it and complain because you do. Or worse, never answer these questions at all, read it, and feel that a "bad book" was imposed on you.[64]

At the very least, Blair does not want her readers to read something because they think she liked it, and then to complain that she has failed in her duty as "taster and tester" if they dislike it. Taste is individual, and the opinions of neither the "elite" critics nor the popular critics supersede individual predilections.

Blair's embrace of reader-driven tastes is, perhaps ironically, the logical result of popular book culture *as well as* a reaction to modernist wagon circling and the growth of gatekeeping academic literary criticism in the early twentieth century. While Blair's columns are largely concerned with literature that her cultural elite contemporaries would have termed "middlebrow," chapters 3 and 4 demonstrate that she proposes and deploys the same readerly attitude, and validation of individual tastes, toward *all* of the texts she discusses—even and especially the few works she mentions that were embraced by the insider readers of the little magazines. She is, in effect, already demonstrating for her audience, and encouraging them to embrace, a notion that Nicola Humble sees at work in the late 1930s: that the designations "highbrow" and "middlebrow" do not inhere in text themselves but in the ways that readers approach those texts.[65] Thus while Blair obviously functions as "mediation" for her readers, she is profoundly skeptical of prescription. In January 1928, she even goes so far as to undermine her own recommendations because they have, by necessity, been predicated on *her own* responses to texts:

> After all, the reader—and here is the rub—must bring himself as well as the writer to his reading of the book. Here I have introduced these books as this one reader found them. But my readers, all too unfortunately, I do not know. What they make of these acquaintances, if they follow them up,

rests with them. How I wish I could know not only how many like what I like, and hate what I hate, but also—and this knowledge would be equally valuable—how many hate what I like and like what I hate! Please, some of you, write and tell me.[66]

In other columns, both prior and subsequent to January 1928, Blair regularly takes on the persona of a particular "type" of reader in order to speculate that that "type" might enjoy or be disappointed with a particular work. But here, she seems to caution that even skillful readerly ventriloquism might be faulty. In the final analysis, she is herself—and as herself, can only read the books as she has read them. Such a caveat, particularly when paired with the warning that preceded it, may well have been sparked by reader complaints; by offering this disclaimer, Blair may be protecting her recommendations from running afoul of the *Good Housekeeping* "money back guaranty."

She is also performing critical transparency, something she and her readers find lacking in other "critics" and "judges." We will see in chapter 4 that Blair accuses "the critics" of perpetrating a "racket" that promotes the kind of literature that will require their services for comprehension. To distinguish her own work from theirs, Blair abjures the role of interpreter in favor, as the January 1928 title insists, of "summary" that will enable readers to "choose for themselves." Sometimes this extends to a summary of various critical takes on one novel, which is the strategy when she describes recommending Virginia Woolf's *Orlando* to her good friend Francis Parkinson Keyes. Blair frequently mentions Keyes in her columns as one model of an ideal reader-user, but she was more than a casual personal friend; she was an associate editor for *Good Housekeeping* who was instrumental in arranging Blair's position with the magazine. The women wrote to and about each other in multiple mass-circulation magazines. In chapter 4 I argue that their mutual professional support, translated into anecdotes and book recommendations in Blair's review columns, functioned as a model of feminist literary networking that went beyond specific titles to introduce an engaged readerly lifestyle to the *Good Housekeeping* audience. It is no accident that Blair's most explicitly Keyes-centered column finds her discussing *Orlando* and Rebecca West's *The Strange Necessity* as books she will give to her friend, implicitly drawing a parallel between their literary and professional friendships. West's modernist critical practice, which is interspersed with a narrative of a shopping trip in London, is an explicitly *feminine* practice that gets rejected by the modernist boys' club of Eliot et al.; Woolf was, like Willa Cather, not accorded stable "highbrow" status by her contemporaries. Woolf and West, like Blair and Keyes, become a feminine alternative to the critical "racket," as Blair invites her majority-female *Good Housekeeping* audience into a parasocial relationship with herself, Keyes, Woolf, and West. This column, thus contextualized, can be seen as a feminist intervention into literary culture that wants to resist the external pressures of cultural hierarchies and render intellectual life accessible and useful—and attractive and desirable—to all in the modern era.

Each November, Blair devoted her column to children's literature. She framed these discussions more explicitly as a "service" to the parents in her audience, her guidance on the selection of appropriate books for children analogous to the Test Kitchen's support with selection of useful household products and pure, healthy foodstuffs. Medicalized rhetorics are prominent in Blair's November columns; one needed to proceed cautiously, to thoroughly "inoculate" children against an "addiction" to the wrong kind of books. In chapter 5 we will look closely at the first title Blair recommends to parents, not a children's book per se but a guidebook to children's book selection: the American Library Association's *Winnetka Graded Book List* (1926). The compilers of the Winnetka list initially seem to be centering children's preferences; they polled thousands of children about their book preferences and envisioned a resource in which children's voices would be paramount, with representative peer-to-peer recommendations printed for each title. They found it necessary, however, to empanel a group of librarians to designate which books had "unquestionable literary merit" and which were "trashy," and the resulting list ended up explicitly excluding many books beloved by children but abhorred by the librarian panel. If not offered as an option, perhaps these books would simply cease to be read. Similarly, Blair encourages her readers to carefully curate their children's literary explorations; they should be allowed to *think* they are discovering their preferences on their own, but they should not be given the leeway to find books that will prime them to enjoy "silly" books when they are adults. It is in these children's columns that Blair shows her hand a bit more explicitly about the kinds of adult books she does *not* like, as well as the logic behind her silence toward rather than condemnation of such titles.

The epilogue briefly reads several of Blair's late columns, in which she acknowledges and responds to reader challenges, which were either growing more frequent or with which Blair was growing less patient. If, as I suggest in chapter 4, Blair's early columns encouraged the audience to enter into parasocial relationships with her and her friends, the risks of this move emerge by the end of her run when their admiration and emulation turn to rebellion and dismissal. Finally, I wander a labyrinthine path in trying to understand the dynamics behind Blair's final recommendation: Zora Neale Hurston's first novel, *Jonah's Gourd Vine*. In this last recommendation, I find breadcrumbs leading back through the columns to 1926 as well as a speculative rationale for Blair's unheralded departure from *Good Housekeeping*, a departure that marked the end of the Department of Tasting and Testing Books.

CHAPTER ONE

This Is Your Guaranty

You can absolutely trust every page in Good Housekeeping.
—Advertisement, February 1926[1]

A reader who turned her attention to Blair's inaugural column in February 1926 might not have read the preceding pages of the magazine in order, or even fully. She may have ignored the Old Dutch Cleanser ad on the verso of the playful Jessie Willcox Smith cover and may have skipped the editorial on child labor laws in favor of the article about considerations when building your own home, or the first installment of *The Wondering Moon*. But all these elements of the magazine, read or unread, contributed to *Good Housekeeping*'s overall ethos of care, of responsibility, and, simultaneously, of independent judgment. To begin to understand the consistent horizon of expectations shared by Blair's audience, despite the endless possible variation in their paths to her column, it is crucial to first look at the magazine as a whole: the distribution of editorial and advertising content throughout, the placement and tenor of the fiction offerings, and the visual dimensions of the codex.[2] What did it feel like to receive *Good Housekeeping* in the mail in 1926? Or to purchase it at the newsstand? Or to pick it up and peruse it in the home of a friend or employer?[3]

The inaccessibility (or, perhaps, absence) of editorial archives for *Good Housekeeping* might be considered to complicate this task to a certain degree— without internal memos or meeting minutes to substantiate any claims of intentionality on the part of the editorial staff, we have only the text itself, and a few stray documentary scraps in disparate archives, to piece together the overall project of the magazine and its editorial stance in the 1920s and 1930s.[4] But this is also, on some level, precisely the point of approaching the magazine from the position of prospective readers. Absent the kind of publishing industry scuttlebutt that is more prevalent in the twenty-first century, a reader in 1926 approached the magazine with a set of expectations determined by her knowledge of women's magazines in general, and of *Good Housekeeping's* specific reputation, and would then read the advertisements, the editorial content, or the fiction through that lens—if it even was such a strongly established identity. Regardless of internal editorial negotiations, then, the magazine's public face, and the version that appeared in homes and on newsstands, *was* the magazine that its readers experienced. *Good Housekeeping* engaged in considerable self-historicizing during the period and after, so we can follow the public editorial stance fairly easily. *Good Housekeeping's* editor in chief from 1911 through 1942, William Frederick Bigelow, referred to his magazine's readers as the "normal families of America."[5] Who were these readers? The best evidence we have for this comes to us from the advertising industry, which was rapidly expanding in the 1920s and relentlessly surveyed markets to see whether and how their advertising copy was landing.

As one of the "Big Six" women's magazines in the interwar years, *Good Housekeeping* competed for its audience with *Ladies' Home Journal*, *McCall's*, *Pictorial Review*, *Women's Home Companion*, and *Delineator*. While all these magazines covered similar topics, each cultivated an editorial specialty to carve out market share and to combat the looming specter of market saturation. Some looked to patterns, others to fashion advice, and all published fiction to appeal to readers. *Good Housekeeping* took the early lead in the service departments with its Experiment Station in 1901, which led in 1902 to a pledge that the magazine would only accept advertisements for products whose claims had been tested and approved by the magazine. This began first with new appliances, but ultimately expanded to include all manner of household products—soaps, foods, even building materials.[6] Katherine Fisher narrated this move in an article in the fiftieth anniversary issue of the magazine:

> Little was known of these new machines. Questions about them began to pour into GOOD HOUSEKEEPING. We soon found out that to answer these questions satisfactorily we must begin a program of extensive investigation and research to develop first-hand information. There was no other source to which we could turn. For this pioneer work, Good Housekeeping Institute was extended to include testing laboratories. Our purpose was, first, to offer a list of household equipment that, when tested, had been found satisfactory; and, second, to develop and pass on to housekeepers information as to how to use these new labor savers to advantage.[7]

From the start of the twentieth century, then, *Good Housekeeping* touted itself as the consumer's researcher and advisor. Deploying the language of science, the institute empowered women to think of their domestic labor as an extension of—or even the foundation of—modern American life. Scientific approaches to homemaking provided a "domestic fantasy for the new century,"[8] in which women's essential role was to make the house an efficient, up-to-date base for the raising of children and upkeep of the labor force.

The magazine was also the homemaker's personal assistant, a replacement for the domestic servant that she might not be able to employ in her home. An internal advertisement for the magazine in the October 1928 issue highlighted this aspect of the institute's work: "Nowadays there is scarce an intelligent woman, servantless though she might be, who cannot have leisure and more time for her children, her friends, her garden and books and clubs. The secret of this new freedom is to run one's home in a fashion as modern as one's clothes. And the key to this secret lies in the pages of Good Housekeeping."[9] This marketing tactic doubtless appealed to the aspirational reader, who might desire, but be unable to afford, domestic help.

The institute did not stay unique for long, as other magazines began to see the advantages of testing programs and launched their own. But being first held a particular cachet. The seal extended the reach of the *Good Housekeeping* brand beyond the subscriber base, with manufacturers printing the Good Housekeeping Seal on their products as a sign of quality. Market research by the J. Walter Thompson Company suggests that this strategy paid off for the magazine; *Good Housekeeping* garnered a significant circulation despite the fact that it charged the highest annual subscription rates (three dollars) of all the Big Six during the interwar years.[10] Even more striking was its ability to grow its circulation when consumers, for the most part, did not purchase multiple homemaking magazines. As Daniel Starch put it in an August 1928 meeting at the J. Walter Thompson Company, if they purchased ads in only five women's magazines (minus *Delineator*), "You would reach about one third of the homes of the United States" because of this pattern of nonduplication.[11] A study of newsstand purchasing in the 1930s found a similar pattern of nonduplication, "showing that 65 percent of women purchasing a women's magazine at a newsstand bought only one such title in a given transaction, 23 percent bought two, and under 10 percent took three."[12] Nationally, *Good Housekeeping* was purchased more through subscription than at the newsstand, with reported 1923 numbers of 443,527 and 381,070 respectively, but that proportion could vary widely by locality. In the Cincinnati metropolitan area, far more 1923 readers had gotten the magazine on the newsstand

(2,799) than via subscription (1,428).[13] On the other hand, the Lynds' *Middletown* study, conducted in 1925, found that roughly as many Muncie, Indiana, homes subscribed to *Good Housekeeping* as to the other Big Six magazines, although far fewer (only 220) bought the magazine on the newsstand compared with its rivals (who generally sold over a thousand newsstand copies).[14] The actual readership may have been larger and may have overlapped with other titles more, of course, with magazine swapping between households and readership in libraries. Such things are difficult to track contemporaneously, and even more so at a historical distance, but occasional anecdotal evidence of these practices does exist.[15]

Evidence indicates that women's magazines were more accessible to middle-class readers than general-interest magazines; the J. Walter Thompson Company found in 1927 that 17 percent of women's magazine subscriptions went to homes with annual incomes of more than $5,000, while that segment accounted for 24 percent of the subscribers to general periodicals and between 42 and 51 percent of the "class" magazines like *Vogue*.[16] Still, the practice of subscribing to a magazine skewed toward wealthier and more socially prominent households. In the 1923 Cincinnati survey, for example, the J. Walter Thompson team notes that newsstand purchasers of "quality magazines" might not be as wealthy or as well educated as the subscriber base and that newsstand purchasers of "lower-quality" periodicals might be wealthier and more socially advantaged than their subscribers.[17] This was all about perception—was a magazine considered "class" or "trash"? The mode of the magazine's delivery (whether subscriber based or newsstand based) was one mark of this quality. *Good Housekeeping*'s competitor, *The Women's Home Companion*, served as an example of this dynamic in the J. Walter Thompson Company survey. The authors of that survey observe that the canvassing practices of the Crowell publishing company resulted in the *Companion* being purchased by less well-off households: "When large crews of canvassers are sent out to sell magazines in clubs, on short term rates, installment plans, etc., canvassers are practically certain to make their sales along the lines of least resistance. It is difficult for a canvasser to get his foot in the door of a high class home and it is much easier for him to get an audience with a woman of the middle class and downwards who does her own work." As a result, they speculate that "it may well be that the editorial character of these two publications would attract a higher quality of newsstand circulation than the Crowell subscription sales organization would secure."[18]

While *Good Housekeeping*'s editorial content suggests that it nominally strove to remain relevant to households with a wide range of budgets, its readership seems to have been considerably larger among households in upper-middle-class brackets; this is true across all of the magazine surveys in the J. Walter Thompson Company archives and is not terribly surprising given the periodical's relatively high cost. The 1923 Cincinnati study found that 71.4 percent of *Good Housekeeping*'s audience fell into its top (highest-paid) occupational bracket;[19] similarly, a 1931 survey of 810 households in Rochester, New York, found that *Good Housekeeping* was the magazine most frequently read by women in "homes of cultured people with large incomes. At least one servant," and "homes of people with education and discrimination, but with moderate incomes. Servants are sometimes in these homes, but usually the housewife does her own work."[20] When the 810 Rochester housewives were asked what magazine they would choose to read if they were limited to only one, out of the 426 (53 percent) who were able to make such a choice, 102 (24 percent) named *Good Housekeeping*; the next most frequently chosen magazine was *The American Magazine* with 49 (11 percent). The closest competitors among the women's magazines, *Ladies' Home Journal* and *Women's Home Companion*, were each named by 23 (5 percent) of the women. A note appended to the survey results suggests the influence of the growing financial crisis in 1931: "34 of the 102 women choosing Good Housekeeping were not reading it regularly at the present time, either because its price is higher than other women's magazines or because it is not a 'family' magazine and is, therefore, something of a luxury."[21] The magazine seems, by this point, to have become something of an aspirational brand; this could have happened by dint of its wealthier audience, its higher price, or its editorial and advertising content. While these are just the results in one metropolitan area and should not (as Starch noted in 1928) be considered generalizable nationwide,[22] in Rochester, at least, *Good Housekeeping* had eclipsed *Ladies' Home Journal* in popularity and desirability. By 1934, a survey commissioned by the *Journal* reinforces this trend, and the qualitative comments that were recorded suggest that *Good Housekeeping* was now considered the more politically progressive and scientifically modern of the two. "Better and more stories. Too Much Sentiment in stories"; "Good Housekeeping has better cooking sections. Also more diversified and more interesting type of fiction"; "Stop conservatism in editorials"; "Likes the real photographs accompanying special articles in Good Housekeeping"; "Good Housekeeping covers so many different phases of home life—how to press clothes, remove stains, etc. And all are scientifically as well as interestingly told"; "Good House-keeping's editorials and services are far superior to those found in the Home Journal."[23] Coolidge-era Rochester and Cincinnati were apparently the kinds of small metropolitan areas with burgeoning suburbs for which *Good House-keeping* was particularly relevant.

These surveys exist because magazines and advertisers needed to know about various audience demographics for advertising space buys and editorial decision-making. It is easy to see how a feedback loop could develop in which certain readers were presumed and targeted and then found themselves repre-sented throughout the magazine. Anyone falling outside the target demographic would likewise be systematically excluded from representation. The advertising department's 1928 presentation for potential clients, *"Good Housekeeping:" The Shortest Route to the National Market*, is an example of this in action.

> Picture to yourself an intelligent, progressive woman at the time of life when she takes an active interest in her home and family, her social con-tacts, and the affairs of her community. Her point of view is distinctly modern. She is guided by the thought and opinion of the present, rather than by prejudice and tradition. She is eager to learn new things. She is a familiar figure at women's club meetings, in welfare organizations—and at social gatherings. She is equally at ease in a house dress, an afternoon gown, and a party frock. She enjoys an income sufficient to permit the car-rying out of new ideas, to permit the proper development of both herself and her home, to leave a margin for recreation. She sets standards.[24]

The advertising department knows this is the typical *Good Housekeeping* reader how? Well, first they try to say they can tell simply by looking at the editorial content of the magazine. "Note how definitely the editorial appeal is to women of the type we have pictured above—how little there is to attract the woman too old (or too old fashioned) to take an active part in modern life, the woman whose training and social background hopelessly limit her mental horizon, the woman whose income barely covers food, shelter, and clothing in their simplest forms."[25] The aged, the unimaginative, and the poor could not possibly have any interest in this magazine—this is, of course, not a particu-larly persuasive argument, but it is striking to hear just how condescending and demeaning is the rhetoric about non–*Good Housekeeping* readers. There is no quarter given for a woman who does not have the financial wherewithal to, say, "leave a margin for recreation"; she is likely insipid, too, and aged.

To further substantiate these claims (or, to merely substantiate these claims),

30 CHAPTER ONE

The Shortest Route does reference consumer surveys; the majority of the folio is composed of statistics, maps, and charts to indicate market distribution based on the May 1928 issue (in which Blair discusses books to give as commencement presents) and on data compiled from surveys like those in the J. Walter Thompson Company records. The overall argument of the piece is that national advertisers should buy space in *Good Housekeeping* because it is the magazine that most appeals to the wealthiest households in the "Principal Trading Centers" of the United States. Even if its circulation overall is somewhat less than other (unnamed) magazines, *Good Housekeeping* is the best place to advertise because "an overwhelming percentage of Good Housekeeping's circulation is among prosperous, progressive people," which account for a large proportion of the "literate native white families" in a given urban area. Using Trenton, New Jersey, as an example because it has more "foreign-born mill hands" than "wealthy factory owners," the analysis concludes, "It is significant that in a place where less intelligent and poorer people predominate, Good Housekeeping's circulation is comparatively low."[26]

Since the surveys undertaken throughout the 1920s and into the 1930s concluded that the *Good Housekeeping* reader was most likely a white, upper-middle-class housewife, probably on the younger side, and almost certainly a parent or expecting—or expected—to become one,[27] the magazine's attention to parenting, and its inattention to women of color, could be seen as following logically from (and in turn reproducing) these demographics. The magazine presents itself somewhat differently, that is, as less obviously disdainful of anyone whose income does not qualify them as upper-middle class, when the audience for such a presentation is the general public. The *Good Housekeeping* reader is described in a 1932 *Christian Science Monitor* profile of editor William Frederick Bigelow as someone who "has never seen New York and never expect[s] to," but lives in suburbia, small towns, or medium cities, "where people still . . . water their lawns after the sun has gone down. And don't fume if they can't have a new car every year, and believe everything that happens in the movies could only happen in the movies."[28] In an October 1936 profile in *The Quill*, Bigelow is cited explaining his decision to live in suburban New Jersey rather than in New York City as a way to stay in touch with his readership: "Living in a small town and filling offices that bring me in touch with every sort of family problem has brought me closer to the lives of normal families of America for whom we edit *Good Housekeeping*."[29] These suburban homes had room for the new appliances and were the ideal laboratories for the modern homemaker of the 1920s. *Good Housekeeping's* matter-of-fact presentation of domestic competence, while it owed much to the advertising and editorial models developed by *Ladies' Home Journal* in the earliest decades of the century, would emerge from the Great Depression years with a stronger reputation for innovation and consumer advocacy. In the February 1926 issue, we can see that work in process.

Trusting in the Advertisements

When an issue of *Good Housekeeping* arrived in a subscriber's mailbox, it may have been read immediately, or piecemeal in stolen moments. After being purchased on a newsstand, it may have been read cover to cover, or selectively with articles and advertisements chosen deliberately from the table of contents or the index or through desultory flipping. In any case, the whole of the issue needed to cohere to create and respond to a particular set of reader expectations, and when Emily Newell Blair began writing for the magazine, her columns would need to fit seamlessly into its editorial and advertising culture.

By the mid-1920s, *Good Housekeeping* was printed on slick, quarto-size paper, and it was a very thick book, frequently comprising as many as 350 pages that necessitated a solid, nearly half-inch-wide spine. It could be stored upright on a shelf with little problem, and the title was easily read from a distance. But many purchasers would probably not choose to store the book on a shelf, at least not at first—the covers were a draw in themselves and begged to be displayed on coffee tables or sideboards. Popular illustrator Jessie Willcox Smith illustrated every *Good Housekeeping* cover from December 1917 through April 1933; collections of these illustrations sold briskly in her lifetime and were offered for purchase in the back of each *Good Housekeeping* issue.[30] "Certainly no other artist is so fitted to understand us," claimed the magazine's announcement of Smith's upcoming tenure in the November 1917 issue, "and to make for us pictures so truly an index to what we as a magazine are striving for—the holding up to our readers of the highest ideals of the American home, the home with that certain sweet wholesomeness one associates with a sunny living-room—and children. We are sure our friends will consider themselves privileged among magazine readers to look forward to cover designs done each month by this famous artist."[31]

The February 1926 cover, depicting two apple-cheeked children on a sled, is a perfect example of this ethos—there are children, there is sun, and one suspects that after their healthful outdoor exercise they will be welcomed into a warm kitchen and a comfortable living room. Like many of Smith's covers, this one has also had a significant afterlife as the "winter" scene on a series of collectable tins.

The cover, the high-quality paper and abundant colorful interior illustrations, and the heft of the book were all part of the package that would justify *Good Housekeeping's* relative expense to the subscriber. By the time Blair began writing her column, circulation had surpassed one million copies; it would double over the next twelve years, despite the onset of the Great Depression. Historian Frank Luther Mott termed its success "no less than phenomenal," noting that "for 1938, the magazine showed an operating profit of $2,583,202—more than three times the profit of Hearst's other eight magazines combined. This was a recession year, in which magazine advertising as a whole dropped off 22 percent from the 1937 figure, and many small periodicals died."[32] The longevity and consistency of Jessie Willcox Smith's contribution to the magazine were mirrored by the loyalty and consistency of the magazine's subscribers and, equally, its advertisers. The secret to all three was the money-back guaranty, which both reassured reader-consumers and enlisted advertisers as partners in the editorial project.

The advertisements that appeared in *Good Housekeeping*, in the February 1926 issue and throughout the period of this study, were often identical to those that appeared in the other Big Six magazines at the time. The J. Walter Thompson Company placed advertisements for one particularly well-known campaign, the 1928–29 Woodbury soap contest designed by Willa Cather's partner Edith Lewis and featuring F. Scott Fitzgerald, Cornelius Vanderbilt Jr., and John Barrymore, in at least twelve different periodicals—all of the Big Six as well as the *Saturday Evening Post*, *Photoplay*, *True Story*, and a number of the smart magazines.[33] By the middle of the 1920s, stylistic overlap between the advertisements and editorial copy had become a commonplace of women's magazines; both deployed scare copy and an emphasis on "advice and instruction," and in general the advertisements "blended in with and often could scarcely be distinguished from the editorial matter."[34] If anything, the money-back guaranty and the monthly index of advertisers doubled down on *Good Housekeeping's* integration of advertising as a key feature of the readerly experience. Nearly all the advertisements, even the smallest ads that occupied much of the column space in the back of the book, touted national brands; this was probably due in no small part to the magazine's well-publicized "testing" of all advertised products. At the bottom of each ad in the February 1926 issue is printed an advisory: "In using advertisements see page 6," which was an index to the advertisements in the issue arranged by subject. The index's placement very close to the front of the book, and the editorial table of contents signals the advertisements' significance. It even suggests that the ads are editorially chosen, as does the "Guaranty" printed in bold font at the bottom of the advertising index page.

This guaranty, if read without suspicion, serves to reassure the reader that the advertisements in *Good Housekeeping* are there as a service to *her*, not for the pecuniary benefit of the manufacturer (or of the periodical). The advertisement narratives reinforce this stance: the reader-consumer's personal needs are paramount at all points. *Good Housekeeping* would eventually run afoul of the Federal Trade Commission, which opened a complaint in August 1939 against the magazine for "misleading and deceptive acts and practices in the issuance of Guarantys, Seals of Approval, and the publication in advertising pages of grossly exaggerated and false claims for products advertised therein."[35] The magazine would ultimately lose this fight, and in 1941 it was

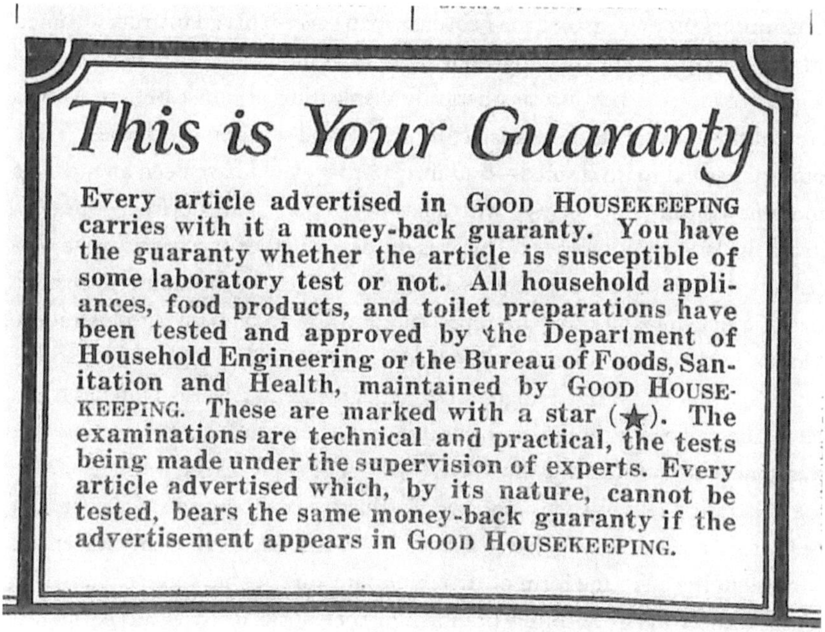

This is Your Guaranty

Every article advertised in GOOD HOUSEKEEPING carries with it a money-back guaranty. You have the guaranty whether the article is susceptible of some laboratory test or not. All household appliances, food products, and toilet preparations have been tested and approved by the Department of Household Engineering or the Bureau of Foods, Sanitation and Health, maintained by GOOD HOUSEKEEPING. These are marked with a star (★). The examinations are technical and practical, the tests being made under the supervision of experts. Every article advertised which, by its nature, cannot be tested, bears the same money-back guaranty if the advertisement appears in GOOD HOUSEKEEPING.

FIGURE 2. The 1926 version of the *Good Housekeeping* guaranty (*Good Housekeeping*, February 1926, 6). Credit: *Good Housekeeping*. Hearst Magazine Media, Inc.

directed to cease and desist claiming that advertised items had been "tested and approved."[36] During Blair's tenure at the magazine, however, this claim remained uncontested, and the mantra of "tested and approved" made *Good Housekeeping* the most trusted magazine on the market.[37] If anything, *Good Housekeeping's* close association of its own brand with the advertising that appears in its pages rendered the ads more essential to the contemporaneous reading experience, more an inseparable part of the whole.

Many scholars have discussed the ways that scientific housekeeping, while elevating the social status of homemaking on the one hand, simultaneously ratcheted up the demands on the scientific housekeeper herself on the other. In her study of the *Ladies' Home Journal* during the opening decades of the twentieth century, Jennifer Scanlon traces the career of Christine Frederick, who argued for the adoption of Taylorist efficiency principles in the home. Frederick's "new housekeeping" philosophy, as published in the *Journal*, had the goal of proving the worth of women's work in the home, although Scanlon argues she ultimately "promised something she could not deliver, namely social status for unpaid household work."[38] The mingled promises of respect and additional work are easily seen in the advertisement for Old Dutch Cleanser that appears on the verso of the February 1926 cover. This ad instructs women on the importance of cleaning their laundry equipment: "That troublesome ring of scum" was not just aesthetically displeasing; it "must be removed to prevent the annoyance of unsatisfactory results and spots on the clothes."[39] The laundry needed to be cleaned—and in 1926 this would have been an arduous and time-consuming task even with a few new labor-saving devices—but now, so did the laundry equipment. This was the case whether one was using an old-fashioned washtub, a more advanced laundry sink, or the most current mangle washing machine; all three are represented in the accompanying illustration. Moreover, the ad cautions that if you were to use (or had been using) something besides Old Dutch it might scratch the surface, and those scratches could catch dirt and make things less healthful in the long run. Once the visible dirt was gone, one had to tackle the invisible dirt. The smile on the woman's face in the illustration notwithstanding, the Old Dutch advertisement might not have been truly reassuring to a harried woman.[40] And yet, there is an element of whimsy in the ad in the form of two miniature, one might even say elven, Old Dutch Girls, who are faithfully brandishing their sticks to "chase dirt" from this lady's laundry sink and washtub. The potted plant on the windowsill and the hint of foliage outside the window likewise suggest a fantasy world of peaceful, natural beauty—as soon as this woman finishes with the grimy ring around her laundry tub, she will thank her tiny helpers and enjoy her garden. The ad is ultimately not admonitory, but aspirational; a "funhouse mirror," as Roland Marchand puts it, which "distort[s] reality to show a society as some people wish it could be."[41]

By contrast, the ad that appears on the first interior page of the issue offers a cautionary tale. At the top: a photo of a young woman sitting at her desk, apparently working on her household budget and paying bills, with a look of distress on her face. Artfully haphazardly overlaid on the photo is a text box proclaiming, "She didn't cook with the gas off." And then the teasing story header appears in bold font just under the photo, "She thought she was economical . . . ," with the clarifying subtitle, "yet she wasted $300 every year in her kitchen with old-fashioned equipment" (1). The dramatic story that follows tells of Mary Ellen's distress on finding her checking account balance perilously low at the end of the month. It is the kind of story one might find in the fiction offerings of the magazine.[42] She "muster[s] up enough courage" to ask her neighbor, "pretty Mrs. Henderson," how she can manage on "less money than John gave Mary Ellen." Fortunately for our heroine, Mrs. Henderson is as well educated as she is attractive, and she tells of the lessons she learned in her college economics course—not *home* economics, mind you, but standard microeconomics. "There I learned that the difference between success and failure in business is often the economies that can be made by buying modern equipment that can, over the period of a year, pay for itself and show a handsome profit in its savings." Again, this was not a course about running a home—it was a course targeted to those who would run a business—but Mrs. Henderson takes the ideas and turns them into her philosophy for running her household *like* a business. "Everything I buy," Mrs. Henderson explains, "is bought on the basis of its savings in time, energy and money, even though the first cost is a little more." By the time the whole story is told, with a teaser that cooking with the gas off "reduces food shrinkage," the reader might well follow Mary Ellen's example by sending off for information about how the Chambers Fireless Gas Range can save them money and time.

The Chambers ad is not the only one that follows the narrative model—another particularly striking example is an ad for the Women's Institute, a correspondence course for dressmaking that doesn't announce itself until the very end of a story titled "Secrets in the Tower Room" (11). This full-page advertisement is formatted just like the stories later in the magazine, with author and illustrator credits. The ad's illustration, like the illustrations for the stories later in the issue, features a phrase from the copy as a call-out caption ("Like a cool, sparkling snowflake under the black of her partner's sleeve"). Only the box at the bottom of the page, which may be clipped out to mail in for a free information pamphlet, differentiates this ad from the short stories that surround it in the magazine.

Good old-fashioned fearmongering was not beneath the dignity of the advertisers, however, as in the Nujol advertisement that appeared in the February 1926 issue with the terrifying headline "And to think I was poisoning my own baby!" (148). A small caption nestled in the negative space in the illustration over the shocking headline asserts that "This woman's experience is typical of thousands. Ask any physician." So, how did she poison her baby? By being constipated. By taking Nujol, she would ensure that "poisons in the blood from sluggish intestines" would not pass to her baby in her breastmilk. Taking Nujol becomes a necessity, because without it the nursing mother might inadvertently kill her baby with toxic milk. In chapter 5, we will see how Blair sometimes echoes the histrionic language of the magazine's health and medicine advertisements as she "prescribes" books for children.[43]

This ad offers more to our understanding of the culture of *Good Housekeeping* and Blair's book recommendations than just this reflection of the intense pressure on modern women as well-educated, scientifically savvy mothers, however. Like many other women's health advertisements in the magazine, the Nujol ad presents itself as an extension of the informal advice once available via folk wisdom and other women's networks in the period before the medical profession's twentieth-century establishment of authority.[44] The illustration shows two women talking as one holds her presumably imperiled newborn; she is not receiving the health information from her well-dressed interlocutor but is passing it along, through the feminine network, as a cautionary tale. The representation of an intrafeminine network of advice here is paralleled by Blair's feminine network; while it does not circumvent the authority of male professionals, it does supplement it and validate it— the speaker here heard the diagnosis from her doctor, and can confirm that Nujol solved the problem of her baby's failure to gain weight. Similarly, Blair will augment, amplify, or moderate the advice of "experts" external to the magazine, while retaining her informal insider status.

This Is Your Guaranty   37

Sound Advice for All Aspects of Home Life

Most of the household advice content of the magazine appeared later in the book, and most of these features were authored by women. Covering home furnishing, home construction, nutrition, and sanitation, these articles work together to insist that all aspects of the home can benefit from modern rational domesticity. My goal in working somewhat deliberately through this single issue of the magazine is not to argue that *Good Housekeeping* is exceptional (many of the "Big Six" magazines featured standing "departments," for example), but working to characterize the expectations for a "women's magazine" that were thoroughly met by *Good Housekeeping*, so as to better understand how Blair' columns might work in context.

Furnishings, Home, and Fashion

"A Woman Learns How to Build" is the first installment of a promised three-part series. After reflecting on the dream of home construction, our intrepid reporter (the eponymous "woman") goes on to interview architects, building planners, and construction experts. She learns how to choose the right type of house for a given plot of land, how to draw a floor plan, and how to select building materials. The author of this piece clarifies that her readers need not feel compelled to embark on a project of building a home from the ground up. Rather, a familiarity with proper building materials and techniques will enable readers to assess homes accurately, and will prevent their falling victim to shoddy construction practices. The latter are such a consumer hazard that they have already been flagged by the American Construction Council founded by Roosevelt and Coolidge. By connecting this advice to a national governmental initiative, *Good Housekeeping* demonstrates how essential the home, and the work of the home, is to the greater aims of the polity. As Sarah Leavitt argues, domestic advice was a way for advisers "to interact with and to help construct national ideologies"[45]—demanding quality construction practices was just like demanding quality clothing or quality food products. Consumer advocacy and activism was also, inherently, political activism, and the reference to the American Construction Council serves to remind the reader of her crucial role as a citizen-consumer.

As important as the overall structure of the home is the material that goes inside it. There are two articles in the February 1926 issue focusing on furniture and home decoration: one on the way the Good Housekeeping Studio furnished a model home for under $900, and one on the history and uses of chests. The article on chests offers a brief course in furniture history, with detailed discussion of chest manufacture in Flanders in the seventeenth century, complete with tips on how to identify chests from different eras based on their wood, their finish, and their decoration. Such an article would appeal to women who might have heirloom chests in their homes—they would be able to relate to the history of these furnishings and would have more appreciation of their possessions. It would present a topic for conversation, as well, whenever in the presence of a chest—the reader would be able to offer her observations and expertise and would have increased interest in others' possessions.

A reader would easily be able to duplicate the work of the Good Housekeeping Studio in her own home after reading "Four Rooms Furnished for Nine Hundred Dollars." The article offers details of upholstery, furniture finishes, rugs, paint colors, and wallpaper choices. It even reimagines the home from the initial room layout, dispensing with a dedicated dining room in favor of a nursery—"a room that children may have for their very own is quite as important as a room where we eat three meals a day" (45)—and converting other rooms into multipurpose spaces: "Beyond the bedroom and bath was what might have been just a sun-porch. We made it into a 'three-in-one': a guest-room, for it had a day-bed that opened out, a breakfast porch (a delightful place for meals with the aid of the tea-wagon), and an additional living-room at all times" (45). The parenthetical commentary on the idea of the "breakfast-porch" both convinces the reader of the attractiveness of the idea and gives her language with which to describe the porch to others and a story into which she can insert herself.

An extensive fashion section appears before any other household advice, lavishly illustrated and offering advice for the dress of older women and young girls ages four to eight years and discussions about how to remake old dresses by remixing tops and bottoms and through the addition of new fabrics. These are some of the only pages that do not have a sense of narrative, but they do offer abundant specifics about the minutest details of clothing design and construction. "Coats on the whole flare less than they did. Sports models are quite straight, and for street wear a model which is straight in the back and folded over on a diagonal line across the front, like the model from Premet on p. 52, is very smart. This coat is really quite wide, but when worn folded over in this manner it gives a straight effect" (53). These kinds of details might enable a skilled seamstress to emulate the fashions shown, as the heroine of "Secrets from the Tower Room" does. But the magazine's suggestions about "How to Use the Fashion Department" focus more on purchasing rather than on construction:

> *If You Would Dress Smartly*, study the pages of the Fashion Department each month, for there we show models actually being worn by the smart women in New York and Paris. *If You Would Shop in New York*, let the Shopping Service buy for you by mail the pretty clothes from Fifth Avenue shops which are illustrated and which we know to be smart and of good value. *If You Would Shop in Your Own Town*, buy there what you would buy in Fifth Avenue shops by purchasing trade-marked ready-made clothes which we recommend and which a reliable manufacturer protects. (54)

Good Housekeeping offers to tell its readers where in their area they can find the "trade-marked" fashions they show in their pages; the fashion spreads, more than any of the other editorial content, actually function as specific brand advertisements. The shopping service is effectively a clothing catalogue; prices are shown for various pieces, and readers are directed to send a check or money order to the magazine and the item will be found and purchased.

"Dressing Our Daughters" announces in its lede that it is less concerned with fashion than with the other governing interests in the magazine: health, economy, and efficiency. After consulting "buyers in New York department stores," "doctors and nurses with decided ideas on what is healthy and unhealthy," and "mothers whose incomes vary from an almost infinitesimal amount to a bank account that never has to be considered," Virginia Dibble expostulates on all manner of children's clothing issues from hem lengths to undershirts and socks, and the fabrics and colors that suit each complexion and eye color ("If your child has blue eyes, always hold a piece of material near them to be sure they are not killed by the frock" [113]). For the items illustrated in the children's clothing article, one may either send away to purchase them ready-made or patterns are available from the Good Housekeeping Pattern Service (61). Patterns are also available in connection with "Remodeling, an Art," which suggests the judicious use of velvet for refreshing previous seasons' clothes and offers detailed instructions for widening sleeves. The fabric arts section closes with a discussion of needlework designs, which discusses one designer's aesthetic in some detail and offers, once again via the shopping service, to send design transfers or patterns and other needlework materials to interested readers.

This fabric arts section emphasizes the reader's skill and her ability to reproduce the items pictured herein; in it the magazine also serves as a go-between for the reader who might live at a great distance from the centers of fashion or even from a place that would sell the more specialized materials necessarily for fancy needlework. There is an overriding sense as well that all dressmaking and needlework is really an *art*—it's fabric artisanship and appreciation, and in this way is not unlike the aesthetically inflected discussions of furnishings and antiques from earlier in the magazine. The reader is being advised by the magazine, but her tastes are still being appealed to, and she has the freedom to mix patterns, shapes, and fabrics at her will. The overall effect is very different from twenty-first-century "get the look" fashion advice—while elements of construction are there to be emulated, the interpretation will be largely individual.

Pure Foods and Efficient Kitchens

Good Housekeeping is most associated in the twenty-first-century mind with cooking and kitchen advice; this material, however, does not appear until relatively deep in the magazine each month in the 1920s and 1930s. Even feature articles or editorials about safe foodstuffs and kitchen equipment appear very late in the book. Food advertisements are not clustered in this way, however, and that might lead to the impression that the magazine as a whole is primarily concerned with kitchen concerns. But when one looks at the magazine overall one actually finds a subtle, but important, shift in tone when it comes to the kitchen arrangement, menu planning, and food safety advice: the ethos of creativity and improvisation that was so marked in the fashion section, and the support for readers' individual judgment that we will see in the personal advice articles and in Blair's reading advice columns, are replaced in these articles by prescription and regimentation. There are absolutely correct and incorrect ways of proceeding in the kitchen, and deviation from the scientifically approved paths laid out by *Good Housekeeping* can result in illness and even death.

We have of course already seen this attitude in the Nujol advertisement, which warns that a mother might poison her baby with toxic breastmilk if she is constipated. This is also a rhetorical strategy with a history reaching back at least to Catherine Beecher's nineteenth-century domestic advice literature. Three feature articles in the February 1926 issue covering kitchen topics are similarly exacting about the management of meal delivery in the home and make it clear that the consequences for failure in this area could be serious. The bad news is sometimes delivered lightheartedly, however—in "The Cottage across the Way," Dorothy B. Marsh describes the *Good Housekeeping* display at the recent Eastern States Exposition and observes that most of the visitors to the model kitchen were less interested in the room's setup than in the nutrition advice on offer. "They wanted us to tell them what they should eat, and were particularly concerned about their weight. Many were fighting surplus avoirdupois, while a small minority was in need of more weight" (68). The most helpful materials on offer at the exposition were the charts of hundred-calorie serving sizes, and Marsh describes the horror that many experienced when realizing just how small a portion would deliver one hundred calories. This response, she offers, "told us only too well of the need for greater help in planning balanced meals" (68). One tool for this is the "Daily Diet Card" and "Daily Diet Diary," available to all readers on request, which helps the homemaker calculate the specific caloric requirements for each member of her household. The level of specificity of this diet card, as it is explained in Marsh's column, does not allow for much leeway—this is a rigid calorie counter and, frankly, just reading the column is an exercise in anxiety and guilt over the "normalcy" or "abnormality" of one's family. "If your family is of normal weight, you need not concern yourself with the daily calories consumed. . . . If, on the other hand, upon checking up weights for age and height, we find that members of the family are abnormal in weight, it will be our problem as housekeepers to consider their calories with care" (69). The rhetoric of "problems" and "responsibilities" here is difficult to parse as empowering, particularly when what is at stake is the reader's family's "normalcy," its very membership in the group of families for which the magazine is produced. Her belonging in this magazine community relies on her family's consumption of the proper number of calories, and tracking this is her sole responsibility.

Good Housekeeping comes to the rescue in the February issue with a detailed weekly menu, which is keyed to a recipe booklet offered by the magazine on request. The institute's testers were able to determine that the sample menu was able to "deliver" exactly 10–15 percent protein and the proper calories for a "typical family of five, consisting of a professional man of moderately active work, a woman doing all her own housework except the most strenuous tasks, a boy of sixteen, a girl of thirteen, and a girl of ten years" (72). The exacting calculations of nutrition goals aside, the model family and its "typicality" become a mental burden for the reader. Are differently constituted families atypical, and what might that mean for the homemaker who is being very closely constrained in this section of the magazine? While there is some latitude for difference in other sections of the magazine, the sense in the food preparation section is that there is very little. This sense of rightness and wrongness, of typicality, would surely make a reader who does not have this model form of family second-guess her choices. The "Market-Basket Wisdom" article, with its picture of an ideal cauliflower juxtaposed with a spectrum of substandard cauliflowers, has the same spiritual weight. Exacting inspections must be made of every fruit and vegetable to ensure that the individual item chosen will deliver the optimal nutrition and will be worth the money spent on it. No woman should choose a "poor" cauliflower, or cabbage, or celery; to do so might be to ensure that her family is not "normal."

Little surprise that the child-rearing article for February is entitled "Is Your Baby Normal?" This regular feature, the Health and Happiness Club penned by Josephine Hemenway Kenyon, is written as if it were a letter addressed to the members of a "club," but unlike many of the other regularly occurring advice columns it does not cite reader letters. February's edition describes developmental milestones each new mother should look for in her child and offers a booklet (by request) for "mothers of babies who are long in learning to behave like other children of their age" (86). These regimented expectations for infant development are typical of the period, but my interest here is in noting once again the rhetoric of normalcy and the impetus that this places on the mother to produce a "normal" child through nutrition ("Rickets may cause definite retardation" [86]) or stimulation ("The nursery window is an all-important affair to the young person dwelling in the room" [94]). This difference in tone will return in Blair's annual children's books columns. Rather than the language of choice and the emphasis on individual tastes that infuse the vast majority of her recommendations to adults, the note of prescription, the elevation of "normalcy" and a pronounced wariness about aberration, will be the governing ethos in these columns.

Two reader-letter-driven features appear regularly in the magazine and are generally the final features in the book: a household hints column called the Institute Forum and Dr. Wiley's Question Box. The Institute Forum combines reader-discovered tips (for example, how to use the iron griddle on a stove to freshen stale biscuits and crackers) and institute answers to reader queries ("Are the vitamins in food destroyed when cooked in a pressure cooker?").

Good Housekeeping's solicitation of these questions promises two dollars for every letter printed. These letters come from all corners of the United States, and their questions run the gamut of household advice in the magazine. When placed in dialogue, they also signal the social expectations and possible class aspirations of the *Good Housekeeping* reader; she might worry about the eroded enamel on her bathtub and hope that it does not necessitate a replacement; she might also have a home in which dinnertime guests are present even in her absence, as in this February letter from Mrs. R. V. H. in Massachusetts:

> When either my husband or I have to be absent at a meal I ask one of the children to sit in the vacant seat, look after the welfare of the others at the table, see that the service is carried on as usual, in short, assume the duties of the missing parent. I find the responsibility quite a help in teaching good table manners and thoughtfulness for others, and I was greatly pleased to receive a note from a guest who had dined at the house in my absence, congratulating me upon the pretty dignity with which my five-year-old daughter looked after her comfort and acted as hostess. (88)

Mrs. R. V. H. presents as a clever mother, but also as a socially active woman (she and her husband both dine outside the home fairly regularly); her household dinners are presented in "service," and her guests respond to her hospitality, even in her absence, with thank-you notes. Her letter is printed without comment, standing alone as a "helpful hint." It offers, for the keen *Good Housekeeping* reader, a cluster of significations and an array of behaviors to admire and, possibly, to emulate.

Dr. Wiley's Question Box, a discussion of nutrition and the content of processed foods, became an iconic feature of the magazine, largely because of the prominence of the eponymous adviser. Harvey Washington Wiley, the former chief of the Department of Agriculture's Bureau of Chemistry and the animating figure behind the eventual passage of the Pure Food Law, became the director of the Good Housekeeping Bureau of Food, Sanitation, and Health after his departure from government service in 1912.[46] Wiley's column ran in the magazine from July 1912 through his serious illness at the end of 1929.[47] Wiley's very public career as a crusader for purity in food products made him an excellent fit for the magazine, which offered him the "smallest salary" among several post–public service offers, as he recounts in his autobiography, but which "appealed . . . the most."[48] Wiley relished the "increased freedom of speech" at *Good Housekeeping*, where he saw his role very much as it was before; "What I thought would be good for the people at

CHAPTER ONE

large and for the readers of *Good Housekeeping* in particular, I was at liberty to express in my own way."[49] One of Wiley's main duties at the magazine, he writes, was "the censoring of advertisements submitted to the magazine." As he describes it, the greatest fault came from advertisers who claimed too much for their products.

> This duty has been arduous and highly exciting at times. I have censored the advertisements relating to health, sanitation, foods, beverages, toilet articles, and the like. The work has involved numerous investigations to determine if products advertised were free from injurious substances. One would think that business men engaged in the conduct of a great magazine and wishing to make it financially remunerative would have objected to the rejection of the many articles offered for advertising that have come under my ban! However, they have loyally followed out their contract and *Good Housekeeping* has never advertised any articles under my censorship unless approved by me. I will confess that on not a few occasions I have had very difficult problems to solve. There are so many products which are just on the borderland of acceptance or rejection. I have had very little difficulty with the quality of the product. The principal trouble has been caused by the extravagance which the writers of advertisements think is necessary to introduce into the advertising text. In seventeen years more than a million dollars' worth of advertising offered *Good Housekeeping* in my department has been rejected.[50]

Wiley's reputation for fighting the food industry and his past as a governmental leader gave his pronouncements the imprimatur of authority and worked to authorize the rest of the magazine as well. In the February issue, for example, Wiley authors a lengthy and technical essay decrying the Coolidge administration's disregard of an open letter he had published in the September 1925 issue of the magazine. The essay, "No Pure Food Action—Now," is an explanation, a rebuke, and a call for readerly action; the "now" of the title presumably holding open the possibility for change later, if his *Good Housekeeping* readers organize. Wiley details the government's current inaction and Coolidge's defunding and deplatforming of the Bureau of Chemistry. After describing the strategies he pursued to try to get his concerns heard, Wiley accuses Coolidge and his secretary of agriculture of dereliction of duty, reporting that both took lengthy summer vacations and left the concerns of state behind for assistants and deputies to conduct. The *Good Housekeeping* reader, of course, went on no such vacation in her concern about governmental screening for adulterated foodstuffs—and the government's failure, from the secretary of agriculture to the Supreme

Court, which ruled in favor of several food manufacturers, is no less than a "miscarriage of justice."

A twenty-first-century reader, with preconceived notions about household magazines, might at first doubt that the 1926 reader of *Good Housekeeping* should be expected truly to pay attention to such minutiae. But Wiley goes so far as to offer a legal lesson and a full printing of the Supreme Court ruling, albeit one that he also has to justify as crucial to his audience. "While I am aware of the fact that the readers of GOOD HOUSEKEEPING do not like to read quotations from legal documents, I think I must acquaint them with this opinion of the highest judicial authority in the country. I beg, therefore, to print the exact language of the Supreme Court on this point" (84). It is not an easy read, but the premise of the article is that Wiley is working both for and with the *Good Housekeeping* audience in this matter. The magazine becomes an instrument of his activism, and the readers become activists with him by virtue of their reading. Many of these readers may not have turned to the article's continuation on page 183, choosing instead to turn directly to the more easily digested Dr. Wiley's Question Box, the page number for which is offered at the end of this initial page of Wiley's essay. Nevertheless, their significance to the movement, and their importance as coworkers in the cause, is already established through the candid discussion of governmental failures on this first page of the article.

That monthly Question Box advice column, to which the weary reader of "No Pure Food Action—Now" may have quickly turned, was clearly a major draw for the magazine in general, especially if one is to take at face value the effusive reader testimonials that appear elsewhere in the magazine. "I am a great admirer of Harvey W. Wiley. I was interested in his work before he was connected with *Good Housekeeping*, and would take the magazine for his articles if nothing more," reads one encomium attributed to Mrs. R. V. B. of Silver Creek, New York. Miss W. M. G. of Alapha, Georgia writes that "We are devoted to Mr. Wiley . . . he has personally advised us in making an exceptionally fine boy of a baby who was sick almost the entire first two years of his life" (246). This "personal advice" may have come through the option offered to readers in the end of the "Question Box" feature, where the audience is encouraged to send personal questions, but cautioned that "prescriptional advice can not be given, nor can samples be analyzed" (90). At the same time, the magazine also offers a series of pamphlets that seem to be less personal advice than compendium, "FAQ" offerings.

46 CHAPTER ONE

Another of the testimonials about Wiley highlights his social prominence (and the social prominence of the letter writer!): "I have frequently met him at the — Club, of which I am a member. Dr. Wiley absolutely lives the life, according to which he advises his readers" (246). Mrs. L. G. of Washington, DC is both demonstrating her own authority and praising Wiley's on the basis of his being exactly who he seems to be—he "lives the life" and is therefore an apt adviser. This form of legitimation will come back in the person of Emily Newell Blair, who also will show herself repeatedly as "living the life" of an active, networked reading woman. As we will see throughout the study that follows, Blair's political and social insiderness, like Wiley's, is performed and leveraged throughout her columns to bestow worthiness and legitimacy on her reading recommendations.

The Question Box is a surprisingly technical feature, where many of Wiley's correspondents flex their own education in home economics in challenging advertisements they have seen or even advice given in previous issues of the magazine. The letters frequently use highly technical language: "Is it bad to mix farinaceous foods with protein: for instance, eating meat with potatoes, or meat or eggs with bread?" Wiley's replies are not always as technical: "Evidently, according to some professional dietitians of today, the Lord made a fatal mistake in mixing proteins with starch and sugar in foods, as, for instance, in milk and in cereals. But this having been done in natural foods, then I think we poor cooks should be permitted to do the same thing" (90). On the other hand, in a response just before this one, Wiley explains that malted milk actually has some benefit over regular milk because of the maltose sugars it contains. In another answer he goes into detail about the body's burning of fats and storage of energy from carbohydrates, to contradict a reader who explains that "in all my food classes at the State University I have been taught that vegetable oils were 100 percent fat," and assumes that they would therefore be fattening. The overall feel of the column is respectful, authoritative, and even a little cranky—Wiley is exasperated with the bad information that is out in the world, especially when the bad information comes from university faculty, and with the poor behavior of food producers. "Licorice is a laxative and should not be used as a candy. I do not know anything more harmful to the children than such combinations as these. . . . Will physicians ever learn?" He even takes the time to answer, albeit with some acidity, a query from a reader who has been told that she should swallow sand to improve her digestion and wonders where she might find sand fine enough to avoid injuring her system. "I think if the gentleman whom you quote had in mind the figurative meaning of sand, his approval of its use would be highly beneficial. In common language, the man who is brave, vigorous, and full of pep is said to have 'sand in his craw.' However, the human stomach is not suitable for grinding grains. If you still think you should eat sand, if you will apply to the firms selling building material, you can get the price per ton." Wiley is like a caring and knowing but sarcastic uncle, and he had clearly been in the pure food trenches for years fighting on the side of the consumer. It is no wonder that his column inspired admiration in the *Good Housekeeping* reader.

Personal Advice

Even though Wiley is the sole male voice in the household and maternal advice arena, much of the lifestyle advice elsewhere in the magazine was delivered by prominent male voices. Editor in Chief William Frederick Bigelow led off each issue with a standing column on current social events. In February 1926, he turned his attentions to child labor laws and religious instruction in the public schools. The focus here on children's issues is typical of Bigelow's columns; his service on his local school board and in his local church undergirds most of these columns and get frequent legitimizing mention. This page also frequently serves as a preview for the month's star features; in February 1926, Bigelow's thoughts about religious education promote Charles M. Sheldon's article "The Religious Hunger of Youth." Sheldon, author of *In His Steps: What Would Jesus Do?* was a household name by 1926, in part because *In His Steps* was so widely pirated that, as Erin Smith writes, despite "significant controversy about exactly how many copies it sold, it is likely the best-selling novel of the nineteenth century."[51] The novel tells the stories of twelve congregants in a church who, after failing to prevent the death of an itinerant Christ-like figure, "pledge to take no action for a year without first asking what Jesus would do."[52] Sheldon's authority derives from this already phenomenally popular book; the form of his piece, a series of parables, echoes the novel, and the combination surely rendered his piece even more persuasive than the mere arguments would have managed. He tells several stories about young people coming to him for spiritual advice, frustrated by the traditional forms of religious teaching found in the church, and offers them all as parables in support of his caution that "if we do not

48   CHAPTER ONE

encourage and direct that [spiritual] impulse when it is hungry, the chances
are that the hunger will cease, or will be replaced quickly with the hungers for
power and wealth and pleasure" (24). Sheldon's article is, in other words, an
exemplar of what Erin Smith has termed the Social Gospel form: personal
stories that invite identification and result in personal transformation. Smith
has shown how this worked in the case of *In His Steps*, and it is clearly also
the goal of "The Religious Hunger of Youth."[53]

Several of Sheldon's stories end with his young church members becoming
missionaries either abroad or within the United States. This is one of the
few places in the magazine, outside travel narratives, where race and ethnicity
are addressed, and in all such instances the racial and ethnic minorities in
Sheldon's narrative are very clearly marked as the other. They exist solely to
afford Sheldon's white charges an occasion for their charitable impulses and
to enable the spiritual growth of whites. Sheldon tells of his idea to send his
youth group into a Black neighborhood he dubs "Tennessee Town," because
they were bored simply communing with each other in their home church.
The story of their "missionary" work across the street is couched as heart-
warming and inspirational, not because of any benefit it had on the people
Sheldon's group was ostensibly helping, but because it offers spiritual suste-
nance to young white people. Sheldon reports one of his charges telling him
years later that "I believe those Sunday evening services in Tennessee Town
in the heart of that bit of darkest Africa gave me my first real knowledge of
what Jesus meant when He said, 'All of you are Brothers'" (188). The missionary metaphor is literalized in this recollection and held up as an admirable
revelation.

Sheldon does call out the church community in general, and particularly its
older members, for having "too much race prejudice" and celebrates his youth
group's "mission" to Tennessee Town as an inspiring story of faith's power to
encourage otherwise unimaginable acts. "Of what value is religion if it can not
inspire the believer to do the unusual thing and overcome the insurmountable
barriers that have been reared by the centuries of cruelty and pride between the
different races?" (188). Perhaps inspired readers will themselves go out for social
settlement work, although in this case Sheldon's writing seems less directed
toward that type of action than toward parental lobbying for more religious
education in public schools. The only identifications available here are with
white congregants, as no Black Tennessee Town residents are identified with
any specificity or given any interiority. Ultimately, the article only reinforces

the alterity of the Tennessee Town residents in the *Good Housekeeping* reader's mind, although it does model the application of Social Gospel–style reading practices, and continues to practically erase the difference between the ways readers should "use" fiction and nonfiction in the magazine.

Another prominent, best-selling Christian author, who was incidentally also the principal of an advertising agency, is featured in this issue of the magazine, and he is featured even more prominently than Sheldon. Bruce Barton was himself a guru of the middlebrow, not only as the founder of a major advertising agency (BBD&O) but also as the author of a book that was one of the pillars of interwar middlebrow culture: *The Man Nobody Knows*. This nonfiction bestseller portrayed Jesus as "The Founder of Modern Business," a chief executive who started a company with only twelve low-level managers. The book achieved iconic status within American culture, and, as Erin Smith has argued, became "part of the "lived religion of scores of ordinary Americans,"[54] with Barton's books considered "equipment for living."[55] Barton's Jesus was, Barbara Ryan reminds us, not just brawny (although he certainly was that) but also sociable, "the most popular dinner guest in Jerusalem."[56] Barton's translation of the life of Jesus into the gospel of business also redefined "masculine selfhood" as "the persuasive impact one had on others, rather than ... the monadic integrity of self-reliance."[57]

Barton's leadoff feature in the February 1926 issue, the provocatively titled "Do Too Many People Marry?" benefits from the *Good Housekeeping* reader's certain paratextual familiarity with his work. It may not have qualified Barton to offer marital advice per se, but insofar as his column is primarily concerned with realigning men's outlooks to the long term, he would have clout as the man who made Jesus a man's man. He would also be easily associated in readers' minds with the genre of representative biography, a staple genre in the *Good Housekeeping* editorial mix and one into which this article easily fits. Barton explains that this piece, with its atypical subject matter, came about after a prior article on salary inequalities between men of similar experience, education, and dedication resulted in the editors of *Good Housekeeping* receiving a flurry of letters—from *men*—testifying to the problems particularly faced by those who are married with wives and children to support. "In the old days," Barton writes, "people confided their problems to their pastors or their parents or each other; now the editor of a national magazine is the recipient of confidences more intimate than his readers would ever think of making to anybody else" (19). After reproducing two representative letters, Barton explains that he showed them to an "eminently successful and perhaps a trifle 'hard-boiled'" friend who offers a quick and bold appraisal: "There ought to be a law forbidding any couple to marry until they have at least $5000 in the bank" (163). Their further debate over this proposition, in the form of a dialogue, takes up three subsequent columns, after which Barton, apparently convinced of his friend's proposition, offers four anecdotes of couples who married "too soon" and then closes with "six commonsense conclusions on which most of us might agree."

The article is not immediately prescriptive. Its persuasive power, rather, is built up through narrative examples. Even the initial debate, during which the performatively naïve questioner Barton offers sample reader letters to a friend for assessment, is written as a story; the friend has a distinct character ("eminently successful and perhaps a trifle 'hard-boiled'") and Barton himself becomes a character in the piece, arguing for the exception of the clergyman who will never have $5000 but who nevertheless clearly should marry and have children because of the preponderance of clergymen's sons among the prominent thinkers, businessmen, and politicians of the day. The stories that follow his conversion are narrated with no shortage of pathos, as in this story of Ed Morrell and Jean Pearson's bad decision to marry precipitately:

> Everything might have worked out all right if it had not been for his visit home at Christmas time. Just what happened to Jean and [Ed] we can only guess, but somehow the holiday spirit and the full moon combined to banish caution from their eager hearts. They counted back over the long years of their engagement and forward through the years of waiting that must elapse before he would be a self-supporting member of the bar, and they began to indulge themselves in those incredible budgets with which youthful hopes have so often done violence to arithmetic ... and so, against the warnings of all the old folks, they were married on New Year's day and started their life together in New York. (167–68)

The foreshadowing is as thick as the Christmas Eve moon. This story invites identification and empathy and then reorients the reader toward a critical stance: these two young people made a poor choice. It is hardly a surprise when Ed and Jean's baby, "a loveable, laughing little chap who never had a chance," dies after an unhealthy infancy confined to their "crowded, stuffy little home" (168). As go Ed and Jean, so go Lillian and John, whose attempt to live with John's mother resulted in Lillian having a nervous breakdown.

But these stories are countered by a third, of a couple who married suddenly, across a class barrier, and too young, under a "cloud of parental disapproval," but who managed to make things work; they "carried out their program just as they had planned it, living in an inexpensive part of town, saving a little each month, going ahead with their reading and studies. And they have won" (170). Because of the counterexample, Barton refuses to offer any rigid rules for when to marry, but he does go on to offer "six commonsense conclusions on which most of us might agree," recognizing that they will be "debated, and perhaps refused, around the million firesides to which this magazine goes," and might "give rise, no doubt, to several thousand letters to the editor" (170).[58]

The guidelines are less important, for my purposes here, than the spirit in which they are being offered and the general shape of Barton's advice column, which are both echoed precisely in Blair's reading advice column. The narrative examples Barton offers track closely with Blair's practice of offering representative readers at the opening of each of her columns. Barton's general principles, too, and his expectations that they might be debated or refuted, are similar to Blair's general guidelines for reading; she does not put on the persona of a prescriptive adviser, as we will see, but fashions herself a concierge to her readers. This stated respect for the preformed opinions of the audience even as advice is being offered is a hallmark of the editorial content of the magazine and, when promoted by Blair, helps her to destigmatize middlebrow culture in general.

Representative Biographies/Autobiographical Writing

A frequent figure in *Good Housekeeping* throughout the 1920s and 1930s was Frances Parkinson Keyes, a contributing editor to the magazine and a close friend of Blair's. I will further address their professional and personal relationship, and the networks it illuminates, in chapter 4; as we shall see, Blair frequently recommends Keyes's fiction and nonfiction writings in her columns. She is able to easily reference Keyes's travels because the details of those journeys were presented almost monthly for the *Good Housekeeping* audience. The February 1926 installment of Keyes's around-the-world travelogue is typical of her contributions and demonstrates the way she draws readers into a parasocial relationship with herself, her family, and her friends.

Written like a letter to an intimate friend, Keyes's "Pages from My Scrapbook" is addressed "Dear Sue" in the opening and signed at the close with a reproduction of Keyes's signature. In the letter Keyes narrates an afternoon pasting invitations and memorabilia into a scrapbook, describing all the events she has attended on a state visit to Tokyo. The article features frequent reminders of the intimate premise: "The paste on the Asabukis' dinner invitation has dried nicely to the scrap-book page while I have been writing you about the function itself; and now it is time to put in another card" (200); "Another letter with the Gaimusho stamp from the admirable Mr. Kishi! It fits perfectly on that page beside the invitation to luncheon at the Maple Club" (203). Keyes is a particular friend of the *Good Housekeeping* reader, inviting the reader into her presence during the opulent events she attends and in her private space while processing the events. The *Good Housekeeping* reader sits beside her while she uses chopsticks successfully ("'You deserve a diploma,' murmurs the Vice Minister" [203]), while she experiences the "peace that passeth all understanding" in a Japanese garden, and while she converses privately with the Princess Higashi Fushimi. She offers "translations" to help her reader process the Japanese scenes she relates and even acknowledges the necessity of translating stateside experiences among regions, as in one striking discussion of the tea ceremony, which is worth citing at length:

> As the peace of the garden had carried me back for a moment from Japan to Spain, so the ceremonial in the dim corner carried me from the Japanese tea-house to a New England kitchen—a kitchen with the floor scrubbed white, and a red-checked cloth on the table, and geraniums growing in a sunny window, and a kettle steaming and singing on the newly polished stove; the immaculate, empty kitchen of Saturday afternoon, with a pot of beans in the oven for supper, and no other preparation necessary for two hours at least. Do you have kitchens anything like that in Kentucky? Probably not; probably you never came into one, after scraping the snow off your overshoes, and shaking the snow off your mittens, and standing up your sled by the side of the house, and calling to Cousin Agnes or Cousin Mary to know if you and the others—for in my case there were about a dozen small boys and girls in the "old guard"—couldn't have something nice and hot? ... But you have had, I am sure, something that corresponded to this—something that made you feel, even when you were very young, how beautiful a simple and necessary thing could be. And so I know that you will understand the echoes which the tea ceremonial sent sounding through my soul, and my joy that a great nation has shown the wisdom of so distinguishing a humble and ordinary act. (205; ellipses in original)

In this passage Keyes moves from a Japanese teahouse to a New England kitchen, from adulthood to childhood, from diplomatic wife to domestic goddess to girlhood, and then back out again to comment on national cultures. She acknowledges potential differences between New England and Kentucky, which might indeed be as profound as the differences between Japan and New England, but asserts that all have a "corresponding" scene that impresses upon one the beauty of a "simple and necessary thing." The image of a comfortable, warm, and *clean* kitchen, with flourishing window boxes, dinner preparations complete, and a few hours of leisure to be had by the homemaker, would of course be heavenly not just for the child coming in from the cold outdoors but also for the homemaker herself—for any *Good Housekeeping* reader, given the premium the magazine places on efficient and aesthetically pleasing homemaking. Keyes's ability to envision this scene ties her to the *Good Housekeeping* reader because she recognizes that the work *has been done*, and by someone who now can look forward to two hours without any work to do for dinner. It is not, in other words, a magically cleaned kitchen, a magically prepared meal. Keyes has benefitted from this work being done for her (as a child) and she, it seems, has done this work as an adult, and can therefore appreciate the glory of the *earned* moment of pause. She may be dining with diplomats, but she is "one of us." Similarly, the Japanese tea ceremony elevates and celebrates the work of tea preparation. The national importance of that ritual is something for Keyes and her readers to admire and renders Japan an ideal nation. Japan's priority is *Good Housekeeping*'s priority: "distinguishing a humble and ordinary act."

Keyes also invites her reader into the private spaces of her domestic life, like the car when she is driving home and discussing the evening's entertainment with her husband. "'Well,' said Henry as we drove home, 'if I ever hope to have a better time than *that*! . . . Do you think I can hold these flowers straight till we get them upstairs? Tough luck if I couldn't, wouldn't it?'" (203). Keyes's family's frequent appearances in the letter serve to ground Keyes's exceptional experiences in the everyday; she might be having tea with princesses, but she still has a goofy husband and a silly young son. The "boys" also throw into relief her more sophisticated appreciations of the things she is experiencing. Whereas she (and by extension her addressee, the *Good Housekeeping* reader) can recognize transcendence in the Japanese garden or in a meal perfectly rendered, Henry and her son offer a comically down-to-earth perspective that saves the piece from becoming too reverent. Indeed, Japan's alterity resides in the lack of irreverence Keyes finds there— Japanese women, she remarks repeatedly, are impervious to age, to stress, to time. She offers one of her hosts a poem that likens a Japanese woman to a finely wrought lacquered box; like the box, which has an interior design that "is perfect, whether it is to be seen or not," Keyes argues that a Japanese woman's "greatest beauties . . . are not carelessly revealed" (207). This may be an impressive ideal, but it is not the governing ethos of Keyes's own letter, in which she (ostensibly) reveals all of her own thoughts about her visits, even confessing moments when she feels awkward, complains about the weather, or fears she has gotten lost going to an appointment. It is also far from the sauciness of Keyes's son, presented affectionately at the close of her letter when he calls her out for more rainy-day sightseeing: "The scrap-book is finished—for the time being—and the boys have come busting into my room. 'Put on a raincoat and a bathing suit and a pair of rubber boots and take your umbrella,' says Larry, 'an c'mon. We gotta go out and see Kyoto'" (208). Keyes's proud transcription of her son's contractions, and her reveling in his "busting," rollicking behavior, separates her from the tranquil grace of the Japanese scenes she has described. That she ends on this note returns her and her reader to an American sensibility, which can in true Orientalist fashion appreciate the beauty of the other but ultimately privileges rambunctious bonhomie. She is, indeed, one of "us," and the *Good Housekeeping* reader, presumably, likewise leaves the letter with a reentry into a bustling domestic space . . . or can envision herself doing so. These reminders of intimacy will be echoed in Blair's columns, in which she repeatedly mentions her midwestern home, her husband, her friends, and her children.

The February 1926 issue also contains a biography of Florence Easton, an opera singer who overcame early illness and considerable death in her family (both parents and an infant child) but is still an accomplished singer and has a "sunny disposition." The latter is the moral of her story. While Easton tells her biographer that her disposition "is no credit to me. I was born with it," the article argues that Easton's triumph is her maintaining this outlook: "But how many of us were born with the sunny heart of childhood—and how few of us have kept it in our mature years! Perhaps it is no credit to be *born* happy—but to *keep* happy—that is the task that tries the metal [*sic*] of every one of us." And again:

> It is a simple secret, the formula by which she has won through to peace and poise—simple as all great things are. But it takes a deathless will to use it. And that formula is only this—to live each day as it comes, without fear for the future, without regret for the past. Our days would not be so bad if we did not load them with the sorrows of other days and the apprehension of bad days to come. Live in the present, and life will change its face for you. (160)

A paean to mindfulness may seem disingenuous in the midst of editorial and advertising content that might spark anxiety about one's home and homemaking practices. Just beside this passage, in fact, is an advertisement for metal lath that might make one worry about the material *underneath* one's walls: "Your finest draperies, your most cherished pictures, your distinctive furniture,—all are lost against the ugliness of cracked, unsightly walls" (160). Short of a major construction or renovation project, it would be impossible to heed the warnings of this advertisement or to truly embrace its philosophy ("after all is said and done, the walls and ceilings of your home reflect its Beauty and Permanence"). A *Good Housekeeping* reader might well process this ad as an extension of the magazine's vision of "society as some people wish it could be."[59] Like the article on home building techniques, this ad is about the education of the homeowner, not necessarily an imperative to action. And still, the juxtaposition of concerns about metal lath and psychological "metal" can't help but be mutually reinforcing.

The extensive biographical (and semibiographical) material in *Good Housekeeping* primes Blair's use of representative biography in her columns. Just as she samples from and feeds into the narrative modes of the advertisements, the advice columns, and the magazine fiction, Blair freely adopts this genre by penning biographical sketches of model readers in her columns, Blair asks her readers to identify themselves with and in these sketches, so that they may follow book recommendations that are sure to satisfy.

Well Plotted and Smoothly Written

In 1933, William F. Bigelow attributed *Good Housekeeping*'s continued circulation success not to the magazine's consumer advice content, nor to its living advice, but to the large proportion of fiction in its pages. "I haven't the slightest hesitation in saying that it is next to impossible for any magazine to achieve a circulation of more than half a million without basing it upon good fiction, and that has been the policy which I have consistently followed during the last fifteen years."[60] The fiction that appears in *Good Housekeeping* in the 1920s and 1930s flows seamlessly into and out of editorial and advertising content that closely mimicked fiction. Visually, fiction and nonfiction are practically indistinguishable in the front of the book, and the continuations of fictional pieces are interspersed with continuations of the nonfictional pieces and, of course, surrounded by narrative-heavy advertisements. Thematically, the concerns of *Good Housekeeping* fiction were also the concerns of its nonfiction: "In fiction, [editor Bigelow] looks for stories that reflect the fundamental interests of intelligent women—romantic excitement in far places, and quieter adventures of home and community life—stories of courage and cheerfulness, constructive stories, well-plotted and smoothly written." Bigelow was apparently a hands-on editor when it came to fiction: "He studies each story, and makes many suggestions for improvement."[61] Presumably even the prominent authors who appeared in its pages—John Galsworthy, Ellen Glasgow, Kathleen Norris, and Gene Stratton Porter, among many others—were subject to Bigelow's editorial suggestions.

The February 1926 issue includes five short stories and three installments of serialized novels at various stages in their runs. All but one of these fiction offerings feature young, unmarried female protagonists; as mentioned above, the majority of *Good Housekeeping* subscribers seem to have been married women, but several surveys do suggest that the magazine had more young, single readers than others of the Big Six. These heroines all triumph independently over adversity, but their reward for doing so is always a fulfilling romance that leads to a glad renunciation of independence in favor of marriage. The sole married protagonist in this issue wrestles with a midlife crisis in which she misses her life before marriage; she and her husband both come to value their union at the end of the story and their marriage is saved. Somewhat surprisingly, the fiction all addresses dimensions of female property ownership, particularly the attendant difficulties of women owning their own land or inheriting great wealth. These are stories of intergenerational inheritance that code their protagonists as US-born, nonimmigrant, and white, but in general the protagonists feel uncomfortable with sudden alterations of fortune. While the promise of financial security from the sudden inheritance or the fortunate marriage seems initially attractive, wealth tends to be more of a burden than a boon. The happy ending generally involves an abdication of wealth, or at least a significant diminishment of the inheritance to a comfortable sufficiency rather than a jackpot.

An inheritance is at risk in the featured fiction for this month, the first installment of a new serialized mystery/romance novel, *The Wondering Moon* by George Weston. The story of a young woman whose estranged father dies in a mysterious accident, having uncharacteristically squandered thousands of dollars and leaving the family surprisingly destitute, *The Wondering Moon* is a page-turner. The serial is touted on its first page as "an old-fashioned one-ring love-story with a lost fortune and a mysterious accident on the side" (14), and in general it fulfills those promises; the heroine does end up with her dashing cousin Victor, despite his occasional acts undermining her attempts to salvage her inheritance. The "mysterious accident" that caused her father's untimely death ends up not being a result of murder but of an actual accident, despite the occasional suggestions that it was premeditated. While many of the mysteries do not get resolved by the end of the serial's run in July 1926 (who set fire to the country house and the glen? What happened to the $65,000 of which Ethel's father had been trustee—did he in fact squander all of that money and why? How was it feasible for the destitute family to live in a cave for so long?), one of them does, and the heroine is restored to a portion of her father's money and is primed at the end of the story to marry her stepcousin, who plans to purchase her rural property and turn it into a limestone quarry: "If you *did* sell the place, the Cottage would go to help build other cottages, and factories, and bridges, and all sorts of useful things—improving the country wherever it went, building it up, giving work to people who needed it" (116). While flirting with the more radical possibilities of female inheritance, *The Wondering Moon* finally settles its heroine down to a marriage that will also see the dissolution of her family lands, but this conclusion is written as a happy resolution, not a travesty or a tragedy.

One of the two other serial novels included in this issue, Temple Bailey's *The Blue Window*,[62] similarly sees its heroine embracing her mother's ethical training and rejecting the money and social ambitions of her superficial wealthy father. Hildegarde Carew is the heroine of this piece, who was brought up by her mother and two aunts on a farm in northern Virginia. On the death of her mother, Hildegarde is taken by her estranged father into cosmopolitan society, where she befriends a young woman, Sally, who is about to marry a wealthy man against her wishes. Sally ultimately chooses to leave her wealthy older fiancé, Winslow, at the altar in favor of her relatively less well-off (but still propertied) younger suitor Merriweather. At this point, Winslow tries to blackmail Hildegarde into marrying him by promising to ruin her wealthy, until just recently estranged father, if she does not. The installment for February 1926 sees this dynamic coming to a head, ending on a cliffhanger with Hildegarde's refusal and Winslow's promise to confront her father. But the cliffhanger is resolved very quickly by the header of the final installment in the March 1926 issue: "Hildegarde finds that her little silver key unlocks the door to happiness."[63] This key is, of course, the key to the house purchased by Crispin, Hildegarde's former beau in northern Virginia—and this header therefore completely gives away the ending. Even

58 CHAPTER ONE

before beginning the concluding chapters the *Good Housekeeping* reader knows that somehow Winslow is disposed with and Hildegarde ends up with her preinheritance beau. That Hildegarde must renounce her father is a surprise but is entirely consistent with the general message of the fiction in the magazine; she tells him, defiantly, that "love doesn't mean being weak because others ask it. It means being hard because one is right,"[64] and leaves Baltimore to return to the farm and, eventually, to Crispin. And as it turns out, she does so just in time to save the spirits of her two aunts, who were just beginning to see themselves as elderly and useless: "They needed youth about them and high spirits. They had no initiative when it came to making new interests ... they had lost all that had given zest to their lives."[65] Hildegarde's return is morally, spiritually, and romantically right for her, and a salvation for her aunts. She has lost her cosmopolitan lifestyle and the wealth of her father, but she has gained a home and a husband and reconnected with the spirit of her deceased mother.

A similar move is at work in "A Peacock in the Dooryard," which the *Good Housekeeping* title writers dub "Lois Seyster-Montross's charming story of a poor little rich girl and a man whose motto was, 'love me, love my house'" (27). In this story, the heroine, Meg Faraway, has wealth and charm, and the man, her lawyer, is exhausted by overwork. They are early at odds, so it is no surprise when he faints, and she whisks him away for a springtime drive in the country in her limousine. They end up at a cottage for which she proclaims a passion—she wants to buy it! He avers that the owner would not sell it and that moreover she is not the right person to live in that house: "The earth cares nothing about money. ... Did you ever think that the earth can not be bought? It belongs to those who till it. The rich man's estate does not belong to him, but to the gardener who tends the ground with his hands" (227). Of course, it turns out that this is the lawyer's summer house, to which he someday hopes to retire, and he is the careful gardener. His love for his garden makes her think, "If I could only live here in this serene place ... and do these same quiet, gentle things to the earth that he has done, perhaps this restlessness and ache of lonely spring would go away, and I could be happy for a little while" (228).

He reluctantly agrees to rent the house to her for a month so she can try out this experiment, but she is not a skilled homemaker. Her first solo dinner would be laughable to the *Good Housekeeping* reader: "She bought a great many things at the little grocery store, all she could think of: tabasco sauce, curry powder, camembert cheese, mayonnaise, paprika, bread and butter, and eggs" (228). She can't start a fire or boil eggs, much less keep an elaborate garden thriving. As she adjusts to living in the house and becomes a passable gardener, she reads her lawyer's secret poetry and writes him long letters in response. Inevitably, vicariously living in his dream house leads Meg to fall in love with the aptly named Charles Meadow, more particularly after she discovers a villanelle he has written about her. After he does not respond to her letters, Meg feels rejected; in her anger she invites her fast-living friends to a raucous party during which the cottage is trashed. When she, regretting the destruction, meets back up with Charles in the ruined cottage, she learns that he had not written because he was too busy trying and failing to save her fortune. She objects, "I would a million times rather . . . have had you answer my letters than . . . save a million. . . . And if I can't buy you new things . . . I can at least stay here and work hard and do my best in the garden" (240). Meg and her lawyer-cum-lover will, presumably, make this cottage a pastoral haven; he may still need to work, but he will be able to return to this space in the country to recharge on a more regular basis.

Also retreating from the city is Miriam, the heroine of "Her Job." The story opens with a family reunion at home, during which Miriam feels left out because she is the only one of her siblings not married or engaged. She has instead been working and living in New York while her friends and family have followed a more traditional path, staying close to the family home. Though she feels an outsider to her family, Miriam knows that her father is proud of her: she overhears him telling a friend, "Miriam earns her living, and buys bonds and things—sort of nice for the old man!" (114). After his sudden death, she is similarly surprised and pleased by the message in his will: "To my daughter Miriam I make no gift of money—not that I hold her in less affection, but because I have absolute confidence in her ability to look after herself" (118). Her family expects Miriam to give up her job to look after her mother, but she refuses: "Father wanted me to keep on with it. That was the last thing he said to me" (120). The story ends, however, with Miriam giving up her job "of my own free will" to marry the one man she has met who appreciates and is curious about her work. He has even hesitated to declare his love because he knows she loves her job. He is about to leave her behind in New York, where he has come to visit and see her work and her apartment life, when she runs after him to declare, "Oh Russ . . . you don't know anything about women. A job's a wonderful thing, but it isn't in it with the man you love" (123). The denouement tries to assert that Miriam's independent mindset will maintain itself through her marriage; she and Russ both refuse to speak disparagingly of her job when her sisters try to dismiss it, and he seems to be, still, the only person aside from her father who holds its memory sacred. Miriam's renunciation of her job is of a piece with Hildegarde and Meg Faraway's renunciations of their inheritances and Ethel's renunciation of her family lands.

Throughout these fiction pieces one finds a dominant pastoral strain; while the country may be a place of relative poverty, it is a place of beauty, meaningful work, and spiritual depth. In *The Blue Window*, for example, Hildegarde relishes farm labor: "It was a picturesque crop, and Hildegarde rather enjoyed the days" (210). This pastoral is *not*, mind you, antimaterialistic; Hildegarde is still attracted to the things in her father's beautifully appointed home, reflecting in a moment of loneliness at the farm that "she found herself missing *things*, not people. There was no one at Round Hill, not even her father, whose companionship seemed vital at the moment. The old aunts did very well indeed for company. She missed, as it were, the stage properties—the crystal cat, the bronze turtle, the silver pheasants on the table, Delia's crisp ginghams, Sampson's delectable trays, the scarlet-coated ancestor in the library" (213). She is similarly enticed by Crispin's description of the house he has precipitately purchased for the two of them (precipitately because he has not even proposed to her, and she gives no indication that she would accept such a proposal) and signals her eventual acquiescence to his plans by mentally furnishing it when she goes back to her father's house in Baltimore.

"Emmy and the Door," a short story by Jay Gelzer, is another agrarian romance, but in the "local color" mode. The dialect spoken by the characters signals an Appalachian setting; the title character, Emmy, is looking after her ailing (consumptive) "Pap," who promises her that "Toreckly I'll be well enough ter ride down ter the settlement an' get you a stepmaw, Emmy" (20). Emmy and her father, originally from "Kentuck," are neighbors to Condie Neale, who had previously owned all of the valley before their arrival. Emmy and her father had fled an epidemic of tuberculosis in Kentucky, selling their old farmstead for too little money to someone who knew that there was coal under the land (Emmy's father apparently did not know this). Condie, a brooding Heathcliff type, had avoided Emmy and her Pap until the latter's (heavily foreshadowed) death. They think it is because they are "white trash," but Condie was just reeling from being jilted by another woman.

After Pap dies, Emmy's old horse dies, half of her chickens die and the other half stop laying eggs, and she slips and breaks her leg in the snow.

Things are, in short, bleak—she had refused a gift of grain from Condie in the fall, and she refuses now in the winter to go to him for help, even though he is the only other human anywhere near. Emmy keeps thinking of her father's homespun wisdom, "if you made out the best you could, even if you got up against a blank wall, a door would open and let you through" (257), but she refuses to think of Condie's help as that opening door. Finally, however, when Emmy is near death, Condie comes to her rescue; he sets her leg and then confesses his love for her: "You poor, hurt, proud young thing! You're for all the world like something wild caught in a trap, and I'm going to take you out of it." Emmy's story feels more like a "local color" tale than the stories of Miriam, Meg, and Ethel; where those three heroines are modern women living in relatively developed locales, Emmy's dialect, her Appalachian setting, and her tubercular father work to distance her story from that of the mainstream *Good Housekeeping* reader. Because the story is not as "realistic" as the others, its sudden resolution is more forgivable. We will see, when we turn to Blair's recommendations, the kind of latitude Blair gives to "local color" stories and the acceptable uses to which she believes they can be put.

Similarly unrealistic, although ostensibly set in modern Italy, France, and New York, is "*Perella*: A Novel with a Little Cinderella Heroine and a Hero Who Just Could Not Help Being Prince Charming." The February 1926 installment is the third of the series, which began back in December 1925. This is therefore the third serial novel in this issue of the magazine; throughout the 1920s and early 1930s, there are usually two or three serials overlapping in the magazine at any given time. In this installment of *Perella*, the eponymous heroine's secret fiancé, Anthony, has been invited to travel to Brittany with his wealthy, widowed patroness, and Perella is going to be abandoned in scorching-hot Rome for the summer. He goes because he believes that this residence will make his artistic fortunes, and he does not want to be a starving artist: "I'm not going to be content, Perella *mia*, with love in a cottage. I want passion in a palace. I want everything!" Perella's rejoinder: "She sighed with a sense of death in her soul. 'I'm afraid, Anthony dear, my everything—' she marked on the table-cloth a pitiful little circle with her forefinger—'is too small for you'" (126). Perella is ready from the beginning to renounce wealth for love.

Anthony and Perella are thus separated by Anthony's ambitions, and eventually both marry older wealthy patrons; by the June 1926 installment, the two couples meet up again and the older partners suspect that the younger pair is still in love and meant to be together. They cede the field by pretending

62   CHAPTER ONE

to run away together, and in August 1926 the *Good Housekeeping* reader is told on the first page of the serial installment that "William J. Locke's brilliant novel ends with the best man and the best woman winning—each other."[66] In a twist, the title character learns of the older couple's sacrifice and returns to her older husband, Sylvester; the young cad Anthony does not go back to his older wife, Beatrice, and he is the loser of the piece: "Beatrice stood before [Perilla] tragic, heroic, beautiful, facing life with queen-like courage in acceptance of inexorable verdict. Silvester and Beatrice loomed before her as the real people. Anthony melted into an abstract force that had racked her with delicious and unprofitable thrills. There was no longer an Anthony."[67] The best man was Sylvester, the best woman, apparently, Perella; the older Beatrice, while noble in her loss, presumably should have known better than to try to secure the affections of a younger roué like Anthony. While this is a "Cinderella story," Perella's consistent preferencing of faithfulness over passion or wealth is the thing that helps her end up wealthy, married, and happy.

Stella Raymer in "The Smell of the Sawdust" finds that her renunciation was offered to one who would not honor the sacrifice. She had been a famous European music hall performer but gave up the stage and performing in order to become a more proper wife to Ben in Evanston, Illinois, outside Chicago. The story opens during a dinner party, where Stella is playing a classical piece for the after-meal entertainment of the group while watching her husband flirt with another woman. Piqued, she launches into one of her old vaudeville songs after one of the other guests unwittingly mentions that he had been a fan of a forgotten performer (he does not recognize Stella as the performer until after she begins to sing the original composition). Stella's reveal is not popular with Ben, although it is popular with his social milieu, and Stella feels justified in reverting to type: "If Ben was going to affront her love by his attitude toward another woman, she would stab his pride by resumption of the self she had renounced for him" (243). She had loved her life as Stella Sanborn: "What a joy it was, after all, the knowledge that she had it in her to make men and women forget for the time any world but the one she created for them! What glories the old life had held, with all its hardships, the life she had so willingly given up for Ben!" (244). Her old manager comes to watch her perform for a charity function and invites her back to the old life. Furious with her husband for his flirtations, and chafing at his proprieties, Stella takes up the offer on a trial basis. She is unable to make her sets successful, however, because her whole heart is not in the performance. She now thinks of her singing as a "job in which she was striving to do her best," not "the breathless thing of glory which it had been" (248). Her marriage foundering, she knows that she could go back to the stage if she had to support herself, but she no longer wants to.

Fortunately, Ben comes to see her final show—she sings her signature tune with all the sorrow she feels for her loss, and he realizes that he does in fact love her. She readily returns to him, although the final line suggests that the stage still appeals: "Kiss me . . . so that I won't smell the sawdust" (248). Of course, there is no chance that a *Good Housekeeping* story would end in a divorce and a return to the stage, nor is there any chance that there is supposed to be ambiguity in Stella's ready return to domestication. Her brief stint on the stage merely served to make her caddish husband realize that he had been acting ridiculously and that she was what he wanted all along.

All these narratives provide a marital resolution, but the ultimate goal of each heroine is not the marriage but the self-actualization that precedes, enables, and is finally fully realized within the marriage. This is the hallmark of what Maureen Honey has called the "New Woman romance."[68] While Honey's survey of a broad swath of women's magazines finds a not insignificant number of stories that end in vocational happiness without marriage, that tends not to be the direction of the *Good Housekeeping* story. "Her Job," for example, does not end with an employed heroine—her success comes from finding a man who would have accepted her as a working woman and that acceptance enables her to renounce her job in favor of his partnership. The ultimate goal of all of these stories is to justify and celebrate the transformation of the independent girl into the competent housewife, to validate the renunciation of a life of independence because true self-actualization can only be achieved through marriage, motherhood, and homemaking. The skills that all of these heroines hone in their bachelorette days will serve them well when they need to make the difficult decisions about aluminum siding, or lunch meat, or nursery windows—but there is no question that the latter decisions are the more crucial or that each of these heroines will ultimately become *Good Housekeeping* readers.

The final story in the February 1926 issue has no romance plot; it is a "humorous" piece, which offers racist stereotypes as the basis for humor and presents a highly flawed white woman as the savior of a group of brown children. "Lonch for Two" is set in a classroom filled with Latinx students (coded by their names and the dialect in which their speech is represented). The story focuses on a young white teacher who first tries to politely overlook the substandard hygiene of one of her students and then inadvertently shames him into correcting his habits. Abundio Lopez is the intransigent pupil who seemingly cannot recognize his own shortcomings until his generous gift of a cake is repeatedly, and clumsily, rejected by his teacher. First she tries simply to ignore it, then to feed it to a dog (Abundio sees the dog eating it, rescues it, and returns it to the teacher—apparently unaware that this is unappetizing), then to hide it in the bottom of the class cupboard (two of her other students find it when they are cleaning out the cupboard). When Abundio finally realizes why his teacher is rejecting the gift, he flees the classroom with a bar of soap to scrub himself clean in the nearby stream. Returning to class nearly unrecognizable (aside from the remaining rings of dirt around his eyes), he finds his teacher contrite. She invites him for "lunch for two," and they eat ice cream and cake while he comments on the uncleanliness of his classmates.

The incompetence of the young teacher, Miss Lipscomb, provides some of the piece's supposed humor. She is apparently less than fit for her teaching duties after a long night of partying; after gossiping at her desk while the class squirms impatiently in their seats, her fellow teacher Miss Winters tells her, "Well, if you will dance all night and then sleep until eight-thirty, don't expect me to be sorry for you" (75). This is clearly a young teacher who is not particularly engaged by her classroom assignment, who is not intending to teach school or to abide for any length of time in this community. The *Good Housekeeping* reader is not expected to condemn her for this, however, but to use it as context for her clumsy dealings with Abundio's cake offering. She is not a parent or a skilled teacher and is graceless rather than malicious; the reader (particularly if she is older and a mother) can laugh at these mistakes. Abundio is not to be pitied; while he is not entirely an "unfeeling, noninnocent nonchild[]," [69] his emotions are represented as transient and a little silly, like his reverence for his incompetent teacher. Ultimately it doesn't matter if she has embarrassed her student; his quick conversion to cleanliness is played for laughs in the same way that adaptations of *Uncle Tom's Cabin* offered a Topsy who was comic relief, a "de-childed juvenile" incapable of feeling pain or shame. [70]

The other children offer their "Ticher" foods from plates that are "reassuringly clean," and she eats their food reluctantly: "Hungrily the Third Grade watched as she broke off a minute portion. They marveled at her self-restraint" (76). Watching her eating through the eyes of her adoring class heightens the humor here—the *Good Housekeeping* reader will easily understand that she eats only a small amount because she is afraid that she will not like the food. Not all of the children are dirty, but the teacher *is* hesitant with their food offerings because they are foreign—"tamales" and "enchiladas." She is additionally hesitant with Abundio's offering because he licks his hands and then touches her food; *Good Housekeeping* readers know that her fears are not misplaced, as they have been shown how he dropped part of it on the floor and then picked it back up and returned it to the plate; how he carried it through the streets unwrapped. He is completely unsocialized and is thus an outlier in the classroom—but not by much! Abundio acts like a third-grade boy would be expected to act, but his dirtiness is clearly presented here as a function both of his youth and of his race. His eventual reformation is supposed to be read as a charming story of the unwitting positive influence a pleasant young schoolteacher can have on her pupils regardless of her teacherly skill; the *Good Housekeeping* reader who understands more about children and who has a kindly but critical distance on the follies of youth (young women will make bad choices about dancing too late at night!) can smile indulgently at the conclusion and congratulate herself on her own offspring's superior cleanliness.

"Lonch for Two" locates the teacher's reformatory success in bodily and alimentary cleanliness, which was of course a preoccupation of the magazine's child-rearing advice. The bodies of the white children of *Good Housekeeping* readers were the focus of constant attention, as we have already seen—the things they were putting into their bodies and the things they were able to do with their bodies were constantly monitored and programmed by the watchful white mother. Abundio serves as a stand-in for these white children, and his white teacher's success in bringing him up to a certain level of cleanliness mirrors the white mother's work and plays it as humor.[71]

The other significant nonwhite figures in the February 1926 issue are also children. James Swinnerton's *Kiddies of the Canyon Country*, a long-running regular feature, trades in racist caricatures of Native American children.[72] Like "Lonch for Two," *Kiddies* demonstrates that "Progressive Era fixation with race was intertwined with contemporary obsessions about childhood"[73]; there are no adults in this recurring comic, just children who are the darkened versions of the apple-cheeked sledders on the magazine cover. One child tells wild animals that his father can beat them up. Another is surprised to see a blonde white girl with curly hair ("Her comment is, we hope, well meant / she says 'that girl's hair is awful bent'" [34]). A third child gives himself away playing hide-and-seek with his dog in tow. Any of these scenarios would be understandable juvenile kitsch regardless of the race of the child making the errors, but the strips operate under the ongoing premise

66 CHAPTER ONE

that the Indigenous children "seemed to be on terms of perfect friendship and understanding with all living creatures."[74] Swinnerton's biographer notes that a 1923 collection of previously published *Kiddies* cartoons sold poorly, "but for an unusual reason. Many children across the country had been keeping scrapbooks, carefully pasting each monthly page of *The Canyon Kiddies* [*sic*] in their collection. In effect, they already had the book!"[75]

After page 94 no more new articles are commenced; the editorial content that does appear in the back of the book is exclusively text-only continuations of the features begun in the first third with illustrations and elaborate headings. If a reader opens to any page in the latter two-thirds of the magazine, they will find mostly advertisements; one page in a two-page spread will have a center column that continues a feature piece from earlier in the magazine, flanked on both sides by advertisements, or else one column running down the spine side of the page, with a double-column-sized advertisement next to it; only rarely does the facing page have another editorial column but is much more frequently a full-page advertisement. Many of these back-of-the book full-page ads are printed in full color, whereas the column pages are in black and white; the ads, therefore, draw the eye, and can easily distract even a focused reader who is flipping to a continuation of an article or a fictional piece.

The Five Foot Shelf: Where Advertising, Advising, and Reading Collide

On page 90 of the February 1926 *Good Housekeeping*, in the column flanking Dr. Wiley's Question Box, is an advertisement for Dr. Eliot's Five Foot Shelf of Books. "Which of these women has learned the secret of Fifteen Minutes a Day?" asks the ad, under a pair of illustrations that shows one woman surrounded by eager listeners and another woman sitting alone and dejected. The Five Foot Shelf of Books, which was marketed as a substitute for a Harvard education, has been described by Joan Shelley Rubin as an inflection point between the celebration of genteel culture and the undermining of the notion that "culture required sustained effort."[76] Inaugurated in 1910 by P. F. Collier, the series was impressively bound, could be ordered with its own display shelf, and promised erudition in just "fifteen minutes a day." Advertisements for the subscription-based series were ubiquitous throughout its fifty-year publication history, and appeared in newspapers, general-interest magazines, and specialty magazines—anywhere an aspirant to cultural capital might be found. The ads were keyed to the expected status anxieties of each periodical's target audience; thus this entry in *Good Housekeeping* with its focus on the impact being poorly read might have on a woman's social life. The socially isolated woman who has not learned the secret to fifteen minutes a day is identical to her more popular doppelgänger in every respect but one: she has not purchased the Five Foot Shelf of Books: "Two women live in neighboring homes. They are of the same age. Their husbands' incomes are about equal. They seem to have the same chance of social success and happiness. And yet, one of these women is seldom invited to go out. She belongs to no club or society. She is lonely all day long. The other woman is always the center of a group of friends. Her calendar is full of engagements. She is sought after as a guest and admired as a hostess" (90).

The connection between reading a lot of books and social success is not as oblique as it might initially seem—and the astonishingly minor time investment would not prevent anyone from maintaining an active social life. The woman in this comparison who has used the Five Foot Shelf "has learned how to attract people" by reading widely—"her mind is keen and alert, and people feel instinctively that she is worth knowing." Quite explicitly, this woman is more valuable because of her reading. People are attracted to her because of what she can give them: the secondhand experience of her erudition. Reading of this nature does not lead down a dark path to bookishness or plainness, the ad obliquely reassures its audience. "Any woman who knows something of literature and science, of travel and biography, will find herself becoming more and more attractive." Our woman is not a "scholar" or a "bookworm"—she is not even, necessarily, a "Reader." Her engagement with books is an adjunct to her social interests and duties and is entirely secondary to such concerns. These carefully curated books function, rather, to "enable anyone to think clearly and talk well" in less time than one's skin-care routine might take.

Other Five Foot Shelf advertisements in later issues will highlight the benefits that redound to mothers who read the Five Foot Shelf, to single women in search of a mate, or (more directly than this ad) to women who want to ensure that their marriage remains vital (see chapter 3). These ads, and the implicit *Good Housekeeping* validation of their claims, are an important precursor and context for Blair's columns. In her inaugural February 1926 column, she is becoming allied with the Five Foot Shelf, Old Dutch Cleanser, and the Chambers Range; Bruce Barton and Dr. Wiley; and of course her friend Frances Parkinson Keyes. Just as these advertisements, stories, and advice columns about marriage, homemaking, and pure foods echo and reinforce the narrative model of aspirational identification, Blair's stories about the women for whom she envisions certain texts serve as moments for identification and emulation. The stories that surround her columns reinforce the magazine's interests in inspirational, but ultimately family-focused, female ingenuity—independent actions that ultimately lead to the renunciation of independence in favor of more fulfilling family service. With these values and models in mind, we can now turn to Blair's first column as a response to and extension of the remainder of the magazine.

CHAPTER TWO

Your Taster and Tester

Because of her political work, Mrs. Blair is one of the best
known women in America. Her friends, however, know her
best as a discriminating reader of books and are accustomed
to go to her for advice. Here she tells, for the benefit of all
book-lovers, about the books she has advised her friends to
read. Any one who wishes additional or special titles or
advice on reading, may write to her in our care.

—*Good Housekeeping*, February 1926

Emily Newell Blair's inaugural column opens with a scene from her Joplin,
Missouri, women's study club, which has just closed "a most delightful
season of good papers and good fellowship."[1] The members, tasked with
suggesting improvements for the next club season, initially could think of
nothing, until Charlotte Lennon ventured that they might supplement their
discussion of current events with

> something . . . that will give us the same kind of information about books,
> stimulate our curiosity, you know, so that we'll want to read something
> besides the Best Sellers; help us to pick the best books out of the yearly
> output that so overwhelms me with its quantity that I can't find quality—
> not just fiction or books at the Carnegie Library, but the unusual ones,
> the more worth while and less popular. I try to keep up with at least one
> review, but it is not very satisfactory, for I don't know the reviewers and
> whether we like the same things. I'm often disappointed in books it rec-
> ommends. (43)

When Blair quips, "what you need is a taster," her friends readily agree:
"That's it exactly . . . and you, Emily, ought to be our taster." And so, "before
[she] could protest," Blair was appointed the "committee of one, with the
privilege of adding as many members as I wanted to perform this miracle"
(43). Rather than cursing her impulse to make a clever joke, or devising a plan
to avoid her friends until they forgot about the request, Blair sets to work

69

70 CHAPTER TWO

researching the current book reviews to find things to recommend. This does not go well. "The more reviews I read—and I bought every magazine that carried any kind of book review—the more I realized that reviews by different people with differing tastes and viewpoints mean nothing unless we know and approve the reviewer's taste or agree with the reviewer's viewpoint" (43). None of these reviewers know Blair or her friends; they are "different"—not just in comparison to each other, but in the sense of being "other" than the Joplin, Missouri, women. Like her friend Charlotte Lennon, the purported speaker of the above plea, Blair is interested in the books that are getting a lot of buzz, but she craves the hidden gem. She is intelligent and even worldly but is also from the Midwest and has concerns aside from the purely intellectual. Reading through the reviews, Blair comes to agree with Charlotte that these unknown critics could not be trusted to accurately anticipate and meet their needs. Blair realizes that "what the girls in the club would want to know was what I had read, and how I liked it, and if it was worth their while. Just as I said, what they wanted was a taster, a taster whose taste they admired, a taster who knew their tastes" (43).

Blair's "taste" is both admirable and accurate—she knows her friends' tastes, as opposed to the distant reviewers who may enjoy differently seasoned books. Where the eighteenth-century literati studied by Denise Gigante felt that "the danger was always the potentially 'bad' taste of the economically empowered consumer,"[2] Blair and her Joplin club see a danger to their own reading pleasure in the potentially "bad" taste of the book reviewers in the newspapers and magazines. This opening anecdote establishes one of the key tenets of Blair's columns: the only taste that matters is the taste of the reader, and if the reviewer's recommendations do not suit, one should not try to like the book that has been recommended but should change reviewers. Blair realizes that she has, in herself, all she needs to do this work. She does not need to consult "experts," just her own preferences and reactions to a text. Her qualifications are not advanced degrees—indeed, having an advanced degree would disqualify her—but are, rather, the days and evenings she has spent in fellowship with the women to whom she will recommend books.

By launching into her list of recommendations to various friends and explaining the logic of her choices through quick personality sketches of each of the women for whom she selects books, Blair both becomes and refuses to become like those other reviewers. Blair sets up her column as a monthly answer to her study group's requests, and she explicitly shares her thoughts and their personalities with her *Good Housekeeping* readers. In essence, her readers are eavesdroppers on some future Joplin study club session, brought into intimacy with both Blair and with the women to whom she imagines herself recommending each book. Through witnessing Blair's recommendation thought processes, the reader can know whether Blair is "a taster who knew [her] tastes" and ultimately whether she should follow Blair's suggestions or keep looking for a more kindred spirit.

Blair's columns work very hard to approximate the ethos, tone, and priorities of the rest of the magazine. She echoes multiple other proven, regularly appearing article genres: she is an advice columnist, who encourages her readers to have confidence in their reading preferences. She is a product tester, whose products are books. While the *Good Housekeeping* "money-back guaranty" is not explicitly extended to the books Blair recommends (that applies only to advertised goods and services; there are vanishingly few book advertisements in *Good Housekeeping*), its promise infuses and sometimes spurs her to qualify and nuance her reviews. Blair is personal, autobiographical, and biographical, offering herself and her famous and nonfamous friends as character studies for the kinds of readers who might like each of the books she recommends. And, finally, we can see the aesthetics and the cultural concerns of typical *Good Housekeeping* serial and short fiction carried over into Blair's recommendations—not necessarily because she recommends only books that are continuous with the standard *Good Housekeeping* fiction, but because she reads each text in light of the readerly modes that the magazine has cultivated in its readers and on which it relies. Books are discussed as hewing to or departing from middlebrow expectations (although not in those explicit terms), and Blair frequently performs readings of books that render them consistent with such expectations.

This chapter will focus on Blair's inaugural column from February 1926, which establishes a pattern from which Blair rarely diverges. By reading Blair's recommendations in this column against other contemporaneous reviewers' assessments of the same titles, and then performing brief readings of each of the texts themselves, we can see how Blair embraces multiple reading modes, without judgment or hierarchizing, while offering books best suited for her readers' eclectic tastes and various needs. But first, it is important to understand why *Good Housekeeping* saw Blair as an apt reading advice columnist for its audience. How did she fit into the magazine's cadre of experts, and why would her recommendations be any closer to fitting the tastes of the

Good Housekeeping audience than other reviewers' would? As the header to her inaugural column suggests, her ability to operate as both a nationally significant political operative and a midwestern housewife has a good deal to do with that. Blair's career during the early 1900s and her network of political women rendered her both influential and relatable, an aspirational but accessible ideal for the *Good Housekeeping* reader. The productive paradox of her exceptionalism and her representativeness was the key to Blair's role as a reading advisor, and the rhetorical strategies she deploys to balance these two positions are remarkable.

A Housewife from Joplin

Blair begins her columns in the middle of her peer group in Missouri, as a member of a study club. She is one of them, but she has a particular skill set that her friends admire and from which they hope to profit: "You're always reading. Think up some way you can tell us the books we'll like, the books we ought to read, and what we ought to know about the new books," they (reportedly) entreat her. The service she is called upon to deliver is not substantially different from the service that entities like the Book-of-the-Month Club purport to provide or the implied function of the reviews that Charlotte Lennon found unhelpful. Blair's difference is that she can speak effectively to the "we" of "what books we'll like," despite being one of the "best known women in America." Like her twenty-first-century cognates Oprah, Reese Witherspoon, and Jenna Bush Hager, Blair made a point of being both exceptional and relatable. She is typical of her friends and the *Good Housekeeping* readers, who apparently comprise a "reading formation," as members of a shared "interpretive community."[3] The "we" groups Blair with her readers, or at least indicates that if she is not identical to them, she will know what they like—better than those other reviewers whom Charlotte Lennon does not know and who do not know Charlotte Lennon.

Blair *was* at least somewhat like her readers—we think we can know this because she was presumably a member of a study club located in a town in the geographic center south of the United States—but she was also quite a bit unlike them. At the time of her *Good Housekeeping* work, Blair was serving as the national vice chairperson of the Democratic Party and was one of the leaders of Franklin Delano Roosevelt's presidential campaign. But she was not always at the center of national politics. In her autobiography, aptly titled *Bridging Two Eras*, Blair describes herself as stumbling into her political prominence by virtue of being the most inoffensive woman in the right place at the right time. She describes her surprise at the international recognition she gained from a piece in *Cosmopolitan* magazine about a "contented wife," written in response to "Confessions of a Rebellious Wife," an article anonymously published in *The American Magazine* in July 1909. She credits her husband with the encouragement to write the rejoinder; after her complaint to him that "I'm tired of reading about these unhappy wives. . . . Why doesn't someone write about the contented ones?" he responds with praise of her epistolary style: "The last time I was in New York I read an extract from one of your letters to clinch some point in the conversation, and everyone commented on the way you put it. . . . You could do it if you tried."[4] She does try—and has her husband's stenographer prepare the manuscript—and her shock at being paid $142.42 for the piece propels her into a writing career. "That day was certainly one of the greatest of my life."[5]

Blair's self-effacing autobiographical account of her entrance into the publishing realm echoes the self-abnegation of her "contented wife" in the article she eventually publishes. This epistolary story offers the letters of a woman to her husband from various moments of their married life, beginning just after their honeymoon and spanning twenty years until their oldest daughter is married and (unknowingly) expecting her own child. She writes when one or the other is traveling, for work or for family visits, and addresses all the problems brought up by the "rebellious wife" of the initial *American Magazine* article, modeling the ways a well-adjusted marriage would deal with issues such as the husband's dissatisfaction with his business partners and disagreements over children's education and career paths, or whether to socialize together or separately. The "contented wife" is actually fairly insufferable, to the point where it would be possible to read the piece as a parody of overweening advice or of extreme accommodation: "It seems dangerous for a husband to give a wife a bank-account until she knows [the power and temptations of money], and yet how can she learn but by experience? You, wise man (and dear) that you are, called it a speculation, and surely it has netted dividends. Has not my financial education been a good investment in the long run to you?"[6] She speaks of his profession as "their" mutual job—his judgeship, achieved by the final installment of the series of letters, is a "rung of *our* ladder."[7] She does not have her own profession or goals, aside from the care of her household and children. She is certainly not politically or intellectually active, aside from the letters she sends to her spouse, and she chides herself when she temporarily gives in to any dissatisfaction. Intellectual dissatisfaction was the root of the complaints offered by the "rebellious wife"—the correction for this seems to be not to let that sort of thing bother you.

Blair herself was not unambitious, nor was she particularly careful with her family finances; indeed, her continued writing career was in large part a corrective to her own impecuniosity. After "Letters from a Contented Wife" was published, she became a sought-after writer in general-interest magazines and, consequently, was asked to serve as the editor of a suffrage movement journal, *The Missouri Woman*, in 1913. Her suffrage work then took center stage; in the mid-1910s Blair organized more than 2,000 Democratic Women's Clubs around the country to encourage newly enfranchised women to vote in significant, game-changing blocs (instead of as second votes for their husbands' preferred candidates), and built regional training programs for women party workers. She quickly became prominent in the Democratic Party and in 1922 was elected the party's national vice chairperson; she was subsequently reelected to that post from 1924 to 1928. She was a principal founder of the Woman's National Democratic Club and served the club first as secretary (1922–26) and then later as president (1928–29). Blair's political work continued and even intensified during the years she was writing for *Good Housekeeping*; as I will discuss in the epilogue, she helped Franklin Delano Roosevelt secure the party's nomination for President in 1932, and during the campaign she was one of four women sent by the DNC on speaking tours across the country, culminating with her stint as the national Democratic Party cochair.

In her autobiography, Blair attributes her early successes in political organizing to her understanding of women, rather than any skill in politics. "Little I might know about national politics, but I knew a lot about women, and one thing I knew was that women might follow men directly, but they were not going to be delivered as so many bobheads by an agent of the men. But if I could make them see me as one who could lead them according to tactics they were familiar with, they might treat me as their leader."[8] Blair led by example, but also by demonstrating her similarity to the people she asked to follow her. "I saw that I had an opportunity—it was nothing more than that—to show eligibility for leadership. But the women must know me, they must have evidence of my ability to accomplish things. To show them such evidence, I discovered, was like raising myself by my own bootstraps."[9] She was easy to admire and to identify with, and her name became her most valuable asset in organizing. During the Roosevelt campaign in 1932, she was asked to deploy that exceptional everywoman quality on the lecture circuit, and her listeners responded enthusiastically: "She has a very pleasing platform presence and inspires her hearers with confidence in her knowledge of what she is telling them."[10] As we will see, Blair's reading advice follows a similar pattern.

Blair began her work with *Good Housekeeping* after a particularly dispiriting political season in which she worked for John Davis's unsuccessful presidential campaign against Calvin Coolidge. Home from Washington and overdrawing her bank account, Blair was casting about for writing topics and finding that politics were not interesting to magazine publishers. Her mother, then, came to the rescue, much as her husband had in 1910. "'Why don't you write about books?' she asked me one day. 'You talk well about them, have original ideas.'"[11] Blair's initial hesitation, because "book reviewing was poor pay," was then met with her friends' requests for summer reading, and the thought that she might be able to secure a regular column in a women's magazine. In *Bridging Two Eras*, she writes of contacting William Bigelow at *Good Housekeeping*. Blair cites Bigelow's decision to take her on as columnist as one he had wanted to make for a long time: "He told me he had been wanting this kind of department for ten years, but had never found just the woman to do it. This was not a compliment on my style or knowledge of books. When a literary critic asked him why he did not get a professor of literature, he said he wanted someone who approached books as his readers did, for interest and entertainment." And so, the column was approved—initially for a run of six months or a year.[12] As we will discuss at greater length in a later chapter, Blair's friend Frances Parkinson Keyes, who was a contributing editor at the magazine, was actually instrumental in Bigelow's decision, writing a number of supporting letters on Blair's behalf. Blair's erasure of this feminine network in her autobiography is confusing, but it might be read as a function of her desire to position herself once again as the intercessor. If she has navigated her own way into the influencer position, she has a unique platform from which she can illuminate and uplift other women.

Blair's employment by *Good Housekeeping* initially overlapped with her political activity, although by late 1928 her schedule was so grueling that she resigned from politics for several years. The column required that she read "between thirty and fifty books each month, then re-read ten or twelve until she could write about them." This astonishing reading requirement occasioned

76   CHAPTER TWO

a complete transformation of her home and her personal daily habits. While initially she purchased the books she was going to review herself, for example, she was eventually added to publishers' reviewer lists and was inundated with new books every month. "As our magazine had the largest circulation of any discussing books, publishers were soon sending me everything they published on the chance of my choosing one of their stock." This volume of mail necessitated her hiring a staff to help process, catalogue, and disperse the books: "It took my houseman hours to unwrap them and then wrap up again the ones I did not want. We soon developed a system for handling them and a list of places to send them when through with the ones I used: missionaries in China, tuberculosis homes, penitentiaries. We never, of course, gave them to anyone who could or should buy them." Blair also required secretarial assistance to prepare the article for publication, fact-checking all her references and copy editing her manuscript. She had three secretaries who would help her meet her deadlines, sometimes only just: "The day the article was finally posted was a hectic one. The last possible train—no airmail—went out at nine o'clock at night. Usually Harry [her husband] or a secretary just managed to get the manuscript on the train."[13] Blair eventually rented another small house to use as an office, which she furnished but did not equip with a telephone. This office space was essential to her column, as it gave her a place to do her writing and, perhaps more essentially, her reading.

The reading was the most demanding part of Blair's assignment and had to be performed in the right spirit. While Blair was able to get assistance for the mechanical aspects of prepping and producing the column, all the reading she did had to be her own, and she ended up with a nocturnal lifestyle to accommodate this time-intensive labor. "The time schedule I then followed was to cause me great trouble in later days because of the sleep habits formed by it," Blair notes in her autobiography.

> The reading I did at night. Beginning my book about ten-thirty when the rest of the family had retired, I finished it before I went to bed, at four or five o'clock in the morning. I stayed in bed until ten or half-past the next day. I did this for two reasons. One, I could cover more ground and get a much clearer idea in the night's quiet. Two, I thus got an uninterrupted space of four or six hours, but if I rose at seven or eight I found my morning hours frittered away by telephone calls and questions about household matters. As long as I was "asleep" I would not be disturbed by servants or friends; but if "up and around" nothing would protect me from interruption. At eleven o'clock I went to my office, and my houseman brought

down my lunch at two. When I came home at five o'clock I went over the house, checking up on everything, rested for an hour, and was ready to give my husband the evening.[14]

While she emphasized her similarity to her readers, then, Blair also lived a life that was quite unlike their own. She worked hard to approximate their reading practices in her own very unusual circumstances, however, emphasizing that she tried to read each book first "for enjoyment, as though I had no article to do," because "I knew that if I ever read them as a chore and not as a casual reader, I could not write about them as if their reading was a pleasure."[15] This reading performance was crucial to her column, and, as we will see, she enters into many varieties of "pleasure reading" as she writes about each book she is recommending.

Blair's work here and her self-presentation in her columns resemble nothing so much as the twenty-first-century internet influencer.[16] Just as these highly paid and heavily resourced women present images of effortless homemaking and child-rearing, so does Blair tend to represent herself as an effortlessly voracious reader, just happening to work her way through hundreds of volumes in her spare time between political travel and homemaking. Blair frequently inserts autobiographical details into her column, and her long-term readers get to know her extended family over the course of her *Good Housekeeping* tenure. In the February 1926 column, she mentions her sister in Mexico (for whom she frequently purchases books) as well as her mother, whose special hanging shelf she uses to organize the books she will recommend each month. "And so I got them ready for my friends, placing them on my little walnut hanging shelf that had held the two dozen books Mother brought out to Joplin when she came here fifty years ago, a young bride to a younger mining camp. I took it out of the attic and placed it in my little orange-and-wine living-room over the radio, because the association of the prim little shelf of the seventies with the newest voice of the twenties somehow amuses me" (43). Her preparation for her advisory role is also an occasion for a decorating tip—she is using an heirloom to great advantage, just as readers might pull out their old family trunks for rehabilitation after reading that article earlier in the magazine. Her sister in Mexico becomes the focus of two later columns (May 1926 and April 1928); her husband intervenes on behalf of men in July 1930 ("Isn't it about time that you mentioned us men again?"[17]); her nephew suggests a column topic while she is visiting him in Florida (June 1930); and her son makes frequent appearances as a cheeky interlocutor.

78 CHAPTER TWO

Blair's centering of her midwesterness seems a pointed rebuke to Harold Ross's caricature of the "old lady in Dubuque" for whom he insists the *New Yorker* "is not edited."[18] Blair is neither old nor from Dubuque, but she resembles much more closely the woman to whom *Time* magazine sent a copy of Ross's magazine, tongue in cheek, for comment:

> To an old lady in Dubuque there was sent a copy of *The New Yorker*. She was asked by telegram for an opinion. Replied she:
> "I and my associates here, [*sic*] have never subscribed to the view that bad taste is any the less offensive because it is metropolitan taste. To me, urbanity is the ability to offend without being offensive, to startle composure and to deride without ribaldry. The editors of the periodical you forwarded are, I understand, members of a literary clique. They should learn that there is no provincialism as blatant as that of the metropolitan who lacks urbanity."[19]

Time's "[*sic*]" aside, and of course without being able to know whether this letter came from anyone actually currently living in Iowa (or their age, or gender), this response hands a deft comeuppance to the Algonquin set. As we will see in chapter 4, Blair had to lobby and audition for her column in *Good Housekeeping*, and it may not be a coincidence that she was invited to write the column shortly after this exchange occurred. To respond to its audience, to gain their trust and properly speak to their lives, *Good Housekeeping's* books columnist could *only* hail from the Midwest.

When Blair's columns do make reference to the things that make her different from her readers, those qualities become the differences that make her life interesting, and that make her reading advice both valuable and aspirational. Even better are the times when Blair manages to reference her ambitious reading schedule and her political work simultaneously. For example, the following exchange opens her June 1927 column:

> "Do you have to read all those books?" groaned Minnie Fisher Cunningham as she saw them piling up on the mantel shelf, dresser and tables of my bedroom at the Women's National Democratic Club at Washington.
> "Do you get all those books to read?" drawled Margaret Banister, her eyes roaming the titles in envy.
> And my own attitude, I confess, swings pendulum-like between the two.[20]

All the hallmarks of a Blair column are here: she names her interlocutors, signals her political work, and demonstrates her fallible humanity in the confession that she, too, sometimes finds reading to be onerous. Her friends would have been relatively well-known to her 1927 audience, and would become more notable over the course of the column's run; Minnie Fisher Cunningham, who would become a regular character in Blair's columns, was a member of the Women's National Democratic club, and in 1928 she would run for Senate from Texas (the premise of one of Blair's 1928 columns is her recommending books for Cunningham to read on her travels through the state).[21] Margaret Banister was an editor at the *Washingtonian* magazine who published many short stories in that periodical. If the February 1926 issue makes the *Good Housekeeping* reader a member of the Joplin study club, June 1927 invites her into Washington, DC, feminine power circles.

Particularly in the first three years of her time at *Good Housekeeping*, Blair makes frequent note of her conversations with other prominent political women. "'There wasn't a pleasant character in the book,' said Congresswoman Norton to me," opens the September 1927 column.[22] A frequent interlocutor is Blair's friend and patron Frances Parkinson Keyes, for whom Blair selects a "hamper of books" in May 1929. The July 1929 issue opens with a locally prominent woman specifically asking to be made a part of her column: "'Will you mention me in your article,' asked Reba Boomershine, the vibrant president of the Dayton Business and Professional Woman's Club, on the occasion of my appearance at their annual dinner."[23] Blair's answer—"If you ask me an interesting enough question"—as well as her specification of the occasion for Boomershine's question (Blair was giving an annual keynote at a midsized city's prominent women's club) and the fulfillment of the request are all assertions of Blair's relative power and authority. Prominent men enter as well, as in the opening of her March 1927 column, where William Ullmann, a Treasury Department official (who would later be accused of spying for the Soviet Union while commissioned as a US Air Force officer during World War II) berates her for never directing one of her columns to male readers: "We read all that you write, and take your advice, and borrow your books, and you never so much as recognize the existence of a man reader, much less compliment us as fathers or friends."[24]

By the 1930s, this name-dropping becomes more infrequent, perhaps because Blair herself is more self-evidently prominent and she does not need the reflected glory of others. Her status signals shift to mentions of her frequent lectures (in West Virginia, May 1931; Evanston Illinois and Wichita Falls, July 1931), and she focuses more on her readers' frequent questions about her method. From the first years of her column, Blair has mentioned her secretary and the processes of unwrapping all the books that are sent to her each month; in April 1926 the column is headed by a photo of Blair captioned, "Where the new department of 'Tasting and Testing Books' is conducted, with the Manager at her desk," a caption that clearly winks at the reader's understanding of the lab-like environment of the Good Housekeeping Institute and her appreciation that there is only one "tester" in this whole department, who is also the "Manager."[25]

In August 1928, Blair begins her column by describing the scene in her office on returning home:

> Books to the right of me, books to the left of me! This was the sight which met my eyes on my recent return home from Washington. Regularly during my absence the books had come, been unwrapped, and deposited in a waiting bookcase. Overflowing that, tables had been commandeered by a desperate maid. They, too, soon filled and the couch was utilized. And still books came, until the packages were left to form a miniature mountain range around the border of the room. Gazing at them, I was reminded of the questions often put to me by friends. "Do you read all these books that come to you?" and its obvious answer, "Impossible!"[26]

Where the new department of "Tasting and Testing Books" is conducted, with the Manager at her desk

FIGURE 3. Emily Newell Blair at her desk in the "Department of Tasting and Testing Books," (*Good Housekeeping*, April 1926, 51). Credit: *Good Housekeeping*, Hearst Magazine Media, Inc.

The remainder of this column sees Blair picking up one book after another, pausing at the ones that she feels she should recommend to her readers. Like Frances Parkinson Keyes's column in which she fills up a scrapbook with mementos from Japan, this column brings the reader along in the process of sorting the huge haul that arrived for her while she was gone. The appeal here is not dissimilar from the appeal of twenty-first-century social media influencers or even less-famous YouTubers who make "unboxing" videos, or "PR Haul" videos, where they display for their audiences the results of shopping trips or online orders.[27] It is fascinating to think about having so many books to choose from, to have your home (Blair has not confessed that she has rented another house for her office) turned into a library. Like social media influencer Rachel Parcell, who had an entire room dedicated to "package receiving" in her custom-designed megamansion, Blair's life with all these books is both an outlier and almost imaginable—it is, like the social media influencers, a vision of "attainable perfection."[28]

Interest in Blair's process continues through the 1930s and even intensifies as she becomes more of a quasi-celebrity in her own right. In the epilogue, we will see how that scrutiny will impact Blair's recommendations and, perhaps, will herald the end of her time at *Good Housekeeping*. But for now, we will return to the beginning of her career and the recommendations in her first column.

February 1926

In February 1926, Blair is a new name in the pages of *Good Housekeeping* magazine. The column header, the epigraph for this chapter, describes her as "one of the best known women in America," but she is not yet known as a reader particularly, so the first column needs to work to set up her bona fides in this regard. After introducing her study group, with the narrative about their last spring meeting that we saw above, Blair accepts their charge to "be our taster . . . tell us the books we'll like, the books we ought to read, and what we ought to know about the new books." These three questions delineate nicely the dilemmas presumably facing readers at this moment, which also marked the beginning of the era of academic literary study. How was one to enjoy books, to read the "right" books, and to understand them properly? And exactly how essential was it to be able to do the last two—the notion of "best" books to read and best ways to read them being predicated on the presence, somewhere out there, of professional readers who passed judgment on the reading practices of others? The request both validates the already-formed tastes of Blair's readers and suggests that they know very well that there are books out there that are the ones that they "ought to read"— and Blair's publication of this question signals her acknowledgement of the performative aspect of taste. She will help her study group, and her *Good Housekeeping* audience, navigate the demands on their time, the expectations of others about what they should like, and their own personal, and idiosyncratic, already-formed preferences.

Blair narrates, then, her contemplation of the task, and announces her decision to proceed by "pick[ing] out from the books I read myself the ones I thought each would enjoy, just as I choose the books I send to my sister in Mexico each spring and fall." This suggests that, at least at the start, Blair was simply sharing with others the things she learned while going about her own already-established reading practices. She was already a prolific reader; she would just pick out books from that stack she already had. That the stack seems to include nearly every major title published for the fall 1925 publishing season would perhaps not be apparent to most of her readers. In other words, the professionalism that she will confess over the course of her tenure at the magazine is still hidden in this inaugural column; Blair is still very much an adviser plucked from the audience.

It is the case, in this column as in most future columns, that the books Blair recommends are not necessarily the most recently released titles. Blair probably wrote her columns one to two months in advance of the publication date, so her recommendations do not track the release dates of books the way the major weekly reviews like the *New York Times Book Review* or *The Bookman*, or even more literary magazines like the newly launched *New Yorker*, could.[29] This time lag seems to underscore Blair's separation from the apparatus of books production as well—if we are to trust her account in her autobiography, cited above, she was not initially receiving reviewer copies automatically. But as we will see, this distance from the cultural centers of New York and Boston is also intentional and strategic. Just as Blair is more like her readers, and less like "the reviewers," Blair's columns are more like local newspaper reviews than they are like the larger national reviews, because, as we saw in the first chapter, while *Good Housekeeping* was a national magazine, produced out of New York, it strived for a more suburban or rural tone. In Blair's columns, with her frequent references to her hometown of Joplin, Missouri, and other locations in the middle of the continent, this became also a peculiarly midwestern sensibility.

Your Taster and Tester

This local tone is obliquely signaled by the choice of books, but it is also more explicit in the individual recommendations that Blair makes. One of the hallmarks of Blair's column is her naming of the representative women to whom she is suggesting particular books and the brief character sketches of each. "For dashing little Herma, who loves to decorate her conversation with the latest phrase just as she decorates her drawing room with the latest bric-a-brac, I have 'The Perennial Bachelor,' by Anne Parrish, not because it won the Harper prize, but because of all the year's books it is far and away the most quotable" (43). The *Good Housekeeping* reader may know a Herma, or may consider herself a Herma—if the latter is the case, then she might decide that *The Perennial Bachelor* is the book for her. If not, she can go on to the next book, which Blair will describe in like fashion.

Blair models multiple reading modes in her columns, demonstrating both that she is able to shift among modes that are clearly "out there" and available for deployment and also that she does not make a judgment about the relative value of any of these modes. In other words, she thinks that all of them are fine, are equally appropriate and equally available to whoever wants to use them. The fact that she is able to enter into multiple reading practices shows that she is a savvy reader, and that she is the right person for this job—it also suggests that all readers could do so if they chose that they wanted to read a book in a particular way, for a particular purpose. Individual reading practices emerge as preferences, and as actively chosen by each of Blair's friends in her study group. Like the various types of dress that are offered in the fashion section of the magazine, the trick is just knowing which of the available types is the best of its kind, which book will best repay the kind of reading you want to put into it. And in this column, at least, Blair's personality will take a back seat to the personalities of the readers to whom she is recommending books—and to the books themselves.

The Perennial Bachelor by Anne Parrish

Blair's first recommendation, *The Perennial Bachelor* by Anne Parrish, will appeal, she thinks, to her friend Herma, "dashing little Herma, who loves to decorate her conversation with the latest phrase just as she decorates her drawing room with the latest bric-a-brac" (43). Parrish's novel follows the lives of the Campion family from the 1850s through the 1920s, beginning with the untimely death of the family patriarch and his family's subsequent

84 CHAPTER TWO

decline through genteel poverty to actual poverty. As Parrish puts it early in the novel, "Gently, the Campions slipped from being rich to being 'well-to-do,' from being 'well-to-do' to being 'comfortable,' and from being 'comfortable' to 'having to be just a little careful.'"[30] The Campion women repeatedly forego opportunities to find love and improve their collective lot because of the sole male child, Victor; Mamma Campion refuses a second marriage because of his protests; the oldest daughter, Maggie, ends an engagement because the marriage would take her too far from her little brother; the family's failing prospects make middle sister May a desperate and unappealing marital prospect, and Victor's scorn of her one good prospect leads her to throw him over; Lily is never an eligible woman because of her dowdiness; and finally Victor himself is jilted by a lover because of his family's failure.

For most of its length, the novel does not read as a tragedy despite these disappointments; the family stays together, the sisters caring for each other and sacrificing their own wardrobes and dreams for their hapless younger brother. Blair describes the novel as a social critique on the order of Jane Austen, claiming that "the author cuts through the sham, the hypocrisy, the mock modesty, the sentimentality of the Victorians" (45), but this critique is easy to miss amidst the lovingly described portraits of the sisters' economizing strategies, in which one can hear an echo of Alcott's *Little Women:* "The Campions were so poor that they were all trying to earn a little extra money. Twice a week Maggie drove in to the Women's Exchange with her cakes and May's lampshades and little crêpe paper baskets to hold candies or ice-cream. Such pretty baskets, pale violet with purple paper violets tied with a bow of baby ribbon to the handle, pale green with buttercups, and pink with something charming, though none of them quite knew what."[31]

These crafty endeavors are charming and fit for emulation—they sound like descriptions straight out of *Good Housekeeping's* columns about party hosting on a budget. Similarly, once the family begins to take in boarders, the narration of each boarder's individual quirks becomes a kind of regional piece like "Lonch for Two." The first edition of the novel runs 334 pages; until the 277th page, there is very little to suggest that this is any different from the standard *Good Housekeeping* fare described above. One expects that eventually, May or Maggie or even the unattractive youngest sister Lily will make a suitable match—perhaps that Maggie's former fiancé Edward will return, repentant, or that May will overcome her social snobbery to marry a worthy plumber. The family's resilience will be rewarded, just as Miriam, Hildegarde,

Emmy, and Ethel's resourcefulness and pluck resulted in their happy endings. A reader might even abandon the episodic novel before page 276, expecting this ending and not really needing to see it to the end.

But if a reader does persist to page 277, the novel takes a sudden turn toward darkness as May turns first on her sister Maggie, and then on her brother Victor, finally angry with him for being the barrier to his sisters' successes: "Wadsworth loved me, and I'd have been happy with him, if Victor hadn't shown me how silly he was, laughing and making fun of him. And he kept Mamma from marrying Mr. Lacey, he kept you from marrying Edward—he's done nothing *but* harm, all his life."[32] May's anger turns to depression, and then to humiliation when she is anonymously sent a mocking valentine calling her a "Hopeless Old Maid." The valentine's arrival is never explained, nor does anything else like this ever happen elsewhere in the novel. It seems to serve largely to prompt the next astonishing plot twist: May drowning herself in the bathtub, her body discovered by one of the family's boarders after a comedic set piece in which the boarder anxiously waits for the bathroom to be free and finally goes to knock: "Well, she'd just say something tactful through the keyhole. She rattled the knob a little, and called humourously: 'Anybody drownded?'"[33]

Readers are not ready for this socially awkward humor from a socially awkward elderly lady to reflect a macabre reality. This turn to dark satire is utterly unanticipated by the novel up to this point, but it is actually all the more effective for its suddenness. Complacency has been the most likely readerly attitude up to this point; while the Campions have been slowly becoming more socially isolated and less financially well situated, their familial loyalty and their superior tastes and social mores have made them easy emulation targets for an aspirational audience. The gaudy new-wealth women they encounter, in particular the family of Victor's one marriage prospect, are held up for criticism and scorn. Though they may be poor, the Campions know better than to dress in certain ways—just like the *Good Housekeeping* woman is tasteful on a budget.

May's suicide and the ensuing denouement do tend to mitigate against emulation for the reader who would see it to the end. Blair hints at May's suicide by describing her as "Lady-of-Shalott-like May" (43), but the delivery is so offhand that one could easily miss it. "There is no plot except what the years do to the gentility of that family, what life does to the yearnings of youth, what age does to beauty and strength" (43, 106). Blair focuses instead on the quotable

86   CHAPTER TWO

Parrish, opining, "But who cares for plot when one can read—'The day was like an accordion, First it stretched out ever so long and then swish!—it was folded up to almost nothing'" (106). Likening Parrish to Austen, Blair willfully obscures the rather shocking suicide at the end of the story.

More important to Blair, like Parrish's quotability, is the realism of the portrait of the 1880s and 1890s. She reports that "it took Mrs. Parrish . . . four years of rummaging through attics and magazines and books to gather and digest the material for the background of this novel" (106). It makes sense that Blair would, in the pages of a magazine, validate magazines as the repository of cultural knowledge—and that rummaging in attics after long-stashed popular texts would be the research method that would yield the most accurate portrait of past ages, would enable a writer to capture the "spirit and the life" (106) of domestic history. There are no references to historical events in *The Perennial Bachelor*; the Campion family exists in a relative bubble, and they themselves seem ageless. Rather, the passage of time is marked by the fashions and changing slang of the Campion neighbors and by the mention of popular songs. In the final scene, for example, Victor Campion, now an elderly bachelor and the butt of neighborhood jokes, is walking down the street in front of his former home in which several young men and women are listening to phonograph records. "He and three old maid sisters used to live here," one of the girls says, "One of them went dippy from sex repression."[34] Is this unsentimental summary what Blair is referring to when she praises the book for its "reconstruction of the '50's and '70's seen through the eyes of the 1920's"? That she terms it "delicious" suggests that she did not find May's suicide tragic, or shocking, and that she would not expect her audience to think so either. Instead, May is a pathetic, repressed, "dippy" character, and her brother "that Every Town Institution, easily recognized" (106)—so much for sentiment, or even the notion that the Campion tale is cautionary. To Blair, the Campions were never to be read as relatable or even as objects of pity; they were an anthropological study from the start.

Blair's assessment in this regard parts ways from many contemporaneous book reviewers, both in the major reviews and in local newspapers. Henry Longan Stuart, writing in the *New York Times*, does not shy from terming the events of the novel "tragic." He moreover locates the tragedy not just in May's suicide and Maggie's slow succumbing to cancer, but in Victor's failure to make anything of himself after the family has invested all is hopes in him. "It is all very sterile and heart rending"[35] in Stuart's review—not humorous or charming as in Blair's. Stuart is also less impressed by Parrish's "archaeological detail," with which he feels the novel is "a trifle overloaded." This seems to be an outlier opinion, however. The *New Yorker*, like Blair, celebrated the rich details, "bright and succulent, richly suggestive of the march of time and the sweep of social change from the days of limbs tented in crinolines to these."[36] The focus on period details from both the *New Yorker* and Blair seems to have been suggested by Harper in its press materials; an article reprinted in various newspapers celebrating Parrish's receipt of the second annual Harper Prize for the novel seems to be composed of press release material and tells the story of Parrish's rummaging in attics and magazine research: "I worked for years on the book before I began to write it, trying really to feel the story, really to be inside of each of the characters, and also making sure of my periods. My notebook, typed, is twice as thick as the novel itself. . . . I hunted through attics and museums, read old journals and letters, and had my being in Godey's, Peterson's 'Floral Adornments for the Home of Taste,' old friendship albums, etc."[37]

Most of the newspaper reviewers in smaller markets focused, like the *New Yorker* reviewer, on the sacrifices each sister made in favor of their "maternally narcissized,"[38] "entirely selfish and worthless,"[39] "sluggish-minded and inept"[40] brother, "who wasn't (from the masculine viewpoint) worth any such devotion" and "has his good times at the price of family sacrifice."[41] The family's story is seen as one of tragic waste, albeit beautifully detailed and charmingly written.

Blair is actually most aligned with *Forum*'s Anne Cleeland, who is initially charmed by the period details but eventually becomes "exasperated" by the Campions: "I am grateful to Anne Parrish for the heaven-sent mushrooms that take Mamma Campion away in three days. And I am relieved when May's old spinster spirit passes,—down the bathtub drain. Quirks of humor,—not only I,—cheer the Campion deaths."[42] Blair's take on *The Perennial Bachelor*, while not as crispy as Cleeland's, shares its modern pragmatism; in this, it is also consistent with the *Good Housekeeping* focus on self-sufficient women who would find a way to avoid sacrificing their happiness for the preferences of an "insufferable skirthanger."[43] A more robust heroine than Maggie Campion would appear in the next recommendation, a historical novel of the Oregon territory.

We Must March, by Honoré Willsie Morrow

Blair describes the next book in her column as a profound contrast to *The Perennial Bachelor*, a book that would appeal instead to "serious-minded Elizabeth who divides her interest between our club and her church missionary

88 CHAPTER TWO

society." Honoré Willsie Morrow's *We Must March*, a historical novel about the first missionaries to settle the Oregon Territory in the mid-nineteenth century, might seem an obvious choice for Elizabeth because of the missionary connection—but Blair's recommendation is never actually couched in religious terms. Rather, she focuses on the novel as a historical treatment that recenters a white woman's role in the domestication of the Pacific Northwest and constructs a summary that renders the novel a fairly comprehensive *Good Housekeeping* fiction.

Honoré Willsie Morrow has been overlooked by most scholars, but she was a significant enough author in 1925 to merit the first spot in a compendium review in the *New York Times Book Review*. To some contemporaneous readers she may have been known as the past editor (from 1914 to 1919) of the *Delineator* magazine, the Butterick Company's competitor to *Good Housekeeping* in the women's magazine market. To other readers, she may have been known as Honoré Willsie, author of a number of popular formula Western novels and serial magazine fictions.[44] *We Must March* would be Morrow's first historical novel, and she would go on after its publication to write a trilogy about Abraham Lincoln that would earn her a measure of esteem as an author of historical fiction. Morrow attributed her shift to historical novels to her reading of the diary of Narcissa Whitman, the missionary whose life is the focus of *We Must March*. As with the Parrish book, the repeated story of the discovery of Whitman's diary was probably included in the publisher's press release materials, thus its repetition in several reviews and, indeed, in Blair's.[45] The *New York Times* reviewer notes that Morrow's reliance on the real-life Whitman's journals when researching the novel allows for a different type of historical accuracy than previous tales of the westward expansion. Noting the way Morrow contrasts the "haphazard democracy and its resultant chaos [in] the American trading posts with the aristocratic and efficient government of the Hudson Bay Company forts," the *Times* concludes that "not the least interesting part of 'We Must March' lies in its depictions of the methods, manners, and modes of the period."[46] As with Parrish, then, the portrait of a period is one of the most attractive features of the text.

While Blair tells the same story of the novel that is told by the reviewer in the *New York Times* (again suggesting her shared reading of the publisher's promotional materials), she interprets it in a different key for her *Good Housekeeping* audience. Blair steers away from emphasizing the depiction of social life and manners in the novel, however, in favor of describing it as "the history of action," particularly in contrast with *The Perennial Bachelor*. Her Narcissa Whitman is "another version of the Woman-She myth," "a leader—brave, resourceful, determined," whose story "shows us that by such sacrifices and immolation as hers does the white man build his civilization in the wilderness. [Morrow] makes us see that it was the Woman Pioneer so seldom sung in song and story who conquered barbarism and, bringing with her the idea of continuity and permanence, changed the frontier of the hunter and trapper into a smiling countryside of homes" (106).

At stake is the question of what constitutes "action"—and for Blair, the work of building a "smiling countryside of homes," or the work of domestication, is itself action.[47] Nina Baym describes the romance plot of *We Must March*, "such as it is," as Narcissa's "learning to respect her husband if not his beliefs, and eventually coming to love him. This growth in character makes her a true woman and a worthy martyr."[48] It is a movement similar to those we discovered in our reading of the serial and short fiction in the February issue of *Good Housekeeping*—the companionate marriage would be fine, but the eventual union of woman with home and the consolidation of family is the real happy ending. But this romance does not really figure in Blair's telling of the novel. Marcus Whitman, Narcissa's somewhat hapless physician-missionary husband, barely gets a mention in Blair's column. His heroic final wintertime trek eastward to convince Congress to fight for the rights to lands up to the forty-fifth parallel and to gather more American settlers for the Oregon territory is pivotal in the romance plot—this exertion finally convinces Narcissa that he is a worthy partner—but Blair does not mention it at all, except vaguely and in passing. "The book gave me such an understanding of the geography of the west as twenty transcontinental railroad journeys have not done. I saw plateau and mountain and plain through the eyes of frost-bitten horsemen, and not from a Pullman window" (106). This description taps into multiple threads of interest. First, it promises vicarious travel through a region of the United States for those who might never see the Pacific Northwest, while asserting its accuracy and historical vibrancy to those who have been there or live there. It also resonates with the fascination for "foreign" scenes and people that we have seen in the rest of the magazine; not only is the scenery refreshed in this telling, but "frost-bitten horsemen" are made available for identification. Native Americans are also offered up for the reader's anthropological gaze: "[*We Must March*] gave me another Indian than the one Cooper introduced to me years ago, and yet one

I instantly recognized as the Indian I had been seeing in the flesh." Blair's (and her reader's) purportedly advanced understandings are validated by a supposedly nuanced portrait of Native American people in the novel. But, importantly, it does *not* suggest that the reader will be concerned for the fate of a key character during that journey or that it might be a rare moment when the narrative pulls away from its heroine to focus on her husband, finally making himself into a figure of strength and noble masculinity. The romance plot, oddly, evaporates from Blair's telling in this case, which is all the more interesting since Morrow's previous writing had been in the genre of the Western romance.[49] In this Blair is not much different from other reviewers. The *Chicago Daily Tribune*, for one, notes that the fact that Whitman "was the brains of the group is evident in this story of her life, but that she was also, at times, their moral courage, is evident."[50]

Even without the focus on romance, this recommendation is wholly consistent with the remainder of the *Good Housekeeping* mix. It provides for the audience a narrative focused on white women's role in historical events that valorizes homemaking as both hard labor and as the central work of civilization. There is plenty in the novel to bear out this reading. Whitman is frequently the key negotiator between the missionaries and the Hudson Bay Company, or between her husband and the chief of the Cayute tribe in whose territory they settle. While the mission itself never actually seems successful as a conversion project, Narcissa's domestication projects do convince the Cayutes to tolerate her and her husband's presence for many years. She writes an English-Cayute grammar and opens a school to teach English. She instructs native women on English childcare techniques such as bathing babies and feeding poor nursers with cow's milk, saving many native infant and mothers' lives along the way. She bakes bread and creates a bread craze among the Cayutes, which spurs them to plant wheat and thereby become less nomadic. These projects, along with her beautiful singing voice, make her a much more compelling figure in the novel than her husband or any of the other English characters, and a worthy *Good Housekeeping* new woman heroine. Add to this the recreational enjoyment of a variety of regions in the United States and the opportunity to form judgments about racialized others, and the novel fulfills many of the requirements for *Good Housekeeping* fiction.

Possession by Louis Bromfield

Blair's third recommendation will fit the bill for her friend Harriet, "our aristocrat who comes in a straight line from the Cavaliers and takes her English in the Oxford manner." In other words, Harriet is old-school, aligned with the gentry and the familiar literary stylings of Victorian authors. Blair goes on to name specific authors in Harriet's literary pantheon—Thackeray, Eliot, Meredith, Hardy—and asserts that Harriet has indeed embraced some more contemporaneous authors because of their similarity to this "tradition." "She considers Arnold Bennett in the 'line of succession,' placed there by his 'Old Wives Tale.' [*sic*] Because he may some day find himself in the same line, I shall give her Louis Bromfield's 'Possession'" (106). Blair's analogy functions like a twenty-first-century recommendation algorithm—if you like Bennett and Eliot, you will like Bromfield—but like some recommendation algorithms, the associations are less about any empirical similarities among texts and authors than about readerly *perceptions* of such similarities. Arguments could be made that Thackeray, Eliot, Meredith, and Hardy belong to at least two, if not three, different "traditions," but the only classification schema that matters here is their inclusion in Harriet's personal canon.

This might also account for the (to me) puzzling absence of references to literarily "approved" American realists like Edith Wharton and Henry James. Blair's description of Bromfield's scene takes a page out of Wharton's *The Age of Innocence*, which won the Pulitzer Prize only six years earlier: "After the old tradition Mr. Bromfield creates a world for us in which we can live and move and have our being. We enjoy its 'furnishings' as we do our own, without being aware of them. We enjoy its people as we would acquaintances who knew Society with a big S, who lived in New York's million-dollar apartments and Paris chateaux, won fame and fortune.... Vicariously we savor all of life, eat of the tree of knowledge, overcome evil. Is it any wonder that we enjoy ourselves?" (106)

The New York apartments are certainly Wharton territory, and Bromfield's heroine takes a stage name, "Lilli Barr," that begs, nay, screams, comparisons with Wharton's *The House of Mirth*. But Wharton is not one of Harriet's authors, so Blair does not offer her as an analogue in this recommendation. A mention of Wharton might derail the Victorian-Bennett-Bromfield "line of succession," suggesting a more modern strain than Harriet and her ilk would enjoy (one could hardly say Wharton is more scandalous than Hardy

CHAPTER TWO

or more philosophical than Eliot). The discussion of *Possession* that follows
focuses on tightening the claim that this novel fits in a long Victorian tradition by reading it as one might read one of those novels—it is literary, it
covers similar characters and themes, it welcomes structural analysis and
character study. It also fits in with earlier middlebrow modes of "reading up,"
reading as a means of social and intellectual betterment that is facilitated by
vicarious identification with exemplary characters.[51] Blair's signaling here is a
clear throwback to these earlier modes of popular readings of realist literary
texts. Vicarious identifications are hallmarks of a middlebrow reader from
the beginning of the century, as I have previously argued in my study of the
reading advice in the *Ladies' Home Journal* magazine in the 1900s–1910s. The
resultant discussion follows suit and would not be out of place in Hamilton
Wright Mabie's *Ladies' Home Journal* columns of a decade earlier. The reading experience that Blair explicitly endorses in the passage I've cited above is
one hallmark of what I've called a "reading up" mode: a vicarious identification with characters from a higher social stratum than oneself. Blair writes
not once, but twice, that the pleasure in reading *Possession* is precisely that:
vicarious.

> We strive vicariously with Ellen Tolliver, that child of genius, to escape
> from the Midland Mill Town to Opportunity. We elope with her and
> Clarence Murdock to New York and disappointment; we share her tenac-
> ity; we accompany her to her cousin's Paris home, that house with its back
> to the world and its Caen stone façade. We, too, become Lilli Barr, the
> Great Pianist and, forsaking Lilli Barr, once more Ellen Tolliver, then Mrs.
> Richard Callendar, a lady of the great world, and finally Lilly Barr again.
> We yield with her to love; we deny that love for our soul's salvation. (106)

One might rightly ask what is left to the reader of the novel after this full
recounting of the protagonist's character arc? Truly, Blair's summary covers
most of the novel and does not leave much for surprise. Her summary here
is a signal that the "plot" is not necessarily the most important takeaway for
the reader of *Possession*. Like the taster she is, she is reporting the full experience in order to model it for her audience. The plot seems less important
than the feelings that will be evoked by, and can only be accessed through,
the reading experience itself; her Harriets will know that the reading itself
is the goal.

Blair also engages with *Possession* in a more literary critical mode than she
does with the two novels that preceded it in her column. "The book seems to

me to say that to save one's soul he must escape possession," she opines, at the opening of a paragraph that goes on to trace the theme as it touches the lives of the novel's main characters. Lest her readers go too far in the wrong direction, though, Blair cautions that "it is not a story with a moral. It is a story of life. One must draw from it as from experience his or her own moral." Blair's careful situating of *Possession* in a realist literary canon is consistent with the reading experience that one might expect her "aristocrat" Harriet, "nurtured in the great Victorian school," to pursue. It is also a modeling of that reading mode. Bromfield, finally, is more self-consciously literary than either Morrow or Parrish. *We Must March* and *The Perennial Bachelor* were historical artifacts with clever writing, but by omission Blair suggests that in those novels there were no deeper themes or overarching messages to consider. The mode of reading for *Possession*, in other words, matches its advertised genre: this is a book to be interpreted, and its characters are available for analysis.

Glorious Apollo by E. Barrington

Blair's sole February 1926 recommendation of a massive bestseller is targeted toward "Ethel with her cheerful interest in personality . . . that is, if Ethel has not already read it" (106). E. Barrington's pseudonymously published *Glorious Apollo* is a fictionalized biography of Lord Byron that owed its succès de scandale to the assertion that Byron's divorce was due to his incestuous relationship with his half-sister Augusta Leigh. The reception of the novel was largely caught up with arguments about whether or not this interpretation of the historical record was a valid one, and that is precisely the attraction Blair promises for Ethel. "Every one who likes to roll under or over her tongue bits of not-too-nice gossip must enjoy this romantic biography of Lord Byron." The pleasure goes even further, though, into vicarious vindication of Byron's wife Anne and participation in her "repudiation of her faithless husband." And further still, to the appreciation of the Glorious Apollo himself: "There is a magnetic appeal in the deviltry and daring and rebellion—not to mention the passion—of the Master Minstrel," and readers, presumably like Ethel, will "echo E. Barrington's paeans of praise for his charm his beauty, and throb with sympathy over the downfall of this 'young Apollo, pale with a moonlight pallor, exquisite as a dream of a love-sick sylph on the slopes of Patmos [*sic*]'" (108).

"Throbbing," "thrilling,"—these are descriptors that are simply absent from Blair's recommendations in the remainder of the column. Her purple

94 CHAPTER TWO

prose segues seamlessly into the quotation from Barrington's text, which both gives an example of the type of language a reader should expect and validates (vindicates?) Blair's own indulgent diction. If *Possession* called for a literary critical treatment, *Glorious Apollo* necessitates gushing. The passage Blair cites here can be found in the opening pages of the novel, when a young Byron returns to London after his self-imposed exile to the British countryside, where he has put himself through an extreme diet and exercise regimen to shed his childhood corpulence.[52] Byron's kinsman, Robert Charles Dallas, issues an awed response to the extreme transformation that has been effected by months of extreme dieting: "A daily diet of biscuits and soda water with a meal *de luxe* once a day of boiled rice soaked in vinegar, washed down with Epsom salts, digested with violent exercise and hot baths reminiscent of Trajan and the decadence of Rome."[53] The result was astonishing, and Barrington's description is, as Blair's excerpt demonstrates, lurid—but Blair does not capture that it is *self-consciously* so. The passage quoted above (misquoted, actually, because the reference in Barrington is to the slopes of "Latmos") is both more breathless and more aware of its own excesses when read in full:

> The blockish, moon-faced lout was gone. The marble was sculptured. He beheld the finished achievement. With laughter lurking in brilliant, deep-lashed eyes of hazel grey, there stood the young Apollo, pale with a moon-light pallor, exquisite as the dream of a love-sick nymph upon the slopes of Latmos, haughty, clear-featured, divine. Impossible rhetoric, but most true. The beauty of a beautiful young man, illumined by the summer lightning of genius, may be allowed to transcend that of any woman, for the type is higher; and no higher, prouder type than that of the Byronic beauty has ever been presented to the eye of man.
>
> The comedy of the episode (for it was not devoid of comedy on either side) escaped Dallas at the moment, so thunderstruck was he with amazement. He sat and stared, confused, uncertain.
>
> "Good God!" he said at last, clumsily enough. "What on earth have you been doing to yourself?"[54]

Like their later-century counterparts, studied by Janice Radway in her *Reading the Romance*, it is unlikely that the swooning audience of *Glorious Apollo* would not have a certain self-consciousness about the excesses of the text.[55] On some level, despite the clear lasciviousness of the description of "the Beautiful" (as Barrington sometimes terms Byron), "the comedy of the episode" would not be lost on the readers, just as it is not lost on their representative within the text, Dallas. *The Bookman's* reviewer firmly situates the

Your Taster and Tester 95

book in its romance genre and seems to see it as one of the less problematic of that genre: "Since it was written obviously as a romance, it is perhaps unfair to call attention to its other shortcomings. As sweetly savored romance it is excellent, and it is, on the surface, accurate."[56] Blair similarly refrains from criticism, but implies strongly through her effusive language that the strongly antiromantic should not open the novel. Throughout her tenure at *Good Housekeeping*, her cautions are the most stringent when the book is the most notorious. Like *Dusty Answer*, against which Blair cautioned her readers quite explicitly in January 1928 (see the introduction), *Glorious Apollo* is a hot seller because of its salacious subject matter, but it is certainly not a book for everyone. With such titles, Blair's job is less to recommend a book than to prevent her readers from picking up a book on the strength of its notoriety, only to be disappointed by it in the long run.

South Wind by Norman Douglas

Blair's next recommendation is an outlier in many ways, not least because it was the least "new" book mentioned in February 1926. Norman Douglas's *South Wind* was first published in England in 1917, to mingled success and scandal, and had been brought out in a limited American edition in 1924. The story of an Anglican bishop's gradual acclimatization to the "pagan" social behaviors on the Mediterranean island of Nepenthe (a fictionalized version of Capri), *South Wind* was embraced by the bohemian expatriate community of which Douglas was a particularly notorious member. *South Wind* was written after Douglas jumped bail in England after having been convicted and jailed for pedophilia; he fled to Florence, Italy, where he continued his pederasty but also became the darling of a literary society that would include D. H. Lawrence, Aldous Huxley, and Joseph Conrad. Major modernist writers were also serious fans of *South Wind*, as Douglas biographer Rachel Hope Cleeves writes: "Virginia Woolf sang its praises in the Times Literary Supplement. When the hero of Evelyn Waugh's 'Brideshead Revisited' arrives at Oxford after World War I, he brings with him only two novels, 'South Wind' and Compton Mackenzie's 'Sinister Street.' . . . Graham Greene recalled how his generation 'was brought up on *South Wind*.'"[57] The novel held intellectual cachet, but it was definitely not in the typical run of *Good Housekeeping* fiction.

Blair's recommendation of *South Wind* offers an example of how she dealt with edgy intellectual works that her readers "ought to know about," per the original charge from her study group, but that might not be acceptable to a mainstream audience. She discusses them, and offers an introduction to them, without wholeheartedly endorsing them. There are also hints about the potential problems that many readers might have with the novel, as well as a validation that Blair herself had some questions or issues about the works at hand. After all, if she is seen to be too wholeheartedly embracing an overly edgy text, her relevance to her *Good Housekeeping* audience might erode.

South Wind, Blair writes, is suitable for "Anne, the pagan, who loves life far better than books and reads for the essence of enjoyment and not for improvement and never for advertisement." *South Wind* is definitely not "improving," then, nor is it a book that everyone is reading—though Blair does suggest that the book provides a different kind of cachet: "Only twelve thousand copies have been printed. All the intellectual snob in me was titillated when I realized that there had come to me, before the many had cognizance of it, one of the gems of literature." Blair is a hipster—she is excited to be one of the few in the know, as she imagines some of her readers might also be. This is the recommendation for the reader who will also be convinced by the "tribute of Saintsbury, the great English critic," who Blair confesses is "one of my favorites," who will feel along with Blair that discovering this gem unknown on American shores is "akin to ... the oil prospector who finds a new oil field."

While it will be several months before *Good Housekeeping* begins printing the publisher and the price for every title Blair mentions, it seems likely that the first American edition to which Blair refers is the 1924 Dodd Mead edition. Dorothy Van Doren would hail this publication in *Forum* in June 1925 (quite a bit after the 1924 publication), also citing Saintsbury and adding that the novel "is most certainly a book to be read wherever books are read at all," while acknowledging that the book is wholly taken up by "a never-ending column of hot air,—in short, of conversation. . . . It envelops whatever of the plot the book has, so that the fact that a lady pushes her vulgar and brutal husband off a cliff eight hundred feet high to avoid the consequences of a bigamous union is merely a slight break in the flow of talk."[58] Blair mentions this plot point obliquely and very briefly in the closing sentences of her review, although she does not note, as Van Doren does, that the Anglican bishop witnesses the murder and, "after pondering the matter, decides to go on talking, to the delight of the reader."[59] Instead, Blair provides an overview of the novel's dramatis personae, much as she did in her recommendation of *Possession*, alongside a sketch of a different sort of moral acquiescence: her own. "I am a feminist, a modern of the moderns, a woman politician. And I loved it." This comes after establishing the bona fides of her uncle, to whom she claims to have read the book aloud: "One of the most learned and appreciative of critics, an evolutionized Presbyterian, scientific and theological in one. It is a pagan story. . . . And yet he loved it" (108). There is something about this book that appeals to those who might be expected to be repulsed by it; Blair wants her audience to know that she is attracted to the novel despite this immorality, much as the bishop chooses to conveniently forget the murder he witnesses. "It gives one furiously, as Carlyle would say, 'to think,'" Blair concludes. And that particular intellectual orientation is precisely what she has modeled in her meditation on what precisely she was able to get out of the book.

The novel would be reprinted again in 1925 by the Modern Library, making the book widely accessible—hardly the elusive, elite text that Blair celebrates finding. According to a February 1926 advertisement in the *New Yorker*, in fact, *South Wind* was one of the best-selling volumes in the library.[60] So Blair's celebration of her getting the novel "before the many had cognizance of it" seems a bit disingenuous. It might, instead, be a signal of the novel's cultural position, and of Blair's own ability to step into and out of the intellectual milieu.

The Venetian Glass Nephew by Elinor Wylie

The last of the substantial reviews in Blair's inaugural column recommends Elinor Wylie's *The Venetian Glass Nephew* to "Louise, sophisticated Louise with the wise eyes." Louise "loves the bizarre, the queer. She will enjoy this beautiful fantasy, enjoying more than most. But even if she doesn't understand it all—and I confess I don't—surely she will love the style, as thin and brittle and clear as the glass of the title" (108). Blair's description is certainly accurate; *The Venetian Glass Nephew* is an unusual book. The story of a Venetian cardinal who, lacking an heir, employs a witch doctor to make him a nephew by magically animating a blown-glass sculpture, Wylie's short novel is filled with archaic prose, arcane references to eighteenth-century Italian clerical life, and baffling (even gratuitous) literary references: "The divining crystal upon my watchchain informs me that Virginio has this moment opened a folio of Sophocles, while the noble Querini is giving the best possible proof of his benevolent guardianship by conferring a double blessing and a modest competence upon the betrothed pair."[61]

The novel is really more a fable than a historical novel, with an animated glass protagonist who falls in love with a flesh-and-blood woman, Rosalba, who agrees to have herself turned into Sevres china to sustain the marriage and to avoid being placed in a convent. Wylie herself preferred the term "fairy tale" to describe the text, which ends in a happily-ever-after Venice, "a world of porcelain and Murano mirrors."[62] This is not, in other words, a novel that would immediately strike a twenty-first-century reader as popular fare for a middlebrow reading audience—but it was indeed somewhat popular, and its impact on the cultural scene was long-lasting. The novel was adapted as an operetta in 1931 by Walter Greenough, but ran for only eight performances at the Vanderbilt Theatre in February of that year, closing "abruptly" after what the stage manager told the *New York Times* was a "technicality" but which the *Times* interpreted as "differences over financial arrangements between the management of the theater and . . . Greenough."[63] In 1945, Van Doren chose *The Venetian Glass Nephew* as her novel recommendation for a special three-volume offering by the Reader's Club. An advertisement for the offering cites Van Doren calling the book "a brilliant satiric-comic fantasy," which "taken out of its Venetian setting, . . . would be merely another story of a cool-blooded husband and a warm-blooded wife."[64]

And this, actually, is the tack that Blair takes in her extended review of the novel. While noting that "the sophisticated author would cringe" at her evaluation of the novel, Blair asserts that the story "must remind even the most superficial of readers of those who must make themselves over in pain and tribulation to fit a husband's limitations and fears." This is a far cry from Krutch in the *Nation*, who asserted that "the purpose of Mrs. Wylie's charming fantasy is to capture in a poet's mind a moment of beauty in the declining Renaissance."[65] Rosalba's transformation is not in this reading a reverse Pygmalion that affirms the superiority of art over flesh and blood but is a tragic allegory of unhappy marriages. As allegory, it can remain for Blair a "pretty plaything of the mind," but the version of marital discord that she offers here somewhat in passing is striking and even contains hints of bitterness. If one folds in the characterization of Rosalba at the outset of the novel as an adherent of Sappho and recognizes both Blair's own self-transformation in light of her husband's needs for a government position and Wylie's two unhappy marriages, the couple's meal of "whipped cream and wafers" at the close of the novel seems an overly sweet, nutritionally empty sign that the sacrifice was too costly. The male reviewers' inability to take this perspective on the novel proves Wylie's point even further. Blair chose to alert her readers to this interpretation, however, and to underscore the feminist reading by suggesting that *The Venetian Glass Nephew* is a prophylactic against the "punching bags" of Sherwood Anderson's edgy and lascivious *Dark Laughter*, a darling of international modernist circles which we will take up in the following chapter.

"Books for Several Tastes"

After offering these lengthy treatments, Blair observes that "these are the readers whose tastes are most catholic, who are most likely to enjoy what the many are reading, though not perhaps the 'best sellers.' Their choice is just a grade finer than that. But there are others in our club who read within narrow limits, and the choice for them is not so easy to make" (108). What follows is a comparatively rapid-fire list of recommendations for a number of different personalities. Each of the briefly mentioned titles fits some segment of the population that Blair envisions as her audience, but coming late in the column, printed on a page deep in the interior of the magazine, they definitely seem like an afterthought. These books are offered to the reader who is still at a loss after hearing about *Possession* or *The Venetian Glass Nephew* and who is, yes, intrepid enough to read to the close, but Blair definitely seems less invested in each of these titles, and her one-to-two sentence characterizations of each often feel a little "off."

Take, for example, Barry Benefield's *The Chicken-Wagon Family*. This oddly titled novel will appeal, Blair writes, to "Nim, who reads for diversion." This is all the description the novel receives . . . it is "diverting." To be fair, many of Benefield's other contemporaneous reviewers were not much more effusive. The *New Yorker* recommends *The Chicken-Wagon Family* to "readers who like sentiment better than they do sophistication, provided it isn't of the Tootsie Roll kind, and provided humor, quaintness, and originality go with it."[66] Harry Hansen in the *Chicago Daily News* notes that the novel successfully translates romance into the city (where apparently, for Hansen, it had not lived before)—but that the pat reconciliation ending disappoints. "And there follows—well, you know what follows. A darn good movie, that's what follows."[67] In the *Miami Herald*, on the other hand, Grace Norman Tuttle cites an interview with Benefield that entertains the notion that the final chapter is just a dream sequence and that the narrator never actually does get reconciled with his first love. "Readers who have faith that good old Jim Pickett at last was actually given his beloved Addie and achieved his heart's desire shall not be discouraged by me. Readers who prefer to believe that Jim went 'wandering alone down the lanes of time,' finding as many do, fulfillment of their dearest hopes in splendid dreams—well, I shall not prosecute them."[68] And yet there were fans, like *The Bookman*'s reviewer, who wrote that "I cannot imagine anyone who would not read it with amusement and then honestly fall in love with several of its characters. . . . I don't know when I've had such a good time reading a book!"[69] While effusive, and replete with references to Dickensian pathos, this review does not go far beyond the idea that the novel is best to divert or distract its readers. It is not being embraced as a literary achievement.

The novel's gimmicky "lady or the tiger" model of ending may well have been enough to relegate this novel to Blair's quick-takes section, particularly coming as it does after an already heavily episodic and complicated plot. It opens in a third-shift newspaper room, where Jim Pickett sits mourning the loss of the love of his life and determining to write the whole story as an act of contrition. Taking us back to his youth as a new graduate of the University of Texas at Austin, Jim tells of his chance meeting with the Fippany family, who have been traveling Alabama, Arkansas, and Texas as junk dealers and who are going to relocate to New York City for the educational and social benefit of their ten-year-old daughter Addie. Jim joins forces with the family, acting as Addie's tutor on the road, as they travel with two mules north to the city. The arrival of the family in the city is played for humor, as a fish-out-of-water story in which the Fippanys eventually use their rural skills to succeed in running a boarding house and a building salvage empire. Meanwhile Jim becomes a beat reporter for a fictional New York newspaper, and Benefield indulges in several rapturous descriptions of the joys of journalism.

The narrative of ironically savvy rural innocents in the city takes an awkward turn toward romance after Mrs. Fippany, fearing she is about to die of appendicitis, conducts a bedside "marriage" between twenty-two-year-old Jim and twelve-year-old Addie. Mrs. Fippany does not die, but neither does the marriage promise. Addie and Jim play at being engaged in increasingly less-innocent ways as she grows older, though he insists that, while he is committed to her, she is "free" until after she has completed college. Things turn sour when Jim intervenes in Addie's father's nascent affair with one of the family's boarders, Minnie Febber; Jim becomes in turn entangled with

Febber and eventually marries her after a pregnancy scare. The couple's flight from the multiply betrayed Fippany family sees them leaving New York for points south, and they end up in Dallas for a prolonged episode during which Minnie is tarred and feathered by the Ku Klux Klan for adultery with a prominent local man. After Jim and Minnie's eventual divorce, Jim moves back to New York to resume his newspaper work and to pine after Addie, who has become an actress on the New York stage. After Jim writes the whole story, he bundles the manuscript in a package to be delivered to Addie after his death; as mentioned above, the final chapter of the novel can be read either as a happy reunion, wherein Addie is sent the manuscript, reads it, and summons Jim back to her, or as a dream sequence in which the exhausted Jim imagines a reconciliation.

This was Benefield's first novel, and one certainly gets the sense that it spiraled out of his control. The scenes with Minnie Febber—certainly the Dallas episode with the Klan, but also a prolonged liaison in Atlantic City—are haphazard, in turns overindulgent and rushed. It is a good book for a reader who likes "distraction," and the very things that make it suitable for such a reader would render it an unsuitable text for a long review. But the more likely reason for its demotion is its ambiguity about the romantic relationship between an adult and a child that lies at its heart. Jim as a retrospective first-person narrator is still palpably besotted with Addie, even as he describes her as a ten-year-old child. This can initially be written off as an adult's memory of a beautiful child, until the marriage scene, which reflects backward on all his previous loving descriptions and renders them troubling. Readerly discomfort intensifies in the scene where Jim finally kisses Addie passionately, as opposed to affectionately: "I pulled her closer still and kissed her as men do not kiss little girls," the phrase "little girls" reminding us that this is exactly what Addie was when Jim first met her, and is how he has seen her up to this point. When Addie responds, "Jim, Jim stop; you frighten me. You never kissed me that way before,"[70] it is impossible to forget that she is fifteen in this scene, and while Benefield closes the chapter by asserting that she is now a "woman," it is a determination that does not rest easily. While *Good Housekeeping* is silent on the issue of child marriage in the 1920s, and the May-December romance does not seem to trouble the novel's other reviewers, this element of the narrative may well have contributed to its briefer notice in Blair's column.

The 1920s saw both a rash of child brides and a resistance to the practice, as Nicholas Syrett has documented in *American Child Bride: A History of Minors and Marriage in the United States*. By this point, sexual desire for a child was beginning to be classified as a psychiatric disorder, and the term "pedophilia," while not in widespread use, was becoming known in reform circles.[71] The boundaries of childhood were vexed, however, particularly by the pubescent girl. Melanie Dawson uses the term "child-women" to describe fictional characters whose representations feature "a nonlinear commingling of signs about age." "The child-woman, a quandary in terms of development, possessed the postures, behavior, and assurance of an adult, alongside the naiveté, limited experience, and body type of the very young."[72] The scene of their first romantic kiss sees Addie veering between womanly desire and childish reluctance—"Kiss me again Jim. . . . Now don't do it any more, I am afraid"—and while it finally ends with Jim's assertion that she is a "woman," their final embrace purposefully echoes their previous childish late-night snuggles. While their informal marriage on Mrs. Fippany's potential death-bed is several years old at this point, this adult kiss is what prematurely ages Addie, in ways that disturbed marriage reformers in the 1920s. As Syrett observes, "When children married in a world that celebrated childhood innocence, witnesses saw a rupturing of both marriage and childhood itself." Addie's vacillation between childishness and mature sexuality in this scene would very likely have been distressing for many readers in the middle of the 1920s.

It makes sense, therefore, that the novel works hard to underscore the notion that Jim and Addie's relationship is substantial and emotional rather than prurient and exploitative. Benefield follows this scene immediately with a scene in which Minnie Febber attempts to seduce Jim, on a "hot, sultry July morning when one who had an excuse for sleeping late was glad to take advantage of it" (182). Minnie comes to Jim scantily clad in a silk kimono (contrasted with Addie's cotton nightdress), which keeps slipping off her shoulders, pretending to need a cut bandaged. Her mock-childish request gives her the opportunity to display her very adult body to Jim, who is aston-ished by its voluptuousness and whose hands shake whenever he nears her fully developed womanly body. Her parting words, though hostile in context, actually function as a caution against Jim's pedophilic behavior: "I had better be going, too. Addie will be coming home [from school] soon; and if she saw me in this room, even on so innocent an errand, I believe she would poison me. But she's a darling *child*, is n't she?" (188, italics original). Jim and Minnie both know her errand was not "innocent," just as they both know that the category "child" fails to describe Addie now that she is romantically entangled with Jim. In reminding Jim that Addie is away at school, reminding him that she is technically a child even though she harbors womanly jealously, Minnie is actually voicing many of the concerns leveraged by progressive reformers.

But when Jim does enter into a more age-appropriate relationship with this supposed voice of reason, it is a disaster. Minnie's adult sexuality is licentious, and in contrast to Addie, she does not hold her own or others' marriage vows as sacred. Jim is only able to have a sexual relationship with Minnie while intoxicated. They get married when Minnie tells Jim that their one weekend together has gotten her pregnant, but it turns out that she was either mistaken or, more likely, that she was using this claim to coerce Jim into a union that she wrongly believed would be financially lucrative. Minnie has repeated extramarital affairs, which lead dramatically to her public shaming at the hands of the Ku Klux Klan in Dallas.[73] Jim has by this point become so apathetic to his marriage, however, that he has no recriminations for Minnie: "I did not care even about the tarring and feathering, or about what it signified. Divorce? It never occurred to me. Did it matter what the shadows out there did or did n't do?" (313). When they do finally divorce, to allow Minnie to marry an Alaskan rancher, the transaction is dispatched in a few brief sentences. Marriage, it seems, is more of a failure when transacted by two adults than it is when entered into by an adult and a child; it is held less sacred by a mature woman than by a child-woman. And yet, the novel refuses to consummate a marriage between Jim and Addie until they have both matured. In the final scene, whether one reads it as a real reconciliation or a hallucinatory one, Addie is thirty and Jim forty, and their age difference is no longer potentially scandalous.[74]

Benefield's novel was not the first book recommended in this clean-up section of the column; that spot goes to A. Edward Newton's essay collection *The Greatest Book in the World*. Newton's richly illustrated book is prefaced by an open letter to the founder of a selective men's study club, which had provided, Newton contends, the "only [liberal education] the writer ever received." Newton himself was famous as a bibliophile, although professionally he was an upper-level manager of several electrical manufacturing businesses;[75] the concurrence of the two was of central interest to his book's reviewer in the *New York Times*: "In these and his other books and in his book-collecting hobby Mr. Newton shows the absurd falsity of two notions

104 CHAPTER TWO

concerning American life much cherished both at home and abroad—those invidious prepossessions, now become almost proverbial, concerning the intellectual equipment of the business man and the character of the self-made man. For he is a successful business man and the architect of his own fortune, two facts that every one of his readers ought to keep in mind while delighting in his books."[76]

Newton's pursuits, although presumably more robustly bankrolled than those of many of the *Good Housekeeping* readers, map onto their interests quite neatly. While the essays in his book are more expansive than the travel and furnishing pieces in the magazine, the topics and the tone are similar. Indeed, the book demonstrates the similarity between men's and women's study clubs, a parallel that Blair may be intentionally suggesting to elevate and validate the latter (as she will do more explicitly in later columns). Modeled on the agenda of a study club, the book contains chapters on topics such as a history of the Bible as a printed book; a tour of Samuel Johnson's home in Gough Square in London; the intellectual history of Paoli, Pennsylvania; and a rambling discourse considering the question "Are Comparisons Odious?" It is, in other words, a miscellany, which Blair recommends to "Helen, our dilettante in the arts from music to old furniture, inclusive" (108). Helen seems both a perfect fit for Newton's book and an easy identification for the *Good Housekeeping* reader who can move from discussions of travel in Japan to old chests to child-rearing, and Newton's book a logical nonfiction offering as a catch-all for the readers who have yet to find something they might like in the rest of Blair's column.

Blair's next move is to recommend, very briefly, Willa Cather's *The Professor's House* to "Julia, who never takes any chances on the unrecommended or untried." This is perhaps one of the novels for a reader hoping for a discussion of "the books we ought to read," since Cather was well established as a literary giant in 1926. But the recommendation comes late, and the discussion of Cather is one of the briefest in the columns. In the next chapter, I will take up Blair's treatment of "highbrow" literary authors in more detail; for now, it is enough to note that she is determinedly not a focus of Blair's attentions. Coming right after the Newton recommendation, Cather acts as a different sort of "clean-up" recommendation, an easy one for Blair to make to ensure that most of her readers are satisfied with the coverage in her column.

After Cather, Blair's three final recommendations seem like scattershot afterthoughts. First is Thomas Boyd's *Samuel Drummond* for "Caroline, who appreciates distinction and does not mind a somber theme if it lays bare some truth." Blair suggests that *Samuel Drummond*, which tells the story of a farming family in Ohio during the Civil War period, was considered a disappointment by many others, calling it "the book with which Thomas Boyd forfeits the popularity won with 'Through the Wheat,' to deepen his art." Given that comment, one expects to find multiple reviews disparaging the novel, but in fact it does not seem to have been very widely reviewed at all. It is precisely the novel's distance from the more celebrated predecessor, however, that seems to have made it a suitable pick for Blair's column.

Through the Wheat (1923) had offered a realistic portrait of World War I trench warfare through the eyes of an enlisted marine. *Wheat* was celebrated by the reviewer in the *New York Times* for its political nuance and Boyd's style, "sober, precise, varied—in a word, it is brilliant."[77] Boyd was himself a former US Marine, who settled in St. Paul, Minnesota, after the war and became a reporter and eventually the book review columnist for the *St. Paul Daily News*. The popular column, titled "In a Corner with the Bookworm," made Boyd a literary celebrity; he became friends with fellow Minnesota novelists Sinclair Lewis and F. Scott Fitzgerald, and eventually opened Kilmarnock Books in downtown St. Paul, which became the center of the city's literary scene. With some help from Fitzgerald, Boyd published *Wheat*, his first novel, to considerable acclaim—it was likened repeatedly to John Dos Passos's *Three Soldiers*. Boyd became a member for a time of the Parisian expatriate community around Hemingway and Gertrude Stein, largely on the strength of this novel and his close friendship with Fitzgerald.[78]

Boyd's second novel, *The Dark Cloud*, did not sell well and was termed "boring" by the critics, who hoped it was a sophomore slump "a transition to that splendor of creation which 'Through the Wheat' eloquently foretold."[79] The critical consensus on his third novel, *Samuel Drummond*, was that it did not deliver. The novel does not seem to have been very widely reviewed, and the reviews that were published were ambivalent at best. The reviewer for the *New York Times* accused Boyd of "a restraint so sober as partly to baffle the reader," but grudgingly acknowledged that "as a historical work, it is a superficial, but on the whole accurate, piece of observation" and concluded that "the large public who are intrigued by novels of farm life will find his book true to life and with greater insight than the majority of such volumes."[80] Incrementally more enthusiastic was the *Bookman* reviewer who I cited above enjoying *The Chicken-Wagon Family* so thoroughly: "I do not think everyone will enjoy

Mr. Boyd's clipped style, his careful development, his pages which lack luminosity but gain in understanding and clarity." At the same time, this reviewer compared *Samuel Drummond* favorably to Ellen Glasgow's *Barren Ground* and Edna Ferber's *So Big*, the latter of which had just won the Pulitzer; while Fitzgerald and many of his cohort denigrated the farm novel, it certainly had a presence in the mid-1920s literary landscape.[81]

The novel's historical setting and rural lifestyle both situate it in a sweet spot for *Good Housekeeping* readers. It opens with a farming pastoral; Samuel, the younger son of the family, is not excited that his newly arrived cousin is clearly being set up as his future wife, but he loves the work on the farm.

> The Cochin Chinas, large chickens with yellow feathers which clothed them to their toes, and red, flapping combs, stretched their legs and ran forward with eager caws as Ida appeared from the granary with an apron filled with shard corn; the robins were swelling their little brown throats with cries; the sun beamed warmly; about the earth there seemed to be a great peace and quiet, rather accentuated by the small sounds from the chickens and birds. Samuel was customarily happy on mornings like this, for he had no regrets, and but few hopes. He would have been happy this morning also were it not for Martha Jane.[82]

Samuel eventually marries Martha Jane, and the remainder of the text follows their growing farm and family; Samuel serves in the Civil War, but this portion of the narrative is fleetingly brief compared to the discussion of the Drummonds' attempts to stay independent and continue the farm despite their lack of sons. Samuel is not a good manager, and when he finally accumulates too much debt to compete, he sells the farm and moves to town to live out his days with Martha Jane. The sale of the farm is profoundly melancholy, the departure played for considerable sentiment, with Samuel contemplating the tragedy of his horse's loss of clover-covered hillsides for a barn in town. And perhaps it is this note of loss that drives Blair to relegate *Samuel Drummond* to the briefer mentions in her column. Like *The Professor's House*, it landed too close to the line of the critical, without enough leavening discussion of domestic successes.

After *The Chicken-Wagon Family*, the "diverting" tale of rustics come to the city and a child quasi bride, Blair recommends J. Lucas-Dubreton's brief biography of *Samuel Pepys* for "Ryland, with undergraduate yearnings and a postgraduate brain." This is the final book mentioned in the column, and frankly, her rationale for the recommendation is one of the more baffling ones. Blair

Your Taster and Tester

describes Lucas-Dubreton's rapid-fire narration of Pepys's political intrigues and serial adulteries as "Gallic ruthlessness," which is not really indicative of any scholarly qualities. Truthfully, too, those are not the predominant tones in the book, which is a selective condensation and retelling of Pepys's compendious, and confessional, diaries. As Herbert S. Gorman notes in his review of the book in the *New York Times*, the Pepys described by Lucas-Dubreton is more of a randy arriviste bumbler than an astute political operative. "Pepys might be called the Babbitt of his time," Gorman writes, noting that Lucas-Dubreton tends to speed over the obvious political calculations that would have seen Pepys on the boat that sailed to bring Charles II back to England to unseat Cromwell in favor of "those personal and secret passions that belong to the emotional man."[83] The reviewer for the *Richmond* (Indiana) *Palladium and Sun-Telegram* also tags the book as a chronicle of "early English lack of morals," which "glow[s] with the romantic life of the period"[84]—not a scholarly tome by any stretch. In a brief review, *The Bookman* called it a "racy account of the Restoration," and notes that it is "unexpurgated."[85]

Read in close proximity, *Samuel Pepys* resembles *Glorious Apollo* much more than the biographical sketches and philosophical essays in *The Greatest Book in the World*; it is heavy on extramarital peccadillos and light on intellectual conversations. Why then would *this* book appeal to the reader "with undergraduate yearnings and a postgraduate brain" rather than the reader who "likes to roll over or under her tongue bits of not-too-nice gossip"? Could this be a signal that Blair did not, in fact, finish this book—or skimmed it— or that it did not stay fresh in her brain, as her skeptical audiences in 1931 would speculate? If she did not read the whole book, was Blair's recommendation based on the general idea that Pepys was a significant historical figure, and so his biography should be interesting to a scholarly type like Ryland? Might she have been swayed by the volume's backmatter, consisting of advertisements for critical approaches to Milton, anthropological treatments of Mesopotamia and lectures on "Mental Science"? Surely Blair was not making any reference to the amatory practices of university students, who at any case were not considered as promiscuous in 1926 as they would be by the end of the century, and certainly not in the pages of *Good Housekeeping*.[86] At any rate, there is little of the pedantic in Lucas-Dubreton's poetic conclusion: "History does not tell us if from Samuel's grave there sprouted a bramble which buried itself in the grave of Elizabeth. This phenomenon was observed a short time ago at Tintagel."[87]

108 CHAPTER TWO

Blair closes her first column with a benediction that sums up her recommendation philosophy and points toward her hopes for future columns: "Reading is to some people one thing, to others something else. To some a forgetting, to others a finding. And to each person each book is a different book. I can but offer my club the menu—and leave them to find out for themselves how they like it. They may exchange volumes unread. One tastes for another with diffidence. But I have set the feast before them. And among them some will be grateful" (108). Blair knows that some of her readers will not like the books she has chosen for them, and she accepts this inevitability and even, in accepting it, authorizes this kind of behavior in her readers. There is no need to go on dutifully reading, and trying to enjoy, a book that has not hit the mark. The important thing to Blair is that her recommendations to her club, or her contributions to *Good Housekeeping*, empower her audiences to read and to own their reading preferences. "Once any one begins to read, she will go on. My circulating library is only the 'start'" (108). Of course, Blair's performances of a variety of reading practices could also serve as aspirational models for her readers; a reader might hope, for example, to be able to match Blair's enthusiasm for *South Wind* even if the first few pages or chapters left her cold. Blair does not address in this column the idea of sticking with a book even if it does not initially appeal; even the idea that one will wrangle with Sherwood Anderson's "punching bags" is only a glancing mention, easily dismissed if punching bags do not appeal. The difficult read has no place in the February 1926 column.

In her study of the feminine middlebrow novel, Nicola Humble observes that "a breadth and hybridity of taste was one of the hallmarks of the ideal reader as imagined" by those novels.[88] Arguing that the genre of the middlebrow novel occupies a space "between the trashy romance of thriller on one hand, and the philosophically or formally challenging novel on the other; offering narrative excitement without guilt, and intellectual stimulation without undue effort,"[89] Humble also argues that there is an implied pecking order within the genre, from the "country house" novel to the barely acceptable "racy" novel. Blair's columns are remarkable, however, for her determined resistance to such hierarchies: different books are differently good for different readers. While one might not embrace *The Chicken-Wagon Family*, another might; a reader who embraces that novel might *also* enjoy *South Wind* when she is in her more intellectual moods. The books sit beside each other on Blair's shelf, awaiting their intended reader, but also tradeable and potentially speaking to multiple of her book club friends or *Good House-keeping* audience. The texts that pose some of the greatest difficulty, however, are the more "highbrow" texts that might be read in the middlebrow mode by middlebrow readers. It is to these fictional works by the likes of Cather, Anderson, Lewis, and Dreiser that we turn in the following chapter.

CHAPTER THREE

The Arcadia of the Ozarks

Should I read it, Emily? Is it worth *my* while?
—Natalie to Emily Newell Blair, en route to the Ozarks, October 1926[1]

The question of which books her readers "ought" to read was one of the three posed at the beginning of Blair's inaugural column. That "ought," frequently interchanged with a "should," haunts the first year of Blair's tenure at *Good Housekeeping*, as she establishes the ethos of her columns and the mix of the books she will recommend. The kinds of books that readers felt they *ought* to read, generally, tended to be the books celebrated by intellectual critics as the "best books" of the day—books that for the large part have made up the canon of so-called modernist literature and have continued as the most-studied books of the 1920s and 1930s. These books, however, constitute only a minor proportion of Blair's recommendations, and when they do appear, their significance to Blair's audience is always open to contestation. This chapter will look at two pairs of novels that existed on the periphery of "modernism": Willa Cather's *The Professor's House* and Sherwood Anderson's *Dark Laughter*, and Sinclair Lewis's *Elmer Gantry* and Theodore Dreiser's *An American Tragedy*. All four of these authors were liminal figures for critics in the mid-1920s. Catherine Turner has noted that Anderson "appeared to represent the development of this 'new style' in fiction, even if he was not fully outside the realist tradition and even if they did not agree on what was 'new' about him."[2] Cather, too, was a difficult author to categorize because of her frequent serialization in big magazines; Robert Seguin notes that Cather's self-conscious pursuit of both wide audiences and a reputation as "an uncompromising literary authors" resulted in her reputation "suffer[ing] somewhat in the decades following," particularly among the critics of the 1950s who retrospectively constructed a monolithic "literary modernism."[3] Likewise, Dreiser and Lewis had already been embraced in the heyday of literary realism, so it was unclear to critics in the 1920s whether they were still relevant in this new phase. Blair, ever the consumer advocate, directs her readers to approach these texts with caution—to read these texts if they work *for them* and to avoid internalizing narratives that would make them feel inadequate for disliking the experience. By continuing to direct her recommendations toward her friends, who are midwestern but who do not fit Harold Ross's dismissive paradigm of "the old lady in Dubuque,"[4] Blair deflates other critical debates as self-important and even out of touch and validates her judgments, her friends' preferences, and, by extension, her readers. My chapter title, "The Arcadia of the Ozarks," is a play on H. L. Mencken's infamous essay "The Sahara of the Bozart," which eviscerated the pretentions of anyone purporting to have aesthetic standards while living south of the Mason-Dixon line. I consider Blair's dismissal of such regional snobbery, captured so neatly by her anecdote about explaining the pros and cons (but never the obligations) of reading *An American Tragedy* to her friend Natalie as they motor to an Ozark vacation resort, the inverse of Mencken's move in every way. The process begins in her inaugural column, with her brief reference to Willa Cather's *The Professor's House* and her reduction of Sherwood Anderson's *Dark Laughter* to the status of a punchline.

The Professor's House and *Dark Laughter*

The most recognizable text to a twenty-first-century student of American literature in the whole of the 1926 column receives one of Blair's briefest treatments. In the midst of a closing flurry of recommendations for those who read "within narrow limits," Blair offers Willa Cather's seventh published novel, *The Professor's House*, to "Julia, who never takes any chances on the unrecommended or untried." Blair's whole column—her whole project of "tasting and testing books"—would presumably not be enough of an imprimatur for Julia; Blair's language here clearly indicates that Julia wants a book that has been deemed worthy by recognized cultural authorities. *The Professor's House* is, it seems, one of the "best" of the most recent books, and among those books, it is the one that Blair is going to recommend to her readers. Julia wants a highbrow book—the highbrow book that Blair selects for her is Cather's.

Blair explicitly does *not* suggest that Julia, or any of her readers, tackle Sherwood Anderson's *Dark Laughter*, although she does mention it in the course of her inaugural column, evoking the novel as a foil to another, preferred and recommended, book: "[Elinor Wylie's *The Venetian Glass Nephew*] struck me as a pretty plaything of the mind. And mental playthings we must have, especially if we are to try our mental muscles against many such punching-bags as Sherwood Anderson gives us in 'Dark Laughter,' his story of an individualist who revolts against convention" (108).

As we saw in chapter 2, Blair recommends *The Venetian Glass Nephew* despite the fact that it might baffle the reader; it is stylistically intriguing, a "pretty plaything" of the mind. This is in direct opposition to Anderson's "punching bag" of a novel—also stylistically innovative, perhaps, and one that might be on the list of books one thinks one should "try our mental muscles against," but this is hardly an invitation—more of a caution to readers who might otherwise be drawn to novels about characters who revolt against convention.

Blair seems to have received the go-ahead for her work at *Good Housekeeping* some time after the end of February 1925, when she wrote to Frances Parkinson Keyes that "Mr. Bigelow was sure that he had no opening" at the magazine.[5] She would most likely have had a one-to-two month lead time on the inaugural column, and it would have made perfect sense to work from lists of notable books such as those published in *Life*, *The Bookman*, and the *New Yorker*. *Dark Laughter* and *The Professor's House* were constant companions on such lists throughout the fall and winter of 1925–26, frequently both starred, frequently appearing alongside Wylie, Barrington, Bromfield, and Parrish. In the November 7, 1925, installment of the recurring feature "Tell Me a Book to Read," the *New Yorker* says that Wylie's novel is "a beautiful ironical fantasy. . . . Everyone is saying its style is 'baroque,' but don't let that deter you." Cather's "admirable novel," on the other hand, "holds the 1925 record for making fools of sometimes intelligent book reviewers," while Anderson "once more sees life as sex, and through Viennese smoked glass—but sees it."[6] *The Bookman* ran a compendium review of Wylie, Cather, and Anderson's novels (along with Joseph Conrad's posthumously published unfinished novel, *Suspense*) in its November 1925 issue.[7] *Life* does not include *Dark Laughter* in its September 24, 1925, "Among the New Books" list, although it does list *The Perennial Bachelor* ("The life history of a sheltered male, with a background as rich as a Renaissance tapestry") and *Samuel Drummond* ("Simple characters fictionalized against a Civil War background") alongside *The Professor's House* ("One of our best novelists has an off day").[8] Cather and Anderson are still being mentioned in the same column in August 1926, when *Forum* publishes an I. A. Richards anthology assessment of "Some Outstanding

The Arcadia of the Ozarks   113

Novels"; *Glorious Apollo* and *The Perennial Bachelor* also make the cut for this column, published nearly a year after the publication date for all four.

These two novels, then, would have been expected to be discussed together—and Blair's initial charge, to tell her readers "what we ought to know about the new books," necessitated their mention. But the manner of their mention situates Blair very specifically in this opening column. She is not going to kowtow to the expectations of the standard book reviews, which after all were not satisfying to her readers. *Dark Laughter*, which she glosses as the "story of an individualist who revolts against convention," was also about a whole host of other things—orgies in Paris, marital infidelity, and advertising, to name a few. Blair does not see her way clear to modeling a reading of this "punching bag" of a book. Cather's work, on the other hand, receives a qualified recommendation as a "tragedy of disillusion" that "is almost perfectly told and will make an unforgettable appeal to readers, like Julia, who do not insist that their stories run smoothly and rapidly to their appointed end." In the end, Cather's novel is legible to Blair's readers despite its formal innovations, and Anderson's novel does not seem to repay the mental labor his formal innovations apparently demand. This type of negotiation will be typical of Blair's engagement with texts that self-consciously align themselves with—or are aligned by contemporaneous reviewers with—literary modernism.

Blair's treatment of these "literary event" novels also signals her relative independence from the implicit and explicit pressures the publishing industry was beginning to exert over reviewers in the 1920s. In *What America Read*, Gordon Hutner writes convincingly about the benefits of reading the whole of the *New York Times Book Review* to get an overview of the literary world in a given year, month, week. But he does note that there is a large proportion of positive reviews in the *Times*, both because of the need to maintain advertising revenue and the need to stay on good terms with publishers. Local and regional newspaper book reviews, on the other hand, seem to depart more regularly from the anodyne. Local reviews demanded accuracy when it came to regional representation but also evinced an awareness of broader cultural expectations for readers and reviewers; they tended to engage the "highbrow" literary debates of the day, while also stepping back to note what their readers will want to get out of a book and how they might be expected to approach a book set on home soil.

The reviews for *Dark Laughter* are a case in point. The *New York Times* gave *Dark Laughter* a prominent front-page review, generally positive in tone but not without reservations. Anderson himself is worthy of notice, "a significant writer—a writer for our times."[9] And yet, after an exhausting and exhaustive review that sometimes seems to be trying to ventriloquize the prose of the novel (a constant refrain of "the ground heaves!"), the reviewer concludes that, while the book is not "pornographic," it "is more than marred—it is poisoned from end to end by that strange undervaluation of the human will which has descended like a blight upon the modern school in fiction."[10] Such a review would give H. L. Mencken room to decry the philistinism of the common reader but would also ensure *Dark Laughter's* position as a book with which serious readers should grapple. Anderson, like Cather, was a liminal figure for many critics; his works "appeared to represent the development of this 'new style' in fiction, even if he was not fully outside the realist tradition and even if they did not agree on what was 'new' about him."[11]

Dark Laughter's scandalous moments and its imbrication in literary gossip were probably factors in its relatively wide review coverage in regional newspapers. The *Kansas City Star* initially offers a mixed review of the novel on October 24, 1925; after citing as an opening a long descriptive passage from the novel (a portrait of barges and the banks of the Mississippi River), the reviewer laments that "it is too bad that the man who has flashes of vision like that should have written the whole of 'Dark Laughter.'"[12] The novel is an abnegation of duty, from someone who can write such lovely descriptions of the Midwest, because it has a pessimistic perspective on human nature: "he stacks the cards"; "there is little evidence of progress;" "spinal rigidity in any of his characters would seem shockingly unnatural." Bruce Dudley, the protagonist, "presumably a normally civilized and literate American, apparently can gain nothing from his self-conscious and atavistic quest of primitivism save a certain nonchalance in adultery and a keen satisfaction in doing nothing, or at least as little as possible."

On October 3, 1925, *Dark Laughter* leads off the *Kansas City Star's* anonymous "If You Ask Us" gossip section in the books page: "Sherwood Anderson's new book, 'Dark Laughter,' looks like the ravings of a writer who doesn't know what he's up to. . . . A critical friend of ours, who also finds 'Dark Laughter' disappointing, remarks that 'apparently the modern art crowd has kidded Anderson off his base. He writes about people and life that he doesn't understand, and is smutty in the wrong sort of way. I predict it will be almost as big a flop as 'Many Marriages.'"[13] On this same page, the *Star* reviewers celebrate the new A. S. M. Hutchinson novel; this is where we find Schuyler Ashley's positive review of *The Professor's House*, to be discussed below. The *Dallas Morning News* also hated the novel. "'Dark Laughter' is a disappointment. Mr. Anderson does indeed exhibit a slowly increasing ability to do what he wants to do, but what he wants to do does not seem worth doing."[14] "One really wonders if Mr. Anderson himself is the victim of obsession or affectation. . . . Mr. Anderson tries—and pretty well succeeds—in reproducing the psychological states that accompany the modicum of action in the book. To a degree his psychological analysis is true, doubtless, yet certainly the emphasis upon sex is exaggerated until the people of the story can hardly be said to be typical, and so their experiences seem of little more value than clinical records of morbid types." The reviewer cites Whitman's "barbaric Yawp," but concludes, "Whitman had a message. Anderson? Perhaps; but reading 'Dark Laughter,' one doubts it."[15]

The New Orleans *Times-Picayune* takes the book's edginess as a given: "It is not news any more to announce that Mr. Anderson's new book is shocking."[16] In general, however, this review is positive; even after an opening that seems to validate these assessments, the reviewer criticizes the unfair puritanism of many of the naysayers and recommends the novel as offering an accurate portrait of the city. As we can see, these reviews focus mainly on the novel's regional flavor and on the elements of scandal that make the book a publishing event; formal innovation is lightly discussed if at all and does not determine evaluations either negative or positive. Blair, in contrast, engages in none of these discourses; she registers the formal difficulty of the work ("punching bag") and offhandedly summarizes the novel with the broadest possible brush ("an individualist . . . revolts against convention"). Her brevity reads as dismissal, but not on account of formal "difficulty." I would posit, rather, that it is a function of the novel's uncomfortable relationship with characters who could be said to resemble Blair and her audience: female magazine writers and readers.

Dark Laughter's formal complexity inheres largely in its stream-of-consciousness presentation; the reader lives largely inside the mind of the protagonist Bruce Dudley, whose observations of the world around him open out into meditations on far-flung topics and then circle back to find Dudley having acted without his actions being narrated at all. Anderson is said to have tried to model the novel on Joyce's *Ulysses*, and described the novel to his brother as "a kind of fantasy of modern life—the War, sex

116 CHAPTER THREE

reactions in America, artists, labor, factories. Am trying to make them all dance to slow music."[17] Anderson's own synopsis of the plot describes it as a struggle between two men for the love of one woman, which concludes in the final published version with the woman leaving her husband for a slightly younger interloper, "emphasizing the book's basic theme of the superiority of the uninhibited life to the inhibited one."[18] While the woman in question, Aline Grey, does have more interiority in the novel than Anderson's summary would suggest, she does not have the degree of agency typical of most of the female characters in *Good Housekeeping* or in Blair's recommendations. She leads Bruce to her bed passively; she does not pursue him after he leaves her; and when he returns she makes herself available to him but not obviously so. Her farewell to her husband is similarly passive: "I can't help it, Fred. We are going now. We were only waiting to tell you."[19] While the frequent focus on sexuality might also have mitigated against Blair's recommendation, Blair might have been more likely to avoid suggesting *Dark Laughter* to her general audience because of the novel's more blatant misogyny. After all, as we have seen in the previous chapter, Blair does not shy away from texts that might be sexually controversial (see *South Wind*) or ribald (see *Samuel Pepys*) or focused on ignoble protagonists (see *The Chicken-Wagon Family*).

Another moment in the novel that might have been troubling for Blair and her audience is Anderson's barely disguised parody of Rose Wilder Lane, daughter of Laura Ingalls Wilder and infamous journalist, as a dissipated expat with a predilection for orgiastic partying. "Rose Frank" in Anderson's novel is an "American newspaper woman" who "had made her living by sending smart Parisian gossip to American newspapers, but she had also hungered for—the limit" (*DL* 181). She revels in telling a story about the Quat'z Arts Ball, a Parisian art student party where she witnesses "twenty-nine ways of love-making—all done in the life—naked people" (*DL* 183). Her lengthy and broken narrative of the evening is framed by her neurotic "dark laughter"—the first mention of the novel's title in the text—and her explicit confession of lascivious voyeurism is finally read as pitiable by the audience: "A fool, that woman, for letting anything get her like that, for getting upset and giving herself away" (*DL* 186).[20] Rose Frank has a unique voice, but she is also, in Anderson's representation, a typical American newspaper woman. By analogy, then, all such women, and all of their literary productions, are both shallow "gossip" and the by-products of a mingled sexual repression and voyeuristic inclination. This is hardly a portrait that would appeal to magazine

The Arcadia of the Ozarks   117

writer Emily Newell Blair or her magazine readers, all of whom would have known Lane as a prolific contributor to magazines like *Good Housekeeping*. She had made several appearances in *Good Housekeeping* in 1924 and 1925, including as the author of a featured short story in the December 1924 Christmas issue alongside other famous names such as Gene Stratton-Porter, Alice Booth, Kathleen Norris, and Frances Parkinson Keyes. A novel that connected her persona with psychologically tormented sexual frustration and perversion would not sit comfortably in that forum.

Anderson's explicit primitivism was probably not an insurmountable barrier to Blair's recommendation, although it is one of the more difficult features for a twenty-first-century audience to tolerate. Published the year before Edna Ferber's *Show Boat* and the same year as DuBose Heyward's *Porgy*, *Dark Laughter* has long been treated alongside Carl Van Vechten's *Nigger Heaven* as a specimen of modernist "primitivism" but might also been read on a continuum with those other middlebrow novels of the South.[21] Blair will recommend *Porgy* to her college-educated readers in May 1926, calling it a "masterpiece," which must be read in full to be properly appreciated but which *must* be read, because Heyward has "take[n] a subject that discussion of prejudice has encased in a tradition and [made] you see to its core and suffer and laugh because of it."[22] She also mentions *Porgy* a second time (repeated mentions are very rare in her columns) in August 1930, as well as in October 1926 in reference to *Show Boat*'s adaptation as a stage musical. But *Porgy* and *Show Boat* are both much more amenable to audiences that, as Jaime Harker puts it, "tended to see the African-American community as uniform: primitive, sensual, funny, musical, rhythmic, and simple."[23] In fact, Blair's insistence that *Porgy* be read in full is because her typical summary would not capture the thing that makes the novel work: the dialect. "It would be sacrilege as well as idiocy for me to paraphrase, because it is the way Heyward tells the story that makes you accept Porgy as a great tragic character and so all that happens to him as of significance."[24] Blair's summary would not capture the "rhythmic" or the "simple," which is essential to the effect on the (white, middle-class, middlebrow) reader. We will return to *Porgy* in the epilogue.

Given all the ways in which *Dark Laughter* was unsuitable for the *Good Housekeeping* audience, it perhaps more surprising that Blair mentions *Dark Laughter* at all. The fact that she does signals the degree to which, at least in this inaugural column, she is committed to fully representing the current state of popular and highbrow letters, even when she cannot bring herself to embrace particular texts. The degree to which *The Professor's House* does not require the same amount of hedging both is an effect of and helps to reproduce Cather's uncomfortable relationship with literary modernism. As Janis Stout argues, Cather herself was in continual dialogue with middlebrow literature, in particular borrowing liberally from her friend Dorothy Canfield.[25] Stout also describes Cather as a "modernist by association," who was a member of a network of modernist thinkers and writers in New York and New Mexico.[26] Cather's unique in-betweenness, or both-and-ness, made her an ideal author for Blair's purposes in *Good Housekeeping*.

Stout suggests that Cather was sensitive about her family's relative cultural deprivation compared to her friend Canfield's family. The cultural parvenue is more insecure about being a part of the literary elite, and this registers in her self-conscious policing of the boundaries of her work.[27] It figures too that many of Blair's relatively culturally established friends would have no qualms about spending time reading *The Chicken-Wagon Family*, but that there would be other readers like Julia, the designated reader of *The Professor's House*, who "never takes any chances on the unrecommended or the untried." Julias want to read things that have been validated and approved— and presumably not by Blair. "Unrecommended and untried" clearly signals awareness of a cadre of external gatekeepers, nameless and faceless perhaps, who police the boundaries of what is "good literature" and what could or should be read—and it circles back to the initial charge for the column, to the "should" question. What *should* Julia read? *The Professor's House* seems to be the first text in the column that has both gained the imprimatur of "the critics" and will satisfy a *Good Housekeeping* reader—it has enough in it that resonates with this audience to make it worth her while.

The Professor's House was certainly a known quantity by early 1926; not only had it received significant reviewer attention in the fall of 1925, but it had also run serially in *Collier's* magazine during the summer of that year. The reviews were definitely mixed, some focusing on the formal innovations of the novel and others on thematics. Many reviewer assessments focused on whether they thought that the Outland narrative or the St. Peter narrative should be given primacy, and then on whether Cather had treated that focus character properly, showing said character behaving appropriately or following a fitting story arc. The *New York Times* review found most fault with the Outland section's departures from the standard tone of Western adventure stories—"the adventure is not adventurous, the discoveries are not exciting."[28] *Life* magazine thought that Tom Outland was the "only sparkling character"[29] and assessed the book briefly as "an off day"[30] for Cather. The *Kansas City Star's* Schuyler Ashley characterizes the novel as focused on Professor St. Peter, whose "vigorous masculine color and enthusiasm . . . is deftly centered within a revolving system of feminine selfishness" but finds that "the book closes on a note of tired resignation," speculating that "Willa Cather . . . has grown a little weary of this household." There is only the slightest mention in this review of Tom Outland's narrative, an "experiment" that "gives Miss Cather opportunity for some of her best descriptive prose and . . . concords finely with the rest of the book, revealing as it does the help-lessness of the detached, scientific spirit before the intrenched and practical workaday world."[31]

The *New Yorker's* full review, published in September, actually celebrates Outland's narrative and explicitly rebukes readings like that in the *Times*, arguing that anyone who does not understand that Outland is "the pith of the conception" has "no eye for symbolic intimations and masterly omis-sions."[32] The snarkier comments of the magazine's November book list that I cited above—"For one thing, this admirable novel holds the 1925 record for making fools of sometimes intelligent book reviewers"[33]—focuses more on the reception than the novel itself, and relies on the reader's understanding of Cather's ubiquity and importance.

Regardless of these mixed and occasionally muddled reviews, *The Profes-sor's House* does seem to be a book that the readerly public was expected to read. And thus, this would have been a title that Blair's readers would have expected to have recommended to them. This expectation, fulfilled by one of the briefest of her mentions in her February 1926 column, would have warned Blair's readers that the meaning of the novel was not (as the *Book-man* reviewer put it) "so unmistakable as the dénouement of a detective story, where everything is nicely and tidily explained."[34] But it also would have ticked an important box from the list of things she was expected to do in her column; in alluding to the narrative complexity of *The Professor's House*, Blair was telling her *Good Housekeeping* audiences what they ought to know about it; she does not interpret the book, does not signal that it is "about" either Tom Outland or the eponymous professor, but suggests that the very inde-terminacy of the nonlinear plot is part of the point. Although she will spend more time on the interpretive dilemmas posed by other complex modernist novels in later columns, for this first column it seems that this is an adequate gesture, and one that signals that she will not pressure her readers to follow a highbrow course of study.

Unlike *Dark Laughter*, *The Professor's House* has many inroads for a *Good Housekeeping* reader. Two of the more significant are its attention to the psychic importance of material objects and its sympathy with touristic attitudes toward the American West. Both of these assertions about Cather's novel are under frequent contestation; not every scholar agrees that material objects are important to Cather, and certainly not every scholar thinks that Cather's treatment of Outland's time in the Mesa is touristic. But there are ways to read the novel that make such interpretations readily available, and they are the most likely readings for a *Good Housekeeping* reader because of the attitudes she would bring to the table, having lived in the worldview of the magazine. Cather herself worked on two magazines early in her career; first, as a managing editor and contributing writer for the *Home Monthly* out of Pittsburgh from 1896 to 1900; and then, in the editorial department of one of *Good Housekeeping*'s rivals, *McClure's*, from 1903 to 1912. Both stints are seen by various Cather biographers as both stymying her creative productions and inclining her against magazine fiction in general and women's magazine fiction in particular. But her relationship to the world of the magazine seems more complex than that, especially when one reads *The Professor's House* through its initial serialization in *Collier's* and through Blair's obliging recommendation in *Good Housekeeping*.

Cather's first full-time job in journalism was as managing editor of the *Home Monthly* magazine out of Pittsburgh. As Jennifer Bradley writes, while her precise job title is unclear, Cather "assumed most of the responsibilities for the magazine immediately upon her arrival,"[35] indeed being placed completely in charge of the first two issues after her arrival when the publisher went on extended holiday with his family. Cather oversaw the choice and placement of advertisements and the assignment and evaluation of manuscripts and wrote a large amount of content herself, even after the return of the executive staff. This was a position she held from June 1896 until July 1897, although she continued to write for the magazine until December 1897.[36] Bradley's detailed reading of the *Monthly* issues Cather edited leads her to argue that Cather knew that the magazine was "endorsing a very traditional role for women and that that was an endorsement with which she was not completely comfortable, for she found subtle ways to call into question the role she was also helping to construct." In the short stories Cather wrote for the magazine, in particular, Bradley argues that "Cather, the artist, simply would not create the dependent, consumer-driven heroines or the type of fiction that usually appeared in the women's magazines of the time."[37] And yet, these stories hewed close enough to the *Monthly*'s editorial brief that they could still be included without completely usurping the magazine's ethos. The balancing act Cather effects in these stories can still be seen in her treatment of the upwardly mobile, status-conscious, extended St. Peter family in *The Professor's House*. As in these stories, a redemptive identificatory reading of these characters and their materialistic desires is not entirely foreclosed by the text.

An implicit critique of magazine culture undergirds many scenes in the novel. The opening scene, which shows Godfrey St. Peter in his dilapidated attic study thinking about the myriad frustrations of his old house, reads somewhat like a refutation of many of the upbeat Do-It-Yourselfer articles and advertisements that filled the pages of *Good Housekeeping*. His bathtub takes center stage in the epic of frustrated homeownership:

> He had a deft hand with tools, he could easily have fixed [creaky floor-boards and stair steps], but there were always so many things to fix, and there was not time enough to go round. He went into the kitchen, where he had carpentered under a succession of cooks, went up to the bath-room on the second floor, where there was only a painted tin tub. . . . Many a night, after blowing out his study lamp, he had leaped into that tub, clad in his pyjamas, to give it another coat of some one of the many paints that were advertised to behave like porcelain, and didn't.[38]

Such paints would of course have been advertised and amply tested by *Good Housekeeping*, although perhaps St. Peter's mistake was in not choosing a paint with a money-back guaranty. The influence of women's magazine culture can be easily seen in the women in St. Peter's family—even in his youngest, Kathleen, who watches her mother and sister enjoy spending their newfound windfalls and seethes that she cannot participate in the activity.

In another scene, Lillian and Scott meet up on campus on their way to see St. Peter. They catch the end of his lecture, where he is responding to a student's query about the value of science. St. Peter does not actually find much value in science, as an answer to the important questions of life; he says that it has only managed to "make[] us very comfortable" (*PH* 56). Science in St. Peter's life manifests in two ways: first, as Tom Outland's scientific discovery, which has been monetized by his son-in-law Marsellus and the profits of which are constructing a giant estate on the shores of Lake Michigan; and second, in his own new home, purchased with the proceeds from his research award, which is full of labor-saving devices and advanced plumbing. When he emerges from the lecture, his wife and son-in-law are waiting, the latter to take him swimming and the former to take him to see an electrician. His wife's errand underscores St. Peter's view of science—it touches on his daily life in trips to the electrician and related minor domestic-facing tasks that devitalize him.

The receipts of science also seem to disrupt what St. Peter sees as a pre-scientific domestic perfection inside his family, one that included the prescientific Outland as a key participant. Before Tom became a scientist, he was a traveler from other lands, bringing "princely gifts" to the Outlands and entertaining the girls with his endless stories. "He would spend hours with [the girls] in the garden, making Hopi villages with sand and pebbles, drawing maps of the Painted Desert and the Rio Grande country in the gravel, telling them stories, when there was no one by to listen, about the adventures he had with his friend Roddy" (*PH* 120–21). This idyll, mediated through representations of the West, is of course unsustainable, but St. Peter mainly registers its loss through his daughter's conflicts over the material differences in their lives after Rosamond inherits the rights to Outland's experimental results. He marks, for example, the scorn on Rosamond's side and envy on Kathleen's through their changed attitudes toward each other's clothing. "When they were little girls, Kathleen adored her older sister and liked to wait on her, was always more excited about Rosie's new dresses and winter coat than about her own" (*PH* 71). He contrasts this directly to the envy Kathleen feels when she sees Rosamond's elegant fur coat and lays the blame squarely on the windfall Rosamond and her husband received from the sale of the process.

A reader skeptical of St. Peter's ability to understand his daughters' relationship might question the memory, or his analysis of it—earlier in the conversations Kathleen told him that she was "proud of [Rosamond's] good looks and good taste" and that the problem with her now is the way she inappropriately flaunts her clothes in venues that should be more casual: "I don't like the way she overdresses, I suppose. I would never have believed that Rosie could do anything in such bad taste. While she is here among her old friends, she ought to dress like the rest of us" (*PH* 70). Rosamond's error, then, is in her behavior; Kathleen is hurt rather than jealous, green

The Arcadia of the Ozarks 123

from sadness rather than jealousy. St. Peter cannot understand how or why Kathleen and her friends feel offense if "her things look about like yours"; "if hers are no prettier, what does it matter how much they cost?" He himself enjoyed the aesthetics of Rosamond's coat, appreciated the way it and her other new clothes brought out the purple undertones in her complexion and accentuated her positive qualities. But he does not understand the subtle codes of clothing and cannot read the social faux pas in the same way that he reads conversational faux pas at dinner parties. Even Lillian has cautioned Rosamond's husband about buying things that are out of scale for the Marsellus's life in Hamilton: "Of course emeralds would be beautiful, Louie, but they seem a little out of scale—to belong to a different scheme of life than any you and Rosamond can live here" (*PH* 61–62).

The reader can clearly see that St. Peter is not the disinterested philosopher he frequently affects to be. His attachment to his attic study aside, St. Peter definitely enjoys comfort. He loves Rosamond's fur coat and clearly knows enough about furs that his daughter Kathleen has asked him to help her pick them out. He is delighted by the opulent hotel suite that Rosamond and Louie reserve for him in Chicago. "He was glad to be in a big city again, in a luxurious hotel, and especially pleased to be able to sit in comfort and watch the storm over the water" (*PH* 75). "The Professor had forgotten his scruples about accepting lavish hospitalities. He was really very glad to have windows on the lake, and not to have to go away to another hotel" (*PH* 76). On the other hand, he feels some social compunction after the dinner the Marselluses hold in his honor; he fears that he has "shown up" his professional colleagues, whom Lillian says will envy his luck in sons-in-law. When he goes to the study in the old house, he celebrates that Lillian packed his lunch with "one of her best dinner napkins, knowing he hated ugly linen" (*PH* 85). He is Rosamond's chosen assistant on a shopping trip to Chicago. This last trip, however, exhausts him on many levels; he is overwhelmed by acquisitiveness. "Let's omit the verb 'to buy' in all forms for a time" (*PH* 152). It's Rosamond's "purchasing attitude" that troubles him the most: "She was like Napoleon looting the Italian palaces" (*PH* 153). The novel turns a corner, then, when St. Peter decides he cannot go with the Marselluses to Paris on their shopping/ intellectual adventure. And St. Peter's rejection of this trip—really, of the philosophy that lies behind this trip—might make the novel a less-than-ideal choice for Blair's audience, because the trip that Louie describes sounds very much like Francis Parkinson Keyes's trips around the world. Keyes meets

124   CHAPTER THREE

with significant cultural and political figures on her journeys and discusses things that might be eaten or bought in each locale. The rejection of this agenda might not sit well with a *Good Housekeeping* audience, unless it has already begun to view St. Peter as a bit of a hypocrite.

The potential hypocrisy reading is reinforced by an earlier scene in which Cather skewers the professor for his snobbery about magazine readers. When Tom Outland tells St. Peter that he has sought him out because of a magazine article, St. Peter's response is initially chagrined: "The Professor had noticed before that whenever he wrote for popular periodicals it got him into trouble" (*PH* 97). But then Outland actually turns out to be a brilliant student, one of the few St. Peter gets every year who "kindled him. If there was one eager eye, one doubting, critical mind, one lively curiosity in a whole lecture-room full of commonplace boys and girls, he was its servant" (*PH* 19). The assessment of publication in popular periodicals does not get explicitly revised in the novel, but the implicit revision is certainly available to the reader; magazine readers are not necessarily the philistines the professor previously thought them to be. In fact, magazine readers can be inquisitive, and can bring something unique to the academy—a worldly experience and a sincere connection to art, literature, and history. This moment seems tailor-made to resonate with a *Good Housekeeping* reader, to make her feel that Cather respects her perspectives and potential contributions.

The Professor's House had, itself, been serialized prior to publication in book form, appearing in *Collier's* magazine over the course of the summer of 1925. While the book form of the novel sold around 65,000 copies by the end of that year, Charles Johanningsmeier, in one of several substantive studies he has published about Cather's relationship with serial publication, explains that "slightly over one million copies of each issue of *Collier's* containing *The Professor's House* installments were printed and circulated," and if one accepts estimates of three readers for every periodical, "about three million people read at least part of the issues of *Collier's* in which *The Professor's House* appeared."[39] Johanningsmeier goes on to argue, convincingly, that the *Collier's* audience would likely have not been sympathetic to St. Peter or Tom Outland both because of the accompanying illustrations in *Collier's* and because the magazine's ethos and advertisements would have made readers "more likely to regard these characters' anti-materialist attitudes as almost anti-American."[40] The *Good Housekeeping* audience, similarly positioned to the *Collier's* audience posited by Johanningsmeier, also found St. Peter's

The Arcadia of the Ozarks 125

lament about the creeping vocationalism of the education offered at his school overblown. St. Peter "had resisted the new commercialism, the aim to 'show results' that was undermining and vulgarizing education" (*PH* 120), joining with Tom Outland's physics mentor Dr. Crane against the governing bodies of the school and philistine faculty members who were trying to "abolish the purely cultural studies" (*PH* 121). *Good Housekeeping* readers, on the one hand, would not have seen vocational education at odds with the arts and the humanities; the Good Housekeeping Institute, after all, shared space with fiction offerings and reproductions of classical artworks. On the other hand, such a reader might have been inclined to sympathize with St. Peter and Crane after reading about the sad state of the university's physics building. This description immediately precedes the discussion of their curricular difficulties, and its dereliction, an architectural synecdoche for the problems with the university in general, would have appalled a *Good Housekeeping* reader who valued solid stewardship:

> It was constructed of red brick, after an English model. The architect had had a good idea, and he very nearly succeeded in making a good thing, something like the old Smithsonian building in Washington. But after it was begun, the State Legislature had defeated him by grinding down the contractor to cheap execution, and had spoiled everything, outside and in. Ever since it was finished, plumbers and masons and carpenters had been kept busy patching and repairing it. Crane and St. Peter, both young men then, had wasted weeks of time with the contractors, and had finally gone before the Legislative committee in person to plead for the integrity of that building. But nothing came of all their pains. It was one of their lost causes. (*PH* 141)

Blair's readers would have been shocked by the legislature's behavior—not just because of the abnegation of responsibility in its refusal to follow through with the initial plans for a building that might have been grand but for budget cuts, but even more because the legislature's shortsighted economies made the lesser building that does eventually get built weaker in its fundamentals of plumbing, electricity, and materials. These are the kinds of things valued by the magazine, as evidenced by the series for the woman who is building her own house. Valuing solid construction, rational budgeting, and proper follow-through is concomitant with the magazine's celebrations of the arts, sciences, and cultural studies. Things should be done well, and thoroughly, and with an eye to aesthetics and lasting values. That is emphatically *not* the ethos of the state legislature; readers may not have entirely sided

126 CHAPTER THREE

with St. Peter's denigration of vocationalism, but they certainly would have lamented the need to "show results" alongside him.

Blair's reading advice mitigates against the compulsions to "show results" and the inclinations toward instrumental reading that reading programs like the Five Foot Shelf of Books aimed to satisfy, but she was still responsive to her audience's desires to "read to learn." In the January 1929 column, appearing roughly in the middle of her tenure, Blair surveys multiple reading programs and courses, and along the way she directly discusses the Five Foot Shelf. A reader writes to ask what she would put on her own reading list, not naming but clearly referencing the series: "I wish you would tell me what books you would choose, and in what order you would read or study them, if you were to make a similar list. I want to read books that will show life from all angles and give me a knowledge of history, art, etc."[41] Blair starts by praising the letter writer's definition of "education" and goes on to describe the Five Foot Shelf while demystifying Dr. Eliot as a guru: "In making his selections for the Five-Foot Shelf Dr. Eliot was assisted by a large number of specialists. How many thousand or hundred thousand of these sets have been distributed I do not know. I should prefer to know how many of those sold had been read. For the trouble with sets of books like this is that it is much easier to buy them, and even to pay for them, irritating as the monthly payment plan is, than to continue faithfully, day in and day out, to stick to their pages."[42]

The series, in other words, does not necessarily deliver the results it promises, because despite the "fifteen minutes a day" motto, it is a profoundly difficult regimen to follow. Even Dr. Eliot himself could not, in his preparation of the series that bears his name, perform all of the background work necessary; he had to employ a team of researchers. Be that as it may, the Five Foot Shelf catchphrase, "fifteen minutes a day," clearly had resonance for the *Good Housekeeping* reader, as it was echoed frequently in advertisements for slimming plans and skin-care treatments.

Blair does concede that "for the persevering there is not to be found anywhere more easily available, better courses, more comprehensive, more scholarly in their outline and thoroughness, than those contained in 'The Harvard Classics.'" But having offered this caveat, Blair goes on for seven more columns to discuss alternatives for "the student who wishes to take his education in more homeopathic doses, and to find more variety in the prescriptions." From the American Library Association pamphlet series "Reading with a Purpose,"

FIGURE 4. Many products, like the Battle Creek Health Builder, echoed Dr. Eliot's Five Foot Shelf of Books by promising results in only fifteen minutes a day (*Good Housekeeping*, January 1929, 184). Credit: *Good Housekeeping*. Hearst Magazine Media, Inc.

128   CHAPTER THREE

she moves on to discuss sixteen more books and book series representing myriad approaches to reading courses; some offer lists, some give overviews and methodological guidance, some are brief courses that lead to further reading. As with all her advice, Blair encourages her readers to discern from her descriptions which of these reading courses they are most likely to be able to follow and which might coincide most with their own learning and reading styles.

Blair offers one course that is structured around a method ideologically different from her *Good Housekeeping* reviewing practice and offers a bit of instruction of her own when describing it. The "course of 'Creative Reading,' published by the Institute of Current Literature, College House, Harvard Square, Cambridge, Massachusetts," has the same pedigree as the Five Foot Shelf, but it does not proceed from the logic of a reading list. Instead, it "attempts to teach the reader how to get the most from what he reads though a series of objective reviews by trained reviewers."

> Each lesson, issued in pamphlet form, consists of the analysis of a work of fiction done after the objective method, which means done not from the point of view of its effect on the reviewer as my reviews in Good Housekeeping are done, which is the subjective method, but according to the canons of literature, as to whether the author succeeds in doing what he set out to do, and a criticism of the methods he employs to this end; an essay on some phase of the literary method, a discussion of a work of non-fiction, and a set of questions by which the student is to test his grasp of the lesson. (183)

Presumably, once the reader is trained through these reviews, she will be able to perform her own analysis on literature that has not been framed for her by any instructor. As its name suggests, this course purports to provide its readers with the tools necessary to practice "creative reading"—but Blair is careful to caution her readers that it nonetheless operates under the logic of the "objective method." There is, in other words, a "right way" to read a book, a way that is learnable and that could be practiced by any trained reader. Blair, on the other hand, writes of "the effect on the reviewer"—the "subjective method"—this is the logic behind her evocations of the representative reader (who sometimes is herself).

The affordances of the digital archive enable the twenty-first-century critic to call Blair on an inconsistency here. Two years prior to Blair's January 1929 column, in December 1927, May Lamberton Becker had also discussed the Creative Reading course in her *Saturday Review of Literature* Reader's Guide

The Arcadia of the Ozarks   129

column—in the process revealing that Blair had written the November 1927 Creative Reading course on Cather's *Death Comes for the Archbishop!*[43] A generous interpretation of this discrepancy might be that Blair had changed her mind in the interim; an alternative generous interpretation might be that Blair had taken this opportunity to let loose with the "objective method," just as Becker says she enjoyed writing her own course module because "for once I have space enough to say all I have to say about a book."[44] Finally, knowing that Blair was always on the lookout for writing that would supplement her family's income, and knowing too that she wrote voluminously, we might simply appreciate her hustling and assume that *she* thought it unlikely that her *Good Housekeeping* readers had been two-year subscribers to Creative Reading. One happy consistency, of course, is Blair's devotion to Cather; for this one can easily forgive a sin of omission.

In the narrative of the January 1929 column, Blair finds Frank Luther Mott's *Rewards of Reading* preferable to Creative Reading. "This book always fills me with envy that I did not do it first," she confesses. Mott's mantra of "intelligent pleasure reading" definitely does capture Blair's ethos, particularly when it comes to the more culturally highbrow texts she recommends. So, too, his recommended process of "trying by experiment and accepting on experience." Blair goes on to suggest that her readers seek out certain exceptional books of literary criticism, but not to read slavishly while absorbing those authors' readings. Instead, she tells her audience "to sample, one by one, such examples as are set forth in a good book on criticism." She describes a summer during which she read all the texts listed in the appendix of Bliss Perry's *A Study of Prose Fiction*, dutifully chasing down the out-of-print books and then, in turn, the books referenced in those books. "A year had passed, and two long shelves were filled with books gathered from the second-hand bookstores of the land before I stopped." The hunt for all these books seems to have been a major attraction of this project for Blair (and presumably would be for some portion of her readers)—it is a consumption project as much as a reading project, and the fruits can be displayed on handsome bookshelves. But she finds the actual reading a bit arduous: "Though it was a hard-work way, a tedious way that I should not recommend, in such severity, yet I have never regretted it, for I doubt if with any less concentrated effort I should ever have worked to the point where acceptance of criticism gave way to conscious, informed appreciation." This is one way to think about one's reading "to learn," and it is a way Blair has pursued, but it is by no means the only route. Any reader who prefers the sound of "intelligent pleasure reading" is perfectly within her rights and would get Blair's approval.

This is the mode of reading that we discovered in many other spaces in the magazine—particularly in the travelogues contributed monthly during this period by Blair's friend and mentor Frances Parkinson Keyes. And it is here that we might find another avenue into *The Professor's House* for the *Good Housekeeping* reader: unexpectedly, perhaps, in Tom Outland's story. If a reader does not in fact require that her novels "run smoothly and rapidly to their appointed end," she will find much to enjoy in this embedded touristy tale that covers in-depth the Blue Mesa (based on Mesa Verde in New Mexico) and then journeys to Washington, DC, for a look at the bureaucratic culture that Blair will likewise reference in her future columns. While it is questionable whether the questions of preservation and current Indian affairs will be much on the minds of the 1926 readers of the magazine, by 1929 *Good Housekeeping* will run a series of articles about the situation in the Southwest. The clubwoman spirit running strong in the *Good Housekeeping* audience, such considerations may well have played a part in the interest in the novel.

On a very literal level, the Outland story is filled with concerns about homemaking—cooking in camp, certainly, but also the domestic arrangements of the mesa dwellers whose homes Outland and Roddy explore. "It was evidently a kind of common kitchen, where they roasted and baked and probably gossiped. There were corncobs everywhere, and ears of corn with kernels still on them—little, like popcorn. We found dried beans, too, and strings of pumpkin seeds, and plum seeds, and a cupboard full of little implements made of turkey bones" (208). This moment, like the moment when their cook Henry Atkins claims to be able to recognize a surgical kit because of his wide knowledge of life, is the kind of thing that might be gratifying to the *Good Housekeeping* reader, who would also know what these homely things look like. The makeshift streamside kitchen, the clothes that Tom describes, are all curious but also familiar, acculturation and education inside comforting parameters.

The description of the care that the Mesa dwellers took in their home construction and their aesthetic choices likewise has an easily recognized cognate in the magazine. It reproduces women's magazine prose tonally, and the readers' familiarity with such description might mitigate against any thought that this protracted section is too much of a digression, too self-indulgent, for a middlebrow reader to appreciate. Possibly—but not in the context of a magazine that indulged frequently in meticulous discussions of detailed architectural work. This kind of detail about lintels—the fact that the readers would know about lintels in the first place—is typical of *Good Housekeeping*.

> One thing we knew about these people; they hadn't built their town in a hurry. Everything proved their patience and deliberation. The cedar joists had been felled with stone axes and rubbed smooth with sand. The little poles that lay across them and held up the clay floor of the chamber above, were smoothly polished. The door lintels were carefully fitted (the doors were stone slabs held in place by wooden bars fitted into hasps). The clay dressing that covered the stone walls was tinted, and some of the chambers were frescoed in geometrical patterns, one colour laid on another. In one room was a painted border, little tents, like Indian tepees, in brilliant red" (*PH* 211).

The "tepee" detail could be read as revealing Outland's clumsy understanding of the native culture he is attempting to interpret—why would he parse a border that features triangle motifs as a series of tepees, except for his internal shorthand associations of tepees with all Indigenous American peoples (plains dwellers or otherwise)? If this is a moment where Outland's skill as an anthropological interpreter is to come into question, however, such fine points may well be lost on the *Good Housekeeping* reader who delighted in the Orientalist descriptions of Japanese clothing and pottery in Keyes's travelogue.

When amateur archaeologist Father Duchene encourages Tom Outland to make a report to the director of the Smithsonian Institution, he is relying on the integrity of the institution, which is housed in a building worthy of its charter. "He will send us an archaeologist who will interpret all that is obscure to us. He will revive this civilization in a scholarly work. It may be that you will have thrown light on some important parts in the history of your country" (*PH* 199). This appeal to the government would have been logical to the *Good Housekeeping* reader, encouraged in her faith in institutes and scientific study by the myriad "institutes" in the magazine and by the magazine's intersection with governmental entities such as its employment of Harvey Wiley. Outland is, however, essentially ignored by the bureaucrats in Washington, who are more interested in going out to lunch on the government's dime than in anything scholarly, historical, or anthropological. The Smithsonian building, after which the crumbling Hamilton University

132   CHAPTER THREE

physics building was modeled (*PH* 127), is finally no bulwark against creeping anti-intellectualism or antihumanism. Although it, unlike the physics building, was finished properly and has been kept up to the highest aesthetic and structural standards, an intellectual and moral rot has actually seeped into even that strong edifice. Outland's disappointment in the wake of Duchene's faith in the Smithsonian is that much more profound: the institution has failed him and has failed the former inhabitants of the Blue Mesa.

In February, March, and May 1929, *Good Housekeeping* would run a three-part series about Native Americans in the Southwest penned by Vera Connolly. The first revelation of the series is the state of children in the Indian boarding schools—a tactic that is clearly aimed at most quickly appealing to the motherhood-focused *Good Housekeeping* audience. Connolly is struck that the condition of the children is the most important thing to the male tribal elders: "The other wrongs the race may have suffered in the past at our hands—loss of lands, water rights, and personal freedom—obviously signified nothing in their eyes compared to the sufferings of the 27,000 Indian children in the government boarding schools today. . . . These children, it was explained to us, are taken forcibly from their mothers' arms, as early as six years of age in some Indian communities, and sent away to distant boarding schools to stay till eighteen. There they are underfed, roughly treated, and required to work half of every day at hard industrial labor, in the fields or in the laundry, in addition to the half-day at school."[45]

Connolly's series does not sugarcoat or sentimentalize the situation in the boarding schools or on the reservations, and she lays the blame squarely with the Indian Bureau. Revealing and indicting the practice of pronouncing Native Americans "incompetent" in order to seize their assets, Connolly concludes that Native Americans are "virtual slaves." There is even a wholly unprecedented sentence in all-caps: "THERE IS NO LIMIT IN ANY LAW OF CONGRESS TO THE AMOUNT OF FINE OR LENGTH OF IMPRISONMENT."[46]

To be sure, Connolly's discussion of the health care crisis in many tribal communities is couched in the danger of diseases spreading into neighboring white populations. "At Walpi, an ancient sky-town of crazy, picturesque stone houses flung up in wild beauty against the heavens atop a mesa . . . I saw a gifted people so afflicted with a virulent skin disease (impetigo) that some faces were literally covered with scabs. It is here that the famous Snake Dance is held, to which tourists flock from all over the world. The danger to the white race is obvious!"[47] She refers to native children as "our little Indian wards."[48] But this maternalism, not far from Tom Outland's own sense of paternalism, is at least being served up with the goal of redressing the profound abuses of the Indian Bureau and other governmental agencies. Like Harriet Beecher Stowe, whom she cites in her article, Connolly is appealing to white mothers and encouraging them to identify with native parents. The magazine, in its headings, makes this charge explicit, while distancing itself from muckraking journalism: "This is not a muck-raking article. Current hearings before the Senate Investigating Committee are corroborating every statement Miss Connolly makes. . . . We hope that our readers will ask their Senators for the printed reports of the Committee hearings and then, though their clubs, insist that justice be assured the Indian, now and hereafter."[49] Women reading these articles, then organizing in their clubs—which are official channels—can redress wrongs through official governmental channels, relying on democracy to fulfill its promise of a popular voice.

But as *The Professor's House* demonstrates with Tom Outland's frustrated trip to Washington, DC, and his disillusionment with the careerist bureaucrats he meets there and their utter disregard for the artifacts he offers them (and even greater contempt for the people who crafted and used them), the official channels were dead ends. Cather's novel, then, might be read as an indictment of the decay of the cultural institutions on which the *Good Housekeeping* reader relies. And its potential inappropriateness for that audience, indicated by Blair's reluctance to wholeheartedly endorse the novel or to offer it as a marquee title, inheres, perhaps, in that critique, because expertise and science *are* sacred to the *Good Housekeeping* reader. While she does not have to blindly follow her reading adviser into every text she recommends, she does choose from among a slate of possible texts offered by someone with knowledge and experience. If the experts are being abandoned by the institutions that once housed them, and are being undercut by spurious budgetary and political constraints, what hope is there for those who rely on their guidance? And yet, Cather's openness to the touristic element of white Americans witnessing the Southwest and her meditations (complex as they were) on the relationship between aesthetics and consumption make this novel eminently available to the Julias of the world, who hope that their "intelligent pleasure reading" will distinguish them, mark them as women of culture.

CHAPTER THREE

Elmer Gantry and *An American Tragedy*

In the opening of her June 1927 column, Blair recounts a discussion between herself and her friends Minnie Fisher Cunningham and Margaret Banister, the former of whom considers Blair's monthly reading load onerous and the latter of whom thinks it sounds delightful.[50] That conversation takes a turn, however, when Margaret sees Emily reading *Elmer Gantry*. "Even Margaret's envy gave way to pity when she saw me hard at Sinclair Lewis' 'Elmer Gantry.' 'For I don't want to read it,' she said. 'The reviews have convinced me of that.'"[51] *Elmer Gantry* gives Blair the occasion to discuss what happens to her in a month where she realizes she has to mention a book that she does not like—since if she doesn't "refer occasionally to them, my readers might come to think of me as having lost all sense of discrimination, if not taste itself." *Elmer Gantry* is one of the books that Blair has to tell her readers she did not enjoy, but she does so only after an in-depth survey of Lewis's previous novels, and a robust discussion of their significance to early-twentieth-century American culture.

This survey is a significant departure for Blair; it is the first time she has done an in-depth treatment of one of her focus author's oeuvres, and she will not repeat the exercise in such depth at any other time during her *Good Housekeeping* tenure. *Elmer Gantry*, somehow, is exceptional. For one thing, Lewis's previous work merits attention because *Main Street* and *Babbitt*, both major bestsellers, had become major cultural touchstones during the 1910s and early 1920s. Both books' titles had become widely known shorthand terms for significant phenomena in American life and had been embraced by highbrow and middlebrow readers alike. By virtue of this cultural ubiquity, then, Lewis requires attention, to the extent that a conscientious Margaret Banister thinks he might be required reading.

Banister, by Blair's account, has read the reviews and they have convinced her she does not want to read the book. This might suggest that the reviews were all negative, but this was far from the case. Reviewers were actually quite split on the novel, and this was by design. Lewis's publisher, Alfred Harcourt, knew that the novel would be polarizing and set out to stoke and then foment an argument over its characterizations and plots in the pages of the reviews. Lewis biographer Richard Lingeman cites the plan: "The inevitable scrap about it will heat up between the two groups of readers and go over the publishers' and perhaps to some extent, the author's head."[52] The plan worked, judging by a telegram Harcourt sent to Lewis the day after publication:

The Arcadia of the Ozarks 135

SALES ABOUT HUNDRED THOUSAND. NEWS STORIES EVERYWHERE. KANSAS STAR FIVE COLUMNS, REVIEWS VIOLENT EITHER WAY. CLERGY HOT. REORDERS ALREADY. LETTER AND CLIPPINGS MAILED. EVERY-THING LOVELY.[53]

The usual suspects (Mencken, Bill Woodward) loved the book, clergy pilloried it, and some were sympathetic but found the satire too caustic (Rebecca West, Elmer Davis). But opinions were strong and the novel sold briskly on the strength of the scandal. If this fight was the point of Harcourt's campaign, however, it did turn off some readers like Margaret Banister, who were not attracted to controversy. It was not the reviews' consistent negativity that repulsed her but their argumentativeness.

Blair's strategy in her response to readers like Banister is a model of authoritative negation. Instead of arguing with the subject matter of the book, Blair chooses to short-circuit the fight through a reading that focuses on its worth as literature. In that mode, Blair contends that *Elmer Gantry* is flawed because it does not fulfill the requirements of its first principles; she is not disturbed, she claims, by Lewis's representation of Gantry as a "hypo-crite or . . . a preacher. It is that he is neither a typical preacher nor a typical hypocrite, and yet he is presented, not as an individual character but, after the Lewis manner, as a type—not as a preacher, but as *the* preacher." In other words, Gantry is a strawman, and Blair finds it beneath Lewis's dignity as a writer to construct this strawman for the purposes of an easy satire. *Gantry* is a cop-out, to Blair's way of thinking, and her criticism is all the more cutting because she takes this position that the novel is a shameful outing for the once-great Lewis: "I suppose my complaint is so great because I should have expected Lewis to be able to show us both.[54]

Her survey of Lewis's previous work extends and substantiates Blair's claim that *Gantry* is not just a bad novel but that is also signals Lewis's final fall from grace. *Main Street's* Carol and Will Kennicott, Blair contends, were complex characters—she even argues that Will is the moral center of the book and the "best on Main Street, the best in American husbandhood."[55] She also offers a cogent analysis of the various debates over Carol Kennicott, and whether readers can or should identify with or excoriate her.[56] She goes on to explain that Lewis's second novel is worth reading because its protag-onist, George Babbitt, is similarly complex—Lewis "showed us Babbitt's fine qualities as well as his weak ones." In this, she departs somewhat from Stu-art Pratt Sherman, who "underscored his admiration for the same qualities

136   CHAPTER THREE

Lewis satirized in *Babbitt*."[57] *Arrowsmith* started Lewis's slide "from artistry to tractism," but Blair couches this as simply an instance in which the book "got away from the author." This can no longer be an excuse for *Elmer Gantry*, however: this time, Lewis has chosen to make his main character a caricature. Blair declares that *Gantry* does not merit her usual thumbnail plot summary, in an announcement of this choice that is so uncharacteristically scathing to merit citation in full:

> No, I have not told the story of 'Elmer Gantry,' for it is not necessary. My reader has only to combine all the discreditable things he has ever heard of a man doing, and he has the events of Elmer Gantry's life. He has only to remember the Ten Commandments and think of ways to break them, and he has the plot. He has only to recall all the vulgarities of the most vulgar person he has known, he has only to picture a blatherskite, a glad-hander, a voluptuary, a fool, and an egotist, and he has Elmer's character. He has only to imagine this man as a student at a small college, a convert at a revival, a student thrown out of a theological seminary, a salesman, and then conceive him capturing a female evangelist on sight, becoming an evangelist himself, being taken into another denomination without investigation and working up to a bishopric, to have read the book. I, for one, had thought the fictional fashion of all-black villains and all-white heroes went out with the ten-, twenty-, and thirty-cent shows of my youth, but evidently the all-black villain remains with only, alas! instead of the contrast of an all-white hero, a few drabs and tans that can be called neither heroic nor villainous. A new melodrama, this![58]

This is something like a plot summary masquerading as a character description, but Blair's point stands: *Gantry*'s details are so uninspired as to be easily imagined by even the most casual of Blair's readers. But her approach here is plausibly deniably backhanded rather than overtly confrontational, so she does not enter into the fray that Lewis and his publicists deliberately provoked. Blair does not want to give Lewis the satisfaction she expects he would feel in being denounced for the book. To do so would be to "dignify the performance by attacking it," and this is not the tack she wants to take. Instead of getting angry, Blair follows the suggestion of William Allen White, whom she cites as having said that God had struck "Sinclair Lewis the artist" dead. Rather than attributing the novel's shortcomings to a supernatural smiting, Blair traces a trend toward hyperbole in Lewis's work and through that trajectory announces the regrettable death of Lewis as an artist. The refusal to engage in either celebration or denunciation of Lewis's portrait of Gantry is an intellectual power play, and one bolstered by the performance of critical acumen that precedes it.

The column continues long past Blair's final assessment of *Gantry*, but, again uncharacteristically, keys several of her discussions to the things that Lewis failed to accomplish in his novel: "After reading *Elmer Gantry* . . . [it] is like coming from a kindergarten on to a battleground . . . one book shows life a mere game; the other, a tragic encounter with fate."[59] Booth Tarkington's *The Plutocrat* is "as much a tract in its way as Elmer Gantry was in his," but she concedes that "as a story it will do," while cautioning that Tarkington's point may well be lost on some readers who will certainly choose to empathize with the wrong character.[60] The animating anecdote of the column was, of course, the discussion among Blair, Minnie Cunningham, and Margaret Banister about whether reading large numbers of books is a pleasant opportunity or drudgery; *Gantry* has now become shorthand for drudgery reading, and other books are measured against it in that register. She confesses readily that there are a number of other books on her "to-be-read" shelves that leave her as cold as Lewis's novel, and in connecting *Gantry* to these other books, many of which are undistinguished, and the implication of an equivalence certainly serves to extend her criticism of Lewis. One is a "silly book," others she finishes simply because she cannot go without finding out how they ended up. When she finally reads Edna St. Vincent Millay's *The King's Henchman*, Blair exults in the quality: "All the rejected books were forgotten."[61] Millay restores her faith in contemporaneous literature by writing "such a book as rewards one for many books which had to be rejected, as stimulates hope and turns even Minnie Cunningham's reluctance into Margaret Banister's yearning. . . . Even Minnie F. would find this compensation for the chore of having to read all those books."[62] In her treatment of *Gantry*, then, Blair is both asserting herself as a skillful and authoritative member of the reviewer guild *and* continuing to demonstrate to her *Good Housekeeping* readers that she understands their motivations better than any of the other reviewers could. She did not need to do this kind of heavy background work before she used *Dark Laughter* as a punchline, because she is not picking a fight here with the reviewing establishment.

Theodore Dreiser's *An American Tragedy* receives dramatically different treatment. My epigraph for this chapter is taken from Blair's October 1926 column, published under the title "Some Books Worth While, Selected for Good Housekeeping by a Woman Who Can Read between the Lines." In

138   CHAPTER THREE

this column, Blair recounts a conversation she held with her friend Natalie while they are en route to a resort in the Ozarks:

> The ambitious proprietor had named his camp Lake Lucerne, because he had cunningly entrapped the output of several springs until he had achieved a quite respectable body of sapphire-blue water framed in a circlet of green hills. In this pleasant spot we planned to spend two cold—really cold—summer nights and two idle days; the four of us, Natalie and I, and the men who, husband-fashion, occupied the front seat of the car. What better occasion for threshing out this old question of worth-while literature?[63]

What better occasion indeed? Natalie and Blair are both wives, both women, and are all set to enjoy a weekend at a midwestern resort, but they are also engaged in an epistemological conversation about the value of reading and the degree to which reading can matter, as well as whether and how reading might impact individual lives. This is the moment when Natalie asks Emily, in reference to Theodore Dreiser's *An American Tragedy*, "Should I read it, Emily? . . . Is it worth *my* while?"[64] The emphasized "my" becomes the linchpin for the remainder of this remarkable column, in which Blair doubles down on her commitment to offering reading advice that is centered on individual tastes and that does work on the individual psyche of the reader herself. Natalie's questions presuppose Blair's attitude toward the recommendation process—she asks only for Blair to make a personal appraisal of the possible value of *An American Tragedy* to her, personally, not for a blanket assessment of the novel's value. Implicit in Blair's discussion of her answer is a reassertion of first principles: that books do not have inherent worth but that they are worthy to the degree that they meet their readers in the right way.

As is her frequent practice, Blair prefaces her discussion with a character sketch of her friend. Natalie, Blair writes, is a woman for whom "life" comes first. Books, which apparently in this case are not part of "life," are "valuable only if they enable[] eyes to see more clearly and heart to beat more swiftly." So Natalie's question about whether Dreiser's novel will be worth it to *her* is less about whether *An American Tragedy* is a good book than about whether it will add something to her life personally—not necessarily even whether she will "like" or "enjoy" it but whether it will be valuable in the way that she specifically needs books to be valuable. This is not keyed to any external ideas about value or quality but is, rather, wholly a function of Natalie's personal quirks. And Blair is careful to point out that Natalie is not in fact like all other readers: "To Natalie life comes first, and a book is a representation of it to be judged as it reports truly or not, beautifully or not, life's performers and performances; and to be prized to the extent to which it interprets or explains them. To the others books come first, and life is judged as it accords with the ideas planted by books; and prized to the extent to which it reflects what books have concluded life should be."[65] Since Natalie is taking center stage in this column, there is a slight implicit bias in favor of her approach to reading ("life" first as opposed to books first), although in other spots Blair will validate those who read "for escape." In her February 1928 column, for example, she asserts that "there is much to be said for those books that make the reader forget—books in which he can lose himself. Some people may always want this kind. It is a certainty there are times when every one does."[66] In her January 1928 column, Blair will print a letter from a reader who challenges the idea of "books of escape": "Not to escape life but to extend life, that is why I read. I want books to take me places and give me experiences that I can never hope to enjoy.... She went on to explain. 'I live on a ranch in Oklahoma in an ugly, tiny, four-room house. I look out upon acres of unplowed dirt or unshaded grain. My life is narrow. My days a routine. Love has never come to me. I am just a plain old woman. But let me find the right book and I become a fairy princess, a queen of this world, or a woman longed for and lost, living in palaces, sailing the seas, or heaven knows what.'"[67]

While it is impossible to know whether this is was a real letter that Blair actually received, it is significant because it was a narrative that she felt would resonate with her readers. By reproducing it (or by purporting to reproduce it) Blair gives voice to isolated women in the plains and validates any who use their reading as a means of vicarious participation in the more colorful lives of others. Indeed, she continues in this column to confess to being herself a "'make-believe' person"—she confesses that she loves "books of identification, books in which I can live scenes and feel emotions that I never shall experience in life." She goes even further to endorse vicarious reading as against the variety of reading she has been seeming to praise in Natalie's column—to be a "make-believe" reader is to tap into something unavailable to people who only read to satisfy the intellect or for the purpose of "increasing life, making it more abundant." Make-believe readers, in their identification with the persons about whom they read, are able to experience "the thing that makes life thrilling, wonderful, and not a mere passing of days, that thing in us which accounts for ambition, adventure, which possibly has raised man from a clod."[68] The apparent preference for the Natalie mode of reading herein evaporates.

140   CHAPTER THREE

Blair's recommendation that Natalie should read *An American Tragedy*—and her tacit recommendation that this would be a suitable book for many of her readers—is leavened by some of the caveats she offers. She does caution her readers about the length of the novel and about Dreiser's infelicitous prose stylings, but ultimately contends that the work as a whole is worthy of whatever self-discipline is required to make one's way through it. "He inserts words, scenes, details, ideas, without in any way justifying their presence as parts of themes or characters. . . . But to cavil at weaknesses in a high-powered giant is foolish. And a writer who can leave a weary reader with the impression that he has reared a Colossus and performed an autopsy must be recognized as a literary giant, however the reader might wish him to be different, however he might prefer Milan cathedrals to pyramids, and X-rays to autopsies." The novel was Dreiser's first in eleven years, and the literary reviews of the day took much the same line as Blair when discussing it; the Editor Recommends column in *The Bookman* announces that "literate Americans will wish to read" the novel, despite the fact that "it has the old Dreiser qualities: it is difficult going for the lover of lucid prose, but it is absorbing to him who likes excellent characterization and a novel with real meat in it."[69] Charles R. Walker in *The Independent* finds *An American Tragedy* less encumbered by Dreiser's typical "leaden mediocrities" but nevertheless notes that "there is a tendency to oil the ways with participial constructions in the long passages of emotional conflict and transition. He still keeps his old cacophonies, his abominable *clichés*, his newspaper manner. But, sometimes because of these, sometimes in spite of them, he has built up a great novel that is profoundly tragic and intensely American."[70] Reading through the reviews, in fact, it seems that contemporaneous reviewers quite enjoy indulging in passages of snarky description of Dreiser's stylistic excesses, often mirroring his excesses in their own. The ultimate conclusion for most of these critics, however, is that Dreiser is still worth reading—despite the occasional difficulties of maintaining an attitude of indulgent patience with his idiosyncrasies.

These critics' perspectives seem to presuppose that the reader who approaches Dreiser does so from an already fully formed aesthetic, which will be unassailed by doubts that what they are reading is "really good" because it comes from an author who has been celebrated and elevated by the critical mass. In Blair's column, on the other hand, an engagement with Dreiser becomes an exercise in discerning one's own personal aesthetic preferences. "It is a wise reader who can discriminate between what he likes and what

The Arcadia of the Ozarks 141

he admires. A book may not appeal to him at all. It may even repel him, but an intelligent reader should be able to say of a book: 'I don't like it. It offends my taste, but I can see that this author has skill in presenting his own. I don't like his characters, but I see he has insight and power. Therefore, I admire his work, even if I can't like it.'"[71] To read Dreiser is to come to an appreciation of literature that is not necessarily "enjoyable" but which one could see having merit. This kind of merit is, in Dreiser's case, extra-aesthetic; it lies outside the idea that one might have pleasure in the text and inheres, again, in the way the text helps illuminate the world that the reader navigates. Blair acknowledges that Dreiser's story of Clive Davis is

> Yes, a terrible, a ruthless story, showing a "sordid" life at its worst, yet "worth while" in Natalie's sense. After reading it she will never follow a murder trial on the front pages of the newspaper in just the same way. Bell-boys, waiters, messenger boys, the "riff-raff" of the street will cease to be furniture and become creatures at least as piteous as homeless cats and dogs on winter evenings. She may agree with me that, after Dreiser, may come a greater who can give us all he does with greater economy of word and paper, who can compose a picture, but in the meantime she will accept her debt to Dreiser, now looked upon by many critics as the most powerful writer in America, for widening her understanding.[72]

The reading mode that Blair describes here initially seems to be that of nineteenth-century sentimentality, in which readers learn to feel for others in real life through readerly identification with and sympathy for downtrodden others in fictional texts.[73] The racial and class inequities on which sentimental practices relied also undergird Blair's description of the benefits that will accrue to Natalie from her reading of Dreiser: to wit, that reading *An American Tragedy* will make readers like Natalie have the same kind of sympathy for the homeless that they already do for stray animals.[74] But the identificatory practices of sentimentality are not apparent here; Blair does not suggest that Natalie is going to identify with bellboys and waiters, simply that she is going to see them as animate, sentient, not furniture. She is not going to be spurred to any social justice action by her reading of Dreiser. She will not become an anti–death penalty activist, for example. She will just be able to read the news of a murder trial with more "understanding"—the work of the reading here is wholly work done on the self, not reaching out into the world.

Blair continues, before moving on to discuss other books in this column, that Natalie "will find it well worth her while to read with Dreiser, Elizabeth

142 CHAPTER THREE

Drew's 'The Modern Novel'"; Drew, Blair writes, "sets forth the purposes of literature, what books can and do give to us, and the intention of authors today."[75] On Dreiser, Drew is even more merciless than Blair; he is almost "completely unreadable"; his work "has no picturesque quality, no humour, no subtlety, no elegance—nothing but this ugly solidity of craftsmanship and a terrific determination to express somehow the forms of life and the forces of life which he has seen and felt with intensity."[76] Drew compares Dreiser to Lewis, whom she indicts as "imprisoned stiffly within an attitude" with a satire too explicit to be "art"; and to Anderson, who "seems to be struggling to say something for which at present he has not found the mode of expression."[77] Drew addresses all three as members of a group of artists, also including Upton Sinclair and Edith Wharton in the bunch, who "are in revolt against their material—all are filled with active hatred, or at least active dissatisfaction with the conditions of life they report, and this frame of mind towards their material inevitably affects their work."[78] Drew contends that, while this hamstrings these authors' work from an aesthetic perspective, an awareness of their motivations should temper the reader who might otherwise reject their displeasing prose and shallow characterizations. Blair's recommendation of Drew thus reinforces her own approach to Dreiser; Drew and Blair stand together in their pragmatic approach to the unpleasant authors of the mid-1920s.

In the mid-to-late 1920s, Dreiser, Cather, and Lewis were often considered part of the "old guard," as opposed to the avant-garde of the high modernists to which Anderson belonged. Their reputedly more traditional aesthetics made all three of these authors likely candidates for consideration by Blair. Blair's engagement with Anderson is one of the rare occasions when she does consider a more avant-garde modernist, despite the flourishing of this group during her tenure. Another "experimental" author Blair engages during her time at *Good Housekeeping* is Virginia Woolf; but as we will see in the following chapter, Woolf is the exception that proves the rule. Modernism's misogyny, unnecessary complexity, and performative "reflexive antipathy to the commodity"[79] drive Blair to wage a pointed assault against its pieties. High modernism is not finally "worthwhile" because it is a con game, and as a good consumer advisor, Blair will caution her readers against the scam.

CHAPTER FOUR

The Modernist Racket

Everyone to his taste. The taste's the thing!
—Emily Newell Blair, July 1926[1]

As we saw in the previous chapter, Blair's early columns do engage to a degree with literary modernism. She does not do so in the imperative mode, however, and goes so far as to advise her *Good Housekeeping* audience against the impulse to think about any of their reading as something that they "should" or "ought" to do. Her posture is that of the friend who has read it all and offers opinions but not judgements, who characterizes books in terms that are not necessarily value neutral but are also not prescriptive. This also means that she does not condemn literary modernism to the dustbin; *Dark Laughter* is a "heavy lift, with some problems, but it isn't a must-read" *or* a book to avoid at all costs. And yet, there are works of literary modernism that are contemporary with her columns that Blair never mentions: Ernest Hemingway's *The Sun Also Rises* (1926), *A Farewell to Arms* (1929), and *Death in the Afternoon* (1932); William Faulkner's *The Sound and the Fury* (1929), *As I Lay Dying* (1930), and *Sanctuary* (1931); John Dos Passos's *U. S. A.* trilogy (1930, 1932, 1936); and Gertrude Stein's *Three Lives* (1932). F. Scott Fitzgerald's *The Great Gatsby* (1925) makes a cameo appearance, not in her inaugural column alongside other 1925 works like Cather's *The Professor's House*, but, like Dreiser's *An American Tragedy*, as a foil for other recommendations (more on this curious case in chapter 5).

Something happens, however, over the course of Blair's tenure at *Good Housekeeping*: she begins to lose her patience with apologists for experimental literature, with its complexity, determined inaccessibility, and latent (or sometimes overt) misogyny. The insistence of literary elite reviewers and professional university literary scholars that this new mode was superior to other expressions of modern life begins to grate on Blair, and she takes several opportunities to take on other professional critics, whom she calls out for using

143

144   CHAPTER FOUR

high modernism to "furnish[] them their 'racket,' the material for their jobs."
Blair begins to offer her readers, through her summaries and analysis of various
works, more ammunition to resist the compulsion to read books that have been
approved by the literary elites. In the last chapter we saw how she satisfied her
club mate Julia by proffering *The Professor's House* as a critically approved novel;
as she continues in her time at *Good Housekeeping*, Blair becomes more likely to
try to convince Julia that she really doesn't need to worry about what would-be
cultural gatekeepers think about anything she reads. Eventually, Blair's wariness toward literary modernism segues into an implication that these authors'
and critics' outward disavowal of middlebrow consumer culture is, actually, a
cynical cover for their own form of cultural fetishism. Blair finally accuses these
elite literary critics of being practitioners of misleading marketing who are
only trying to sustain their own status by trying to sell the public on literature
that required intensive critical apparatus for comprehension. As the "Director"
of the "Tasting and Testing Books" department, it is Blair's responsibility to
uncover these misleading claims and to shine a light on this false advertising.

Blair's frustration with elite literary critics bubbles most aggressively to the
surface during her extraordinary discussion of Virginia Woolf's *Orlando* in
the May 1929 column, "Emily Newell Blair Chooses a Hamper of Books for
Frances Parkinson Keyes—and Other Travelers Too." In this column, written as a paean to her good friend (and *Good Housekeeping* editor) Keyes, Blair
recommends Virginia Woolf's *Orlando* but does so with considerable caveats
and an explicit condemnation of the "modernist racket," which she says is sustained by authors and critics alike to bolster their own careers. Blair says she
will send *Orlando* to Keyes *despite*, not because of, its embrace by elite critics,
and asserts that Keyes will be able to make her own way through the novel.
Blair also sends along Rebecca West's collection of critical essays, *The Strange
Necessity*—"selfishly," she admits, because she wants to talk about West's
work with Keyes. West, it seems, is not one of those critics who is engaged in
the racket; she, like Woolf, is worth Keyes's while, but just happens also to be
embraced by the denizens of the little magazine world.

It is no coincidence that Blair sends West and Woolf, together, to her
professional literary journalist friend Keyes. They are two women working
within a male-dominated field, whose relationship *may* be personal but
absolutely looks, to the outside observer, like a mutually supportive professional network. Blair's column, which is just one instance of many in which
she promotes Keyes's work, implies by the association with West and Woolf
that her relationship with Keyes is likewise an alternative to male-dominated

The Modernist Racket 145

magazine publishing hierarchies. But they are not just models to emulate; as we will see, Blair's column, and Keyes's own mentions of Blair in multiple similar articles, implicitly and explicitly invites their *Good Housekeeping* audience into a parasocial relationship of like-minded women.

Moreover, Blair reminds her readers in this and later columns that modernist cultural critics are not divorced from the consumer economy that so clearly contextualizes her own recommendations. By describing their aesthetic judgements and coy preferences as "material for their jobs," Blair is reminding her audience that, like herself and Keyes, all of these other critics work in the material modern world. They are concerned about their own economic and material well-being at least as much as, if not more than, any aesthetic or ideological program they might espouse. There is nothing wrong with work or with a concern about material things—quite the contrary. Blair, after all, highlights the conditions of her labor, just as Keyes does in her travel columns. Both write for magazines devoted to helping their readers navigate the modern consumer landscape. Blair's objection, implied by her thick sarcasm here, is to an ethos of aesthetic and material disinterest, which, in disdaining middlebrow consumer culture for not being intellectual enough, disguises (poorly) its misogyny as intellectualism. Instead, she embraces and recommends Rebecca West, who represents herself working through her aesthetic evaluation of Joyce while on a shopping excursion in Paris, as an exemplar. Blair couples with West a Virginia Woolf who appeared regularly in the British versions of *Good Housekeeping* and *Vogue* and who was closely identified with her domestic situation in Bloomsbury. Woolf and West are important to Blair as the embodiments of a version of modernist literary culture that rendered intellectual life accessible and useful and tied it to women's work and concerns. As I will discuss below, Woolf was already generally considered a "crossover" author, if perhaps more familiar to mainstream audiences in the United Kingdom than in those in the United States. By empowering her audiences to read Woolf any way they liked, and inviting West alongside as a genial literary critic, Blair validated herself, Keyes, and the *Good Housekeeping* audience as full participants in modernist literary culture.

Networking

Blair's May 1929 column is premised on the idea that she is gathering an actual, physical "hamper of books" for Keyes to read on her new cruise, about which she will be writing for *Good Housekeeping*. Keyes would have been very

146   CHAPTER FOUR

well-known to the *Good Housekeeping* audience as the author of several series
of epistolary articles describing her travels and her experiences as a senator's
wife. She was also a novelist, and Blair faithfully recommended her work in
her columns. But in this column centered on Keyes, Blair asserts a bit of priority by taking credit for sparking Keyes's magazine writing career. Her *Good
Housekeeping* readers "may, in a sense, owe [Keyes] to me":

> For long ago, a graceful young matron sitting at tea in a Washington club-
> house, she asked me to advise her how she might secure a regular magazine
> connection.
> "What have you to sell that no one else has?" I asked her.
> And looking under the smart, brown hat at the bright eyes that were
> so soon to win Washington society, and realizing here was one who would
> savor official life to the fullest, I added, with just a touch of envy,
> "Does any Senator's wife write about these official experiences that every
> woman longs to share?"[2]

In 1919, the year Keyes would have been just entering DC society upon
her husband's election as senator from New Hampshire, Blair did indeed
have more extensive knowledge of the world of magazine publishing than
Keyes. By 1919, Blair was established as a frequent contributor to many
national magazines, and she had been editing *Missouri Woman* since 1914.
Keyes's career as a writer was relatively nascent; after publishing two articles
in smaller regional magazines, she broke onto the national scene in 1918 with
"Satisfied Reflections of a Semi-Bostonian" in the *Atlantic Monthly*. Her first
novel, *The Old Gray Homestead*, would be published by the end of 1919, but
Keyes was by no means a known author until her *Good Housekeeping* series
"Letters of a Senator's Wife" ultimately elevated her into prominence.

Blair's account of her early championing of Keyes's career is borne out
by the archive. While letters between Keyes and William Bigelow do not
mention Blair's name at all, a letter from Blair to Keyes dated June 26, 1919,
recounts her outreach to the editors of the *Ladies' Home Journal* on Keyes's
behalf, "as I agreed," and suggests follow-up strategies.

> She answers that she will be particularly glad to see anything you care to
> submit to her. Suggest that you send the manuscript to her with a letter
> saying that Mrs. Blair directed you to her & suggesting that this manu-
> script, even though it may be unadapted to their present needs will show
> your style & what you can do and that you would be glad to discuss some
> new ideas you have in mind if she thinks your style would interest her
> readers. Be sure & tell her about your book. Even if she does not take this
> she may discuss the new article you are planning.[3]

Blair's mentoring advice is solid and, while apparently nothing resulted from Keyes's correspondence with the *Journal* at this early stage, her overtures to William Bigelow at *Good Housekeeping* were more successful. While her initial letter to him does not seem to have survived, his response indicates that she took the initiative to reply to a letter he had written to her husband lobbying for passage of the Sheppard-Towner Bill (for federal funding of maternity and child care). "If the wives of all the senators—for I wrote to them all—get my letter and the magazine, and feel as you do about the Sheppard Bill, I am sure that it will pass." Bigelow also parries Keyes's mention of his previous rejections. "I must confess that I have no recollection of having 'once turned you down, flat as a pancake.' There is nothing in my letter file to show what it was that you suggested. I have no apology to make, however, as I always turn down the things that I do not want, and the name and the reputation of the author makes no difference." But this time around, Keyes's letter seems to have come at exactly the right time for Bigelow, who gives her an assignment: to approach the current secretary of agriculture, Edwin T. Meredith, and ask him "what in his department would be of greatest interest to the American housewife in town and country ... just what is most important regarding our food problem that we should all know and then write it up in your own way?" He cites Keyes's *Atlantic* article—although confesses he did not read the whole thing—as evidence that she is "more human than the average Atlantic writer"[4]—and hopes that she will take on the project. Keyes's access to Meredith is key to Bigelow's idea here; she is both an insider and a representative housewife, and by writing up the interview in her own way she will presumably be translating the language of policy into the idiom of the *Good Housekeeping* consumer. In subsequent letters, Bigelow also enlists Keyes as a lobbyist among the senators' wives in favor of the magazine's legislative agenda. She eventually becomes his woman on the inside on many fronts, and he sends her magazine issues to distribute and talking points for her luncheon chats. The winning combination of her abilities to influence legislation, gain access to prominent officials, and write prolifically made Keyes a major asset to the magazine.

By the time Blair was writing her retrospective account of their friendship Keyes had repaid Blair's favor grandly. In a letter dated January 1925 (one year before Blair's first column would appear in *Good Housekeeping*), Keyes, now an associate editor for *Good Housekeeping*, forwards Blair two letters of introduction to use presumably with other publications (these do seem to be

148   CHAPTER FOUR

in the archive). She then goes on to quote at length from a letter she says she is writing to William Bigelow that day:

> Emily Newell Blair drew me aside the other day and told me she would like to have a talk with me which proved to be on the topic of getting back into the literary field herself. She said she had had some conversation with you which had not as yet borne any fruit. I like and admire her tremendously and she has enormous acquaintance among women who feel the same way towards her, so I can not help venturing to ask if you do not think she might possibly be useful in doing some of the same kind of work that Miss Toombs used to do. Perhaps you have that all taken care of but in case you have not, I can think of no one who would be better for it than Mrs. Blair, provided, of course, she resigned her position as National Committeewoman that there might be no partisan aspect to her work, and this she says she will be quite willing to do.[5]

Blair was at this point, as we saw in chapter 1, trying to return to the writing that had initially launched her in her political career, and Keyes's assurance that Blair would resign her post with the Democratic Party to become fully nonpartisan would be understandably reassuring to a large-circulation magazine editor. That Keyes herself was a Republican, recommending a Democrat, probably also held water. Keyes apparently also suggested editors aside from Bigelow to Blair for her New York trip; when Blair wrote to Keyes in February 1925 with an update and to "thank you for your kindness . . . you are a delightful and a generous friend," she lists multiple editors with whom she had conferred. "Miss Giles was very lovely, but the Editor seemed unwilling to add any new names to her staff at the present. . . . Mrs. Meloney is playing with the idea of my opening the Public Affairs Department for the Delineator. Mr. Bigelow was sure that he had no opening. . . . I do not feel particularly encouraged, but I am hoping that something may yet develop. Please keep me in mind in case you hear of any openings."[6] Had Blair used Keyes's letters of introduction to secure the additional meetings? It is entirely possible; at the very least, she knew that Keyes knew these figures, and that she either might hear of Blair's approaches through her network or that Keyes might be able to offer insight on next steps. Blair also seems to be protecting Keyes's feelings a bit here; when she wrote home to her husband, Harry, about the Bigelow meeting, she quoted Bigelow directly rather than obliquely giving the gist of his rejection: "*Bigelow* was not particularly interested—in fact said politely 'nothing doing' all stocked up etc. tho—did say if I had come to him 1 yr. or 9 months ago just after Eliz. Tombs [sic] died would have taken me to fill her place. Now he has found out he can get along without anyone."[7]

"Nothing doing," slangy and definite, is a bit more deflating than "he was sure . . . ," and Blair diplomatically chooses not to report the direct message that they had been too slow to take advantage of Miss Toombs's death. No need to let Keyes know that her instincts were right but her timing poor.

Although the trail of correspondence now grows cold, and none of Keyes's extant letters to Bigelow mention Blair, something clearly finally convinced Bigelow to publish a books column with Blair as advisor. Keyes privately suggested it was her influence. In March 1926, after the appearance of Blair's first Tasting and Testing Books column, Keyes sent Blair a congratulatory note from Singapore, where she was traveling on her own *Good Housekeeping* assignment. "It has long been my opinion that 'Good Housekeeping' should have a book Department and I have told Mr. Bigelow so time and time again," she writes, implicitly taking credit for the idea of the book department. She continues, "You also know how much I have wanted to have you on the Magazine staff and the frequency with which I have told him that. So it seems to me that a combination of you and the book department is absolutely ideal and I cannot help writing to you from this distant place to tell you how perfectly delighted I am."[8] Blair replies gratefully to Keyes in April: "I do not forget that your interest in my connection with GOOD HOUSEKEEPING may be largely responsible for Mr. Bigelow's hospitality to my idea for the Department and I shall always be grateful,"[9] notably asserting that the department was *her* idea. It is less important to me (despite it mattering to Keyes and Blair) to resolve conclusively the debate about who came up with the idea of the department, however. More significant is the women's mutual acknowledgement of their mutual assistance in navigating the magazine publishing world that was ultimately controlled, in this case at least, by a man. Blair's continued mention of the "many kindnesses" she has received from Keyes in the May 1929 column surely would have been in reference to this ongoing professional networking.

The portrait of their relationship in Blair's column goes beyond the professional, however; the whole premise of the piece is that she is preparing a "hamper of books" for Keyes to take with her on her world travels. As she contemplates giving books to Keyes, she first considers all of Keyes's hobbies and preferences; she knows about her love of gardening and bridge, her appreciation of fine dining. She knows about more than Keyes's professional persona; they are truly friends—just as Keyes, through her columns in the magazine, has presumably become one of the *Good Housekeeping* reader's friends. In other words, Blair is not only narrating a friendship and mutual professional network between herself and Keyes; she is also including her readers in those relationships. Keyes performed a similar move in a February 1928 article she wrote for *Better Homes and Gardens* as part of a series called Homes of Outstanding American Women, narrating Blair's savvy negotiating with a real estate agent for prepurchase renovations on a small house and walking the reader through Blair's home. Keyes tells the intimate details of Blair's decorating, even describing the interior of Blair's bedroom, and knows the economies Blair had to pursue in her renovations as well as an intimate friend might. The house is "partly Spanish and partly Chinese but mostly Mrs. Blair herself," a model of "comfort and convenience, culture and charm; all created . . . from a house condemned as impossible."[10] The correspondence between Keyes and Blair while planning for this article is illuminating; after a series of telegrams making agreements for the profile and arrangements for the visit, Keyes writes a long letter from her next stop in Syracuse, New York, reporting on the success of the article draft, and a possible result of its publication. "I spoke both to Mr. Peterson, the Editor, and to Mr. Meredith about the possibility—and the advisability in my mind—of having you do an article or articles for 'Better Homes and Gardens,' suggesting particularly that if this one *about* you met with a gratifying response that one *by* you might follow it in short order. I know that they are turning this suggestion over in their minds and I hope the results will be in ever [sic] way pleasing to you."[11]

The profile of Blair, in other words, serves both of them in multiple ways. It advances Keyes's profile as an author, a social observer, and a well-connected woman. But Keyes wants to show Blair that it can also work for her as an author and influencer. This profile expands Blair's reputation to the realm of interior design and household management; its success, properly presented (by Keyes) to the magazine's editors, suggests that articles on these subjects *by Blair herself* would be popular with the magazine's audience. This small moment shows how Keyes is always thinking about the angles, both for herself and for others. Each appearance in a national magazine is not an end to itself, but an opportunity for career advancement in multiple forums. After the *Better Homes and Gardens* issue appears in February 1928, Keyes writes to Blair to suggest that she distribute copies of the magazine at her political speaking engagements. It would be, she insists, "good publicity for you," having done the same thing herself in the past with magazines in which she appeared.[12] Keyes is a whiz at self-promotion, but she is also looking out for opportunities for her friend—a friend whose (midwestern?) sensibilities run too far to humility. "I should be delighted to have the February issue of

The Modernist Racket 151

'Better Homes and Gardens' distributed at the close of my speech . . . but don't you think it would seem conceited of me to distribute articles about myself?" Blair responds. "It isn't quite as if the articles were written by me about someone else or something else." Blair has a point, and offers a graceful modification on Keyes's plan: "I am perfectly willing to ask for the copies if you could distribute them as your tribute to me."[13] It isn't clear what was eventually resolved, but this exchange stands as a remarkable vignette of two women navigating together the shifting mores of publication, publicity, and politics.

Since they covered similar beats, the women were careful to keep each other apprised of their assignments, whether to avoid competition or to help each other pitch complementary articles it is not clear. Their friendship seems to rely on full disclosure when there is a misunderstanding. Blair rarely opens her letters without preliminaries but does so in May 1928: "I thought I told you that the King Feature Syndicate had asked me to do some short feature stories for them covering the conventions. I was not sure I would do it until I talked to them in New York the other day but I was not keeping it quiet on that account. It was just that we always have so much to talk about that we never finish."[14] All must have been forgiven, for Blair writes to Keyes in July thanking her for including her as one of "Seven Successful Women" in a *Delineator* article. "I can not tell you how grateful I am for this and every other 'lift' you have given me and you have indeed been generous with them." The portrait is indeed charming, mentioning Blair's new presidency of the Democratic Women's Club and her ongoing literary "activities" ("she is a born booklover," though of course the name of the rival magazine in which Blair demonstrates her bookishness is not mentioned in the piece) and offering this summation: "She is the personification of the old adage that 'the nicest things come in small packages.'"[15] In her letter, Blair is eager to point out that she has tried to reciprocate Keyes's attentions but has been thwarted by the vagaries of magazine publication: "In my September articles on the Conventions, I included an appreciation of you. . . . I regret exceedingly that it was necessary to cut it out on account of space but soon again the opportunity will come and you can be sure I will embrace it."[16]

The correspondence is not exclusively focused on business; a hallmark of the extant letters is a mingling of the deeply personal with the professional. Blair's May 1926 letter responding to Keyes's congratulations on the launch of Tasting and Testing Books is a case in point; she acknowledges that Keyes's even taking the time to write was a gift ("busy as you must be with every moment full and utterly unable to see all that you would like and do all that you would like")

CHAPTER FOUR

and adds that she is "distressed to hear about your misfortune" (what this is is unclear) and that "I follow everything you write with the keenest interest." Her own delayed reply, Blair explains, is due to a move, and then a family wedding, and then a business trip out East—"and the day after I returned my mother died." Blair, of course, hosted the funeral services, and "all my family were here"; her letter to Keyes seems a unique pause in the busy-ness to register her grief: "I find it very difficult to adjust myself to a world without her." After a paragraph break, Blair resumes, "For all of these reasons it has been difficult to give the time to the articles that they require, Mr. Bigelow, however, seems pleased with them and the response from the readers is gratifying. There seems to be no doubt that there was a need for this kind of a Department."[17] Few moments in the correspondence demonstrate the degree to which Blair, and Keyes, approximate the portrait of the "Good Housekeeping Woman" painted by the advertising department in 1928: "She is equally at ease in a house dress, an afternoon gown, and a party frock."[18] The things that have kept Blair from devoting "the time ... that they require" to her columns will have required all of these costume changes, and more (travel suit, business suit). But while she may have been quite *capable* of performing each of these roles, the emotional labor of doing so, and doing them all simultaneously, almost certainly means "ease" is the wrong descriptor.

Schröedinger's Books

Blair does, finally, see a chance to reciprocate Keyes's "lifts" in late 1928 and writes for permission to pen the "Hamper of Books" article. "I have long wanted to find an opportunity to express some of the things I think about your work and personality and this offers the occasion."[19] She queries Keyes about her travel plans, asking whether it might be better for the column to appear in February or March. On November 17, 1928, Keyes replies that she "should be delighted to have you write such an article as you suggest and feel much complimented that you should wish to do so," but she asks her to wait until later in the spring, "even May," so that she would know what her itinerary would be.[20] In December, Blair writes to Keyes: "Thank you for telling me about your conference with Mr. Bigelow. I shall plan to build my article for May about sending you books for your trip." She then adds: "You will be interested to know that Mr. Bigelow did not raise the payment for my articles this year. Needless to say I am *terribly* disappointed."[21] The "Hamper of Books" column, pay freezes aside, appears in May 1929.

Emily Newell Blair *Chooses*

A Hamper of Books

For

Frances Parkinson Keyes—

And Other Travelers, Too

Four years ago, when this picture was taken, Mrs. Keyes was just starting on her round-the-world tour for Good Housekeeping. April 19th she sailed again—by way of Spain—for South America. Her "Letters" will follow soon

IT IS estimated by the steamship companies that an average of one hundred dollars is spent on each saloon passenger for bon voyage gifts. Flowers, of course, to bring a touch of land into the cabin and, too, a touch of color; baskets of fruit to please the eye as well as the palate; books for the quiet, restful hours; surprise boxes with a gaily wrapped package a day to beguile the tedium; games and picture puzzles to keep one company; pictures and even toys to amuse; queer little containers of bath salts or powders; and articles like steamer rugs and pillows, leather traveling trays, bottles, photograph frames, to fill practical needs.

Among those travelers there goes this month a friend of many years and many kindnesses for a tour of South America, a friend shared by my GOOD HOUSEKEEPING readers, whom I like to think they may, in a sense, owe to me—Frances Parkinson Keyes. For long ago, a graceful young matron sitting at tea in a Washington clubhouse, she asked me to advise her how she might secure a regular magazine connection.

"What have you to sell that no one else has?" I asked her.

And looking under the smart, brown hat at the bright eyes that were so soon to win Washington society, and realizing that here was one who would savor official life to the fullest, I added, with just a tinge of envy,

"Does any senator's wife write about these official experiences that every woman longs to share?"

Only the suggestion traces to me. It was the gift for superlative reporting that loses no essential detail while recording only the agreeable, the delightful, the interesting—be the subject a person, an experience, an event—and the editor who ever widened her opportunities to meet people, enjoy experiences, and witness events that have made the "Senator's Wife" into an "Unofficial Ambassadress to the World." And now that she is adding the other America to the countries she interprets to our women, it behooves friends like me to think upon a fitting steamer gift.

I think of her love for flowers, recalling the violets running down her luncheon table at the Congressional Club and the long-stemmed roses in the tall vases in her Washington apartment; of her appreciation of good food, remembering her high praise of Kathie's dumplings; of her enthusiasm for bridge and other games at which she excels; of her search for anything which will increase the efficiency of her traveling kit. Which shall I strive to please? And then I remember the glee with which she confided to me on her departure for Bermuda last year that she was taking along a whole hamper of books. A hamper of books! What more perfect gift? As much color for the cabin as any bouquet, mental stimulus, and food—Mrs. Keyes is not the woman to live by bread alone—a surprise package for each day, a puzzle in each plot, each binding a container of something satisfying, and articles useful to furnish conversation if not, perhaps, information and knowledge. A combination in one gift of everything gifts might offer.

All this provided, of course, that the hamper contains the right books. The right books! That was a difficulty. In the first place they *(Continued on page 173)*

FIGURE 5. Frances Parkinson Keyes, boarding a boat; this illustration accompanied Blair's May 1929 column, "A Hamper of Books" (*Good Housekeeping*, May 1929, 98). Credit: *Good Housekeeping*. Hearst Magazine Media Inc.

154 CHAPTER FOUR

The Blair-Keyes relationship was personally mutually beneficial; its regular invocation in multiple periodicals suggests that it was also valuable to those publications because their audiences found it compelling. Like twenty-first-century social media friendships, Blair and Keyes's mutual appreciation society enabled readers to enter into a parasocial relationship that could be both personally gratifying (readers could feel like they were friends with Blair and Keyes) and could help readers craft their own social behaviors. As a magazine "friend" of both women, who is privy to their intimate exchanges of books and can imagine the professional exchanges that secured both roles in magazine writing, the reader becomes a member of this network of women who have demonstrated their ability to negotiate *for each other* roles in the political and literary spheres of the 1920s and 1930s. The work that Blair and Keyes do in politics, and that they perform for an audience of largely women in their mass market magazine pieces, functioned as a model of feminine literary networking that went beyond specific titles to introduce an engaged readerly political lifestyle to the readers of *Good Housekeeping*. It is through such modeling that Blair extended her goals for the League of Women Voters through the seemingly apolitical reading advice columns she penned for *Good Housekeeping*—women of all political stripes could advise, support, and celebrate each other in their individual tastes and readerly inclinations, through this intrafeminine, and cosmopolitan, network of letters.

Blair's conceit of sending an actual, physical "hamper of books" to Keyes also implicitly encouraged her readers to mediate their friendships through choosing, giving, and talking about books. The gift of a book, as Blair describes it here, is potentially powerful, "A surprise package for each day. . . . A combination in one gift of everything gifts might offer." But this gift is also particularly *intimate*. Books must be chosen carefully. They must interest the recipient but should not have already been read by her. Threading this needle obviously implies a measure of familiarity, but even more importantly it requires mutual trust: "She must feel that she can trust me—trust my taste, and what is more important and more rare, depend on my having given the time and thought to consider her taste." Books take up space and weight on a ship, and the recipient does not have the opportunity to trade books at will; whatever you send will be the thing they have at hand to read, so you can't afford to send something they won't appreciate or want to pursue to the end. Doing so would signal carelessness or, worse, a lack of awareness of either the situation on board ship or the personality of the recipient. In short, the giving of books to a traveler is a particularly

The Modernist Racket 155

delicate act. As if to emphasize this point, Blair assembles a hamper of books for Keyes that many readers would probably not choose for themselves as shipboard reading: a travelogue of Haiti with intense descriptions of voodoo rituals that Blair admits do not "bring joy"; a history of World War I that will leave Keyes, "as I shall warn her it did me, with a depression taking days to lose."[22] Hardly the typical cruise fare; but, as Blair interrupts herself to assert, entirely appropriate for her friend:

> I pay Mrs. Keyes the compliment of choosing serious books, for I know that she is one of those who read for more than escape from life. It is the bored who do that. Her own life is too interesting. Nor is she one to take life under an anodyne. She is far too courageous. Whatever it yields she wants to know, to face. After all, the man who "sees too much of that in life" and wants to forget it when he reads a book is more apt to turn out a broker in real life than a physician or a lawyer whose business is with tragedy. When a person sees tragedy and sin and suffering, he is usually curious enough to hunt for reasons and for them goes to authors who treat of life seriously as they find it.[23]

Blair had, previously, validated reading for escape (see chapter 3), and she will embrace reading as an "anodyne" in future columns (see the epilogue), but here, while Keyes is on vacation, Blair claims she would not want to be given books that would force her to escape the world's tough realities. The tone here is something other than laudatory; Blair does not necessarily seem to hold Keyes up for emulation in the same way that she holds up Natalie or Julia in other columns. Keyes is exceptional, though her way might very well be that of another of Blair's readers.

Or, perhaps, the Exceptional Keyes is as fictional as the "Good Housekeeping Woman" at ease in all her "frocks." There was, indeed, an actual box of books; at least two boxes, in fact, sent from *Good Housekeeping*'s offices to Keyes at several ports of call: "I hope the books reached you in time," Blair writes at the start of June. "There was a delay due to the necessity of holding them until we had read proof but we sent them in plenty of time to reach you. There are still four more to go which for some reason or other were omitted from the first box. Mr. Bigelow though [*sic*] you would want them in relays, as it were, so as not to be burdened with too large a box"[24] (this was, of course, exactly the thing Blair cautions her readers *against* when giving books to a traveler). Keyes does write to thank Blair for—at least the article, if not the physical books; her acknowledgement indicates very plainly

156   CHAPTER FOUR

that she is not going to be doing much reading on her trip. "Your 'Hamper of Books' pleased and touched me more than you can guess and I am sorry to be so long in telling you so. But I have lived a hectic life since I left home, and everytime that I have said to myself 'I will surely write to Mrs. Blair today' I have had to put it off after all."[25] Keyes says she has not been able to make "any mental effort" on her trip, and presumably that would include reading the kinds of books Blair recommended to her, which, as we shall see, were emphatically not light vacation reading. But the value of the article, to both Blair and Keyes, goes beyond the gift of books: it is a gift of tribute, reciprocal professional support, and, perhaps eventually, future publicity.

Keyes speaks in her letter of her exhaustion during the passage to Portugal, and then about her constant work on the article series she has promised to the magazine. "I have got material for five articles in three months, half of which I have spent on the water, so I hope and believe that Mr. Bigelow will be pleased, but it has meant unremitting labor for me."[26] Portraying the real conditions of the writing woman is, however, *also* not the point of Blair's portrait of Keyes—it serves, rather, to prepare Blair and her readers for the recommendations that will come next: a collection of Rebecca West's literary critical essays, *The Strange Necessity*, and Virginia Woolf's *Orlando*. The pairing takes advantage of Hugh Walpole's assertion that West and Woolf are "co-queens of English letters," but it also performs a complicated alchemy with regard to the position of women in modernism and in modernist literary criticism. Woolf and West are paired against the men of modernism like James Joyce and T. S. Eliot in the same way that Blair and Keyes are aligned in navigating the male world of magazine publication. By setting up her literary conversation through her discussion of her friendship with Keyes, Blair recenters the literary field, both for herself and for her readers, in the writings of modern women.

Rebecca West and Virginia Woolf

Blair admits that she is recommending West's book selfishly. She wants to talk to Keyes about the title essay, which is "the sort of essay one must discuss . . . the sort one must reread."[27] In it West takes a broad view of modern aesthetics, narrating her own, flaneuse-style ramble through the streets of Paris while desultorily reading a newly purchased volume of Joyce's poems, *Pomes Penyeach*. As West watches men playing boules, as she shops for dresses and observes the movements of birds, she reflects on the specific pleasures Joyce's bad poetry (she says straight out that it is bad poetry) is able to offer her. Her

The Modernist Racket   157

enjoyment comes not from the poetry itself, she contends, but from the "light thrown on this poem on a certain system of relations, on the nexus of forces which is Mr. James Joyce."[28] Self-consciously and explicitly, West exposes the fact that critical and authorial aesthetic preferences are not *really* about the formal choices themselves (to be allusive or realistic, to be legible or opaque) but are proxy battles over social fields, serving to draw boundaries around those who have "taste" and those who lack it. With Virginia Heffernan, I see in West's criticism a move that anticipates Pierre Bourdieu's work on cultural capital. West explains that she "enjoys" Joyce's poetry, and portions of *Ulysses*, to the extent that they give her access to the cultural phenomenon that is Joyce; they "awaken in West a feeling of mastery over a larger structure," which leads her to understanding how art can "teach us . . . how to read the aesthetic itself as a relation of power."[29] She realizes that she is, at the very least, required to "live in a world where a large number of people are to varying degrees conditioned by a knowledge of *Ulysses*. I shall not be able to analyse any experience of mine in which they take part unless I can fully comprehend their conditioning in this respect. Moreover, I shall find it easier to analyse my experiences with people who have not read *Ulysses* if I can put my finger on the differences in them which are due to this abstinence" (*SN* 180–81). Reading and not reading *Ulysses* are acts that orient people toward each other, but neither choice has much to do with the novel itself—both are decisions made based on discourse around the novel that then refigure the social scene around something that need never be read.

The occasion for this revelation, again, is West's somewhat giddy recognition that Joyce has written, and been allowed to publish, a book of bad poetry. This clear failure provides West with the latitude to return to the whole cultural moment of *Ulysses* with a critical eye—to both the book itself and to the strong opinions that have been publicly expressed about it. West's own criticisms of *Ulysses* are manifold, as are her appreciations; many of both are a function of the difference between her own reading of the novel and the readings offered by Joyce's fans. "It was M. Valéry Larbaud who first detected that the title of the great work was not just put in to make it more difficult, that there exists a close parallelism between the incidents of the Odyssey and *Ulysses*: . . . This recognition plunges Mr. Joyce's devotees into profound ecstasies from which they never recover sufficiently to ask what the devil is the purpose that is served by these analogies" (28). Indeed, West argues, the Greek epic is itself at odds with the Manichean tendencies of Joyce's novel: "For Mr. Joyce to write his Manichean epic with a dove-tailing fidelity to a Greek pattern is as sensible

CHAPTER FOUR

as it would be to write a novel about Middle Western farm life in French alexandrines" (*SN* 29). The critics who are trying to prove Joyce's (and their own) erudition by mapping the events of the novel onto *Odyssey* references are really just exposing their ignorance. She then calls out the critics who explicate the Lying-In Hospital scene as a parodic commentary on the history of British literature. "What they never pause to notice is that even as parodies, and perhaps the parody is the art-form which produces the largest percentage of execrable specimens, these are noticeably bad" (30). West goes on to show that she is a more creative reader than these critics, that she does not need to reduce *Ulysses* to a referential formula but can appreciate its good points as themselves and criticize its excesses when they hamper the project.

West's identification of the social and material investments of a purportedly disinterested modernist aesthetic made her the object of mockery and shunning by modernism's male critics, whom Virginia Woolf portrayed in *A Room of One's Own* as offended by West, the "arrant feminist."[30] Heffernan traces this reception, in particular from Beckett and Williams, who both accuse West of an inability to differentiate between art and other "things" as she "consumes books in the same way she consumes commodities and food—ravenously and indiscriminately."[31] The most affronting element of the essay may well have been that West constantly situates all of her sophisticated literary contemplations in the context of a shopping trip. After a particularly theoretically dense, historically inflected, detailed close reading of Marion Bloom's monologue at the end of *Ulysses*, she interrupts herself to relate that "since my buying of *Pomes Penyeach* at Sylvia Beach's bookshop that morning I had done quite a number of things."

> I had been to my dressmaker and had bought a black lace dress. . . . I had been to a milliner's shop which the head *vendeuse* of a famous house had just started as her own venture and had ordered three hats, and had sat playing with the models, two on my lap, one on my head, changing them about. . . . I had lunched in a divine house that is at the end of the Ile St. Louis like the prow of a ship. . . . I had called at a bank for letters. . . . I had had half an hour with a lawyer discussing an investment. And all the time my mind had pounded away at this matter of *Ulysses*, had refused for more than a minute to relinquish James Joyce. (*SN* 51–52)

While we, her readers, had been distracted by West's thoughts about art, and may have completely forgotten her opening gambit of the walk through Paris, it turns out that she herself was never distracted from her errands. She

The Modernist Racket 159

is actually a little surprised by the degree to which her thoughts of Joyce have been intrusive, since she does "not particularly like *Ulysses* or James Joyce" (*SN* 52), while she does enjoy shopping and eating. "I like dresses, and the wide light *salons* where one buys them. I like hats . . . I like strawberries. . . . Why could I not give the whole of my psychic energy to Paris, on which autumn was lying like very fine eighteenth-century gilt, to dresses and hats and the Ile St. Louis, to my amusing and spurious host and his strawberries, to love and money?" (*SN* 52). Even more irritating, her thoughts about Joyce are overrepresented in her recollections of the afternoon. Ultimately her attempts to figure out why Joyce is still prominent in her memories, despite her trenchant criticism of his novel and the critics who celebrate it, lead her to assert the importance of art—not just because it is "beautiful" or "true," but because it affords the occasion for exploration of the world.

This is the "strange necessity" of West's title; art, West posits, is "at least in part a way of collecting information about the universe" (*SN* 89). West both recognizes the artistic in the quotidian and shows that mundane tasks are essential intertexts for her own critical practice. Her stylistic choices when narrating her walk through Paris contrast with Joyce's use of "gibberish" in relating the thoughts of Leopold Bloom (frequently appropriately) and Stephen Dedalus (completely inappropriately), thus underscoring the critique of Joyce and, presumably, demonstrating the experience that spurs that critique. Later, West writes about how the interruptions of a talkative electrician spark in her a deeper understanding of the Pavlov she has been reading:

> He was a garrulous person and bored me very much; and it happened to occur to me that there was a comical contrast between my boredom and its grandiose ultimate cause. For the man would not have been in my house on this occasion if countless millions of years ago a species had not developed in ways that made them avail themselves, for the better prosecution of their function of living, of certain vibrations in the atmosphere which they discovered would impart certain spatial knowledge if approached with the right tissues, thus adding the eye in themselves and light in their environment. This thought co-existed in my mind with the sentence I had just been reading . . . and I felt this pleasure which comes from the simultaneous awareness of two similar victories over the universe, in admiring the eye for making itself, in admiring the brain for making itself. (*SN* 124)

The accuracy (or inaccuracy) of West's characterization of the evolution of the eye is unimportant for our purposes here. Essential, however, is her reporting of the impact of events external to, and even antagonistic to, her

CHAPTER FOUR

reading on her comprehension of, interpretation of, and reflection upon that reading. Without the presence and interference of the electrician—if, in other words, she was a cloistered thinker as opposed to a multitasking home tender—she would not have been able to take this step in her thinking about the importance of art to humanity. The intellectual pursuit and the consumerist pursuit are not contradictory or in conflict but coexist, and West is able to engage in both simultaneously. Moreover, as Heffernan argues, this is a distinctly *modern* critical practice. West would later describe "The Strange Necessity" (the title essay contained in the volume) as a "copy" of "the form, killed stone dead since by T. S. Eliot, of criticism in a personal and almost fictional framework, such as Remy de Gourmont and several other French writers had used."[32] Regardless of her formal homage to a symbolist innovator beloved by Ezra Pound, West's essay was vigorously disdained by her male contemporaries, who had a social investment in controlling the discourse of high modernism and whose lionization of Joyce she had so acerbically mocked. West's essay certainly demonstrates that there was already a pervasive sense in 1926 that "the value of literature was formed not internally but in relation to other forms of culture (middlebrow poems, for example) and was expressed in cultural forms (a bookstore transaction)" and that New Criticism was only one possible response to modernist literary production, not an inevitable or the sole response.[33]

Blair must have found West's essay, and the remainder of the collection, particularly validating. Like West, Blair's literary musings were situated in the middle of consumer concerns—dress patterns, recipes, housekeeping tips, parenting advice—and was accompanied by professedly middlebrow literary productions. Her column was indeed a relative outlier in the magazine. Here, however, was Rebecca West! Demonstrating, even celebrating, the kind of multi-brow-level thinking, the intellectual multitasking, that Blair and her readers had been performing all along. Blair's practice was not a refusal of the modern, not a throwback, but was in fact the most modern practice possible. It makes sense that West's method, the discussion embedded in an "afternoon jaunt," is particularly compelling for Blair. Little wonder that Blair wants so badly to recommend this book and that she wants to discuss it with her literary colleague Keyes. "Miss West wanders out of a little bookshop in Paris up and down, one might say, the street of literature, stopping for a little time here before Marcel Proust and there before James Joyce, those two incomprehensibles whom the literary critics tell us to our utter scorn

The Modernist Racket   161

and abhorrence are the greatest writers of our time; scorn, because we do not understand them; and abhorrence, because they so greatly shock us in our tenderest sensibilities."[34] West is, for Blair, a flaneuse on the one hand, and on the other, in the style of the *Good Housekeeping* test kitchen, a scientific investigator of the world of high criticism, analyzing both texts and critical biases while keeping her own critical distance. "With the detachment of a scientist looking at a brightly colored butterfly with a sting in its tail, Miss West studies the color of the wings and the grace of their movement, detaching them, for the purposes of her study, from her fear of the sting. In other words, she indicates what it is that attracts and holds the critics without denying the danger of the sting."[35] West's criticism thus enables her readers to avoid the "sting" of the highbrow critic's scorn and to understand what it is they liked about texts that might otherwise seem too difficult, too "incomprehensible," or even too repellent, to attempt.

And while Blair does not explicitly note it, she mimics West's concept of "necessity" in her description of what the *Good Housekeeping* reader, whom Blair fashions as the tourist to West's tour guide, might be able to take away from her reading of West's book. "Much of it the sightseer will, perforce, forget, but certain points of it will stand out in his memory, so that when one mentions, for instance, sentimentality or art, there will arise in his mind certain ideas by which he may, perhaps, measure them."[36] The takeaway for the general reader may not be a detailed exegesis of any particular text, or the ability or desire to perform such exegesis for his or herself, but will be rather "certain ideas" that can be cross-applied, can become useful, for the reader in future situations. The criticism becomes necessary in the sense that it enables the reader to comprehend and use texts, as well as, then, to live in the world not through these texts but in the light of her understanding of them. Blair admits that "it is not an easy book, nor one for everyone to read," but on some level that does not exactly matter because the reader will be able to retain from it the useful bits. Just as West might be said to predict Bourdieu, Blair might be said here to predict Michel de Certeau's "reader as poacher," the reader who does not "assimilate" their reading by "becoming similar to" some proper notion of interpretation but who "'mak[e] something similar' to what one is, making it one's own, appropriating or reappropriating it."[37] This is a keynote of Blair's advice—the reader is central, ultimately, and her needs and experience of the text trump any other critic's assessment. Blair asserts that "Mrs. Keyes, I know, will want to read and ponder" West's book;

CHAPTER FOUR

so, too, should the reader who hopes to model herself on the exemplary senator's wife. But she also gives this reader, who might hesitate for fear of being daunted, permission to think about the essay and to decide for herself what is worth gleaning from it.

This discussion leads directly into the next addition to Keyes's "hamper": Virginia Woolf's *Orlando*, "which has been breveted as one of the 'two most remarkable English books' of the season."[38] Blair introduces Woolf as the "co-queen of British Letters" along with Rebecca West, attributing that coronation to Hugh Walpole. By deploying the language of monarchy, Blair implicitly satirizes Walpole's presumption in assigning Woolf and West such a (gendered) distinction. She continues that Woolf is "one of the leaders of a literary coterie known as the Bloomsbury group, daughter of a well-known critic, Sir Leslie Stephen, whose 'Hours in a Library' are beloved of club-paper writers." Woolf's bona fides are thus established not simply by Walpole's validation but, more importantly, by familial and domestic relations that are simultaneously literary *and* middlebrow. Her father is a clubwoman's favorite, and she extends her literariness into her intimate domestic relationships, much like Blair herself with her network of friends in Joplin. Blair interestingly does not identify Woolf as a magazine writer, despite the fact that Woolf began her career as a literary journalist and continually published magazine pieces in widely circulated venues (not exclusively "little magazines") even as she focused on her novels.[39] To do so would have been to bring Woolf into a circle alongside herself and Keyes, and perhaps even West. But Blair chooses instead to identify Woolf with another social and literary circle, one that includes West, and in so doing opens up an intriguing new "set" for her readers to explore. This framing of Woolf in fact feels like the kind of introduction one might give to another at a cocktail party; it isn't a professional introduction, not even of the variety reserved for "professional" women in the 1920s—Woolf is framed by her family, what others have said about her, and her social scene, not, at least not *yet*, by her work.

The fact that Blair feels such an introduction necessary cuts many different ways with regard to Blair's audience. It might signal either that Blair does not assume that the majority of her readers will know Woolf as well as they know some of the other authors she discusses or that the additional context is needed—that her readers will either be more inclined toward Woolf with this information or that Woolf is significant enough that they should have such knowledge about her. When Blair writes that Woolf's new novel

Orlando is one that Keyes would want to read because it has been lauded by critics as one of the two most significant works of the year, she appeals to her readers who want to be on the cutting edge of literary trends either because of an intellectual interest or because of a social motivation to be so.

And yet, Blair gently acknowledges that Woolf's stylistic experiments make her works challenging to read; she "ventures beyond the frontiers of fiction," a phrase Blair substantiates through her description of the narration of *Mrs. Dalloway* as "abolish[ing] the reticences that protect the individual from his kind, by revealing every thought as it drifted through the minds of her characters." *Orlando*, she warns, "attempts to abolish time." But before Blair's description of these experiments can either become off-putting to the *Good Housekeeping* audience or take on the cast of veneration, Blair turns on the critics whose approval of Woolf initially opened her discussion.

Without any real transition, Blair asserts?—acknowledges?—that "Woolf is one of those authors beloved of critics, since she furnishes them their 'racket,' the material for their jobs." Like West, who exposes the absurdity of critics who find meaningless parallels between *Ulysses* and the *Odyssey* or who would insist on the Lying-In Hospital as a series of parodies of British authors, Blair is hoisting critics who trumpet their erudition on their own petard. The gauntlet thrown, Blair continues, casting serious aspersions as she goes: "Not that any critic ever condescends to inform his reader author-itatively just what it is all about. But each has his own opinion of *Orlando*."[40] Critics have their own opinions, which they hide from their readers. One insinuation of the critics' lack of directness is that their readers should already know how to read and should already understand the implications of certain types of readerly moves. When the critic is allusive or vague, it is because their readers are already in on the game, and the critic is not going to "condescend" to offer anything like an explanation of the text (the pose that explaining a reading would be condescending is, of course, in itself a conde-scension). Blair's phrasing here, however, also suggests that the critics might not really know what they are talking about and might be being deliberately obscure in order to hide their own lack of clear comprehension of the text. If criticism is a "racket," the con artist critics must remain slippery; the readers, their "marks," need to stay in the dark so that they will not start to question the expertise that is being performed for them.

Blair proceeds by calling out two well-known critics by name, sum-marizing their takes on *Orlando* for the benefit of her *Good Housekeeping*

164 CHAPTER FOUR

readers. She then offers her own reading of the novel, which she frames as a "guess."

> Professor Canby says it is the esthetic history of English belles-lettres, showing the literary mind of England in all its modes from the time of Elizabeth until today. Rebecca West says it is an "account of human experience during that period which historians call modern history: the last few hundred years, which are near enough for us to recognize their parentage of us.[41]

This portion of the column is a real power move on Blair's part. She is glossing the work of two of the most well-known critics of the day, who represent significant strains of contemporaneous criticism; she is making their work known and accessible to her readers; and she is commenting on it and ultimately trumping it with first her own approach and then her assertion that her reader should be able to evaluate the novel herself. Canby's take, as Blair summarizes it, is indulgently metafictional—*Orlando* is about "esthetic history," a history of "belles-lettres." The terminology Blair chooses here deliberately implicates Canby in elitist gatekeeping behavior, which she has already characterized as a racket. Henry Seidel Canby may have been already familiar to Blair's readers as a former Yale professor who left that position to become a more public-facing intellectual book reviewer who hoped, through that work, to advance the cause of modern literature. Janice Radway characterizes him as one "committed to the idea of finding a literature adequate to the discontinuities and disorientations of the modern age" and explains Harry Scherman's choice of Canby as the chairman of the selection committee for the Book-of-the-Month Club (BOMC) as a function of Canby's "inherent interest in book selling by virtue of his commitment to promoting reading." Even with this procommercial stance, Canby steered more experimental high modernist literature into the BOMC lists, Radway writes. "Although Canby preferred the work of an older generation of writers, including Edith Wharton, Willa Cather, John Galsworthy, and Booth Tarkington, in part because he found the despairing cynicism and 'amorality' of the modernists deeply disturbing, he was also keenly aware of the radical nature of modernist formal experimentation and acknowledged that this kind of stylistic play was often more closely attuned to the tempos and 'deranged' sensibilities of the contemporary age than was the work of the writers he favored personally."[42]

By the end of 1928, the BOMC was a serious cultural force, with a membership of 94,690 subscribers,[43] a significant enough player in the market for

Blair to call it out in her August 1928 column. "From a Flood of Books, Emily Newell Blair Selects a Desirable Dozen," promises the title of this column, in which Blair is confronted with an undifferentiated "flood" of books after a trip to Washington and narrates her process of choosing the twelve for her columns. Her classification scheme, she explains, is "not governed by subject matter, but by my desire to find quickly those books that will give pleasure to one or another of my readers." After the first few titles that immediately catch her eye as worthy, Blair turns to another category of book: "books which have brought pleasure to the critics, books of the Literary Guild or of the Book-of-the-Month Club, but which may not fill my needs."

> Into [this group], on this occasion, went Thomas Beer's *The Road to Heaven*, so admired by the sophisticates but which would, my reading disclosed, in spite of its undeniable art, seem to the respectable frank to the point of brutality; Howard W. Odom's *Rainbow Round My Shoulder*, an undeniable document of negro life, absolutely hypnotic in its power to convince and hold, but repulsive in the savagery it records; Princess Marthe Bibesco's *Catherine-Paris*, Balzackian in its scope and thoroughness, exquisite in its irony, charming in its characterization, altogether a beautiful book, yet depicting manners and situations shocking to the sensibilities of the Anglo-Saxon; and finally Rose Macaulay's *Daisy and Daphne*, which will be a veritable joy to those who can laugh at themselves.[44]

Blair serves her audience by offering a reading of both the book club and its critical selections; she is helping them navigate their memberships as one who has a better idea of their possibilities and limitations. Even these popularizing and supposedly user-friendly clubs, it seems, should be approached carefully and critically. Despite their language of widespread appeal, the "sophisticates" do not properly know the *Good Housekeeping* reader and might well recommend things that are "known from the beginning to be hopeless because of treatment or subject matter, some of them good books, perhaps great literature, but not for popular taste or consumption." And yet these are no better than "sweet, immature, and silly tales whose very titles are a give-away."[45] Both ends of this spectrum are unacceptable for the *Good Housekeeping* reader, and the implication of Blair's column is that they have been offered to Blair for potential review somewhat cynically. Why else would a publisher send her something "known from the beginning to be hopeless"? But Blair does need to help her audience pinpoint such titles, because they have also, potentially, been offered to them in their subscription clubs. In Blair's discussion of *Orlando*, Canby represents this group of popularizers

166   CHAPTER FOUR

who might attempt to sell unpleasurable high modernism to unwitting readers under the guise of sophistication.

His review is actually far more accessible and celebratory than Blair's rather bloodless one-sentence summary would suggest. Yes, Canby sees Orlando's career as a metaphorical history of British literature, but a rollicking one—he calls it the "first readable history of our literature," a "gay and witty fantasy," and derides those who would make "esthetic" arguments for having been unable to convey the "spirit of the age." Canby also offers an analytic plot summary of sorts in his review, telling the reader "what it's all about," at least in his way of reading it, and apologizes if that summary is confusing: "I hope that all this does not seem like nonsense to the reader who has not yet read 'Orlando.' If it does, the fault is mine and not Mrs. Woolf's. The relation between the English mind and its modes in literature is clear enough in her narrative, although one reading will by no means draw out all of her critical subtlety."[46] He also confesses that a thorough commentary on the novel would be as long as the novel itself and that he himself has "not yet unravelled" Woolf's narrative fully. This latter admission is significant coming from the editor of the *Saturday Review* and does begin to offer readers some freedom to be baffled by the book. Still, Canby offers one central reading of *Orlando* as, fundamentally, a narrated literary history, and asserts that the reader must approach it looking for this story to "truly read" the novel. Canby does, then, have a very specific idea of what the novel is "about," and how the reader should read it—and Blair seems to feel either that he has been less than forthcoming in his instructions to the reader or, perhaps, that his reading is wrong or his suggestion of prescription inappropriate.

After the quick nod to Canby, Blair invokes Rebecca West's review of *Orlando* by citing one passage, thereby creating the assumption that this passage encapsulates the review as a whole: "Rebecca West says it is an 'account of human experience during that period which historians call modern history: the last few hundred years, which are near enough for us to recognize their parentage of us.'"[47] In Blair's gloss, West is not just talking aesthetics, but the whole range of human experience—the book, therefore, is not just for the reader who has a taste for discussions of literary history. West would be known to the *Good Housekeeping* audience through Blair's preceding discussion of *The Strange Necessity* if not before, and her "take" would hold weight because of that prior praise. Even after celebrating West as a keen reader of the literary scene in "The Strange Necessity," however, it seems important for Blair to steer her own readers away from a too-trusting acceptance of

West's version of *Orlando*. This suggests that it is less important for Blair *what* or *how* Canby and West write about *Orlando* than that she offer their readings—and her attitude toward their readings—by way of modeling the process of grappling with reviews, rejecting those that do not jibe with one's own readings and refusing to subordinate one's own tastes to those of the professionals.

Blair takes in what other people have said about the novel but engages in her own analysis and is not beholden to the opinions of others—and the implication is that her readers should do so too. Reclaiming the floor from Canby and West, she offers her own take on "just what [*Orlando*] really is all about":

> My own guess is that Mrs. Woolf has imagined in "Orlando" a human being independent of time in order to show that in each individual there are a number of selves all built up, "one on top of another, as plates are piled in a waiter's hand," all of these selves handed down to the individual biologically through the germ plasm which contains all the grandparents to the uttermost generations. If one wants to know how we may read all of this out of a biography, one has only to recall "Gulliver's Travels," a good and amusing tale for children on its face and yet also, to those who read it right, a scathing satire on human beings.[48]

Blair's gloss, with its talk of "germ plasm," would be generously described as idiosyncratic, for sure. Perhaps even so much so that her own faithful *Good Housekeeping* readership might balk—maybe she expects them to? Is it a self-consciously ludicrous "take"? It is certainly quite unlike most of Blair's other summaries or analyses. Regardless, Blair does term her own take on *Orlando* a "guess," thereby underscoring the spirit behind her reading—that no reader should feel absolutely beholden to any one "expert opinion" on the meaning of a modernist text. Each individual reader's imagination is brought into play, individually, when thinking about *Orlando*—and this dynamic is not at all unlike the kind of reader-author interaction that occurs in any other book, which some may like and others may dislike, despite the reverence with which Blair says critics like Canby treat this particular text.

Nicholas Greene and Other Disingenuous Critics

Woolf's own attitude toward literary critics is frequently described as antagonistic. Jeanne Dubino observes that Woolf "repeatedly voiced a desire for an unmediated relationship with the reader and increasingly condemned the literary intermediaries—namely, book reviewers, professionals, and the

168   CHAPTER FOUR

academy—that got in the way of this relationship."[49] This despite the fact that Woolf herself was a book reviewer, indeed began her career writing book reviews, and confessed to a friend in 1904 that her "real delight in reviewing is to say nasty things."[50] In 1932, six years after the publication of *Orlando*, Woolf wrote, but never sent, a letter to the editors of the *New Statesman and Nation* in response to a BBC Radio exchange between J. B. Priestley and Harold Nicholson. Priestley's talk, "To a High-Brow," addressed a stereotypically effete and elitist companion, encouraging him to leave off his effeminate intellectual ways to go out for a pint and relax a bit. "Don't be either a highbrow or a low-brow. Be a man. Be a broad-brow."[51] The transcript of Nicholson's rejoinder, which aired a week later, does not survive, but Melba Cuddy-Keane has reconstructed the gist of the talk through archival detective work and speculates that Nicholson countered Priestley by opining that an embrace of the lowbrow attitude would lead to cultural stagnation.[52] Woolf's letter ultimately argues that the high- and lowbrows have a useful symbiotic relationship, because both actually care about experiencing life to the fullest and are able to enjoy the fruits of each other's labor (lowbrows go to the cinema, highbrows ride on trains and go to restaurants). The problem, in Woolf's view, is with the middlebrows, who cynically play the two off each other and use both for self-interested ends: "The middlebrow is the man, or woman, of middlebred intelligence who ambles and saunters now on this side of the hedge, now on that, in pursuit of no single object, neither art itself nor life itself, but both mixed indistinguishably, and rather nastily, with money, fame, power, or prestige."[53] But, Woolf continues, the middlebrows also have a racket of mediating highbrow literature for lowbrow readers; they deign to teach the proper reading of Shakespeare to people who might be able to read Shakespeare for themselves, and this is the most ruinous behavior of the middlebrow. The popularizer, the reviewer, the writer of books on "how to enjoy literature"—the BBC itself, which she terms "the Betwixt and Between Company"[54]—work to commoditize culture and to separate those who produce literature, film, and other cultural works from those who would consume them. Rather than reading Shakespeare, people read other people writing about Shakespeare. The intercession of the critic is the key problem, particularly when the critic dictates audience response; one might imagine Woolf being concerned when Canby told his *Saturday Review* readers that *Orlando*'s theme is "the philosophy of literary history and the most acute and perceptive analysis of the literary mind. The book must be read for this or it will not be truly read at all."[55] Bloomsbury,

The Modernist Racket   169

on the other hand (Bloomsbury having become her shorthand for highbrow life in the essay, as it had by now in the cultural imagination), is "a place where lowbrows and highbrows live happily together on equal terms and priests are not, nor priestesses, and, to be quite frank, the adjective 'priestly' is neither often heard nor held in high esteem."[56]

While the "Middlebrow" letter will not be written until 1932, Woolf's feelings about the critics are already in evidence in *Orlando*. Nicholas Greene, whom Orlando summons to his estate for writing advice and general literary conversation, is a frustrated poet and a profoundly negative critic—and Woolf suggests that the two identities inform each other. Greene derides Shakespeare, Marlowe, Johnson, Browne, and Donne as hacks who might have written one or two things but whose work would never stand up to the Greeks. Orlando is shocked by these pronouncements but also notices that "the critic himself seemed by no means downcast. On the contrary, the more he denounced his own time, the more complacent he became."[57] Greene thrives on saying "nasty things," much like young Woolf herself. Orlando revels in Greene's literary gossip but is also disquieted by him, thinking him a "plaguey spirit of unrest" (68). Greene's satire of Orlando, who was still serving as his patron, ends up sending Orlando into extreme social isolation, for a time doubting literature and language's capacity for revealing truth. "He kept looking at the grass and at the sky and trying to bethink him what a true poet, who has his verses published in London, would think about them." He is unable to shake Greene's memory, "as if that sardonic, loose-lipped man, treacherous as he had proved himself, were the Muse in person, and it was to him that Orlando must do homage" (75). But then, finally, Orlando repudiates Greene and his ilk: "'I'll be blasted,' he said, 'if I ever write another word, or try to write another word to please Nick Greene or the Muse. Bad, good, or indifferent, I'll write, from this day forward, to please myself'" (76).

There is to be sure an element of class snobbery in Woolf's representation of Greene, and by extension all critics, as middle-class strivers who hope to control the literary productions and assessments of the noble Orlando. Greene's crowded, cluttered, and overpopulated London hovel, the fact that his satirical exposé of Orlando will cover "the expenses of Mrs. Greene's tenth lying-in" (70), code Greene's literary pursuits as crass. He cannot write in the countryside in Orlando's estate; he must return to his cramped kitchen with his egg cup ink pot. This is by no means a celebration of Greene's spirit but is an indictment of the opportunist's shoddy literary practices. He writes gossip,

CHAPTER FOUR

denigrates sincere attempts like Orlando's, and does it all in the service of personal finances. This is why he can never truly achieve the "glawr" he celebrates in the Greek poets—his utter unfitness to do so signaled by his pronouncing the beautiful French word for "glory" into an ugly guttural monosyllable.

When Orlando meets Greene again in nineteenth-century London, he has become "the most influential critic of the Victorian age"; he is a LittD, a professor, an author multiple times over, and has been awarded a knighthood. He is now respectable and respectful, if his dress and manners are "overdone perhaps," an "imitation of fine breeding" if a "creditable" one to Orlando (204). But his critical patterns have remained unchanged; he still laments the passing of the greats, but now the greats are "Marlowe, Shakespeare, Ben Johnson . . . Dryden, Pope, Addison"—all the authors he denigrated during their time as mediocre compared to the Greeks. Contemporaneous authors Tennyson, Browning, and Carlyle he denounces as "in the pay of booksellers. They turn out any trash that serves to pay their tailor's bills. It is an age . . . marked by precious conceits and wild experiments—none of which the Elizabethans would have tolerated for an instant" (205). The Victorian Greene's dislike of experimentation echoes early twentieth-century genteel critical disdain for high modernist formal experimentation, and Orlando finds his respectability "depressing," although he does immediately recommend that she publish her poem "The Oak Tree" because "there was no trace in it, he was thankful to say, of the modern spirit" (206). Greene's approval must be read, from a modernist perspective, as a strike against the poem. Orlando composed it during a complete retreat from the modern world, so it is an anachronism, just like Greene and the critics Woolf is satirizing through him.

Greene and these critics are in league with the publishers, it seems, so Orlando might easily have found a publisher for her throwback poem. Respectability has trumped innovation, and Orlando finds the bookstores filled with the "complete works" of many Victorian authors. Even more remarkable is the ready availability of "works about other works" by people like Greene (209); here Woolf is certainly referencing works like Arnold Bennett's *Literary Taste and How to Form It* (1927) and the books Blair discusses in her January 1929 column (see chapter 3, above). Orlando immediately purchases a large number of critical works and goes out to read them under a tree near the Serpentine, where she is highly distracted by the activities taking place around her—dogs and children playing, boats passing by on the river. Reading *en plein air* had not always been distracting for Orlando, but

The Modernist Racket 171

now it is; "works about other works" are too far removed from both life and literature to hold attention. Turning to think about the conditions of such books' composition, Orlando concludes they must be stultifying:

> I don't think I could . . . sit in a study, not, it's not a study, it's a mouldy kind of drawing-room, all day long, and talk to pretty young men, and tell them little anecdotes, which they mustn't repeat, about what Tupper said about Smiles; and then, she continued, weeping bitterly, they're all so manly . . . though I'm spiteful enough, I could never learn to be as spiteful as all that, so how can I be a critic and write the best English prose of my time? (210)

Not only this, the critics "made one feel—it was an extremely uncomfortable feeling—one must never, never say what one thought. . . . that one must always, always write like somebody else" (210). Critics are in themselves not fascinating writers, and they stymie the individual impulses of the writers whose work they evaluate. Not only this: their work is petty, tantamount to gossip, and it is set in enclosed and airless rooms rather than the vibrant outdoors where Orlando reads. And there is a superabundance of criticism, as well as a superabundance of literature—the critics produce criticism running to "sixty volumes octavo," assessing all of the Victorian literary output—"For, of course, to the Victorians themselves Victorian literature meant not merely four great names separate and distinct but four great names sunk and embedded in a mass of Alexander Smiths, Dixons, Blacks, Milmans, Buckles, Taines, Paynes, Tuppers Jamesons—all vocal, clamorous, prominent, and requiring as much attention as anybody else" (213). It's actually the same dilemma in which Blair finds herself, although Woolf chooses to dispatch of the whole processing of Victorian literature to a quick paragraph-length sentence, which runs longer than the six lines she initially promises but much briefer than the sixty volumes octavo. Orlando's final meditation on criticism dispenses with it altogether. "So that all this chatter and praise, and blame and meeting people who admired one and meeting people who did not admire one was as ill suited as could be to the thing itself—a voice answering a voice" (238).

The perspective afforded by Blair's comment that professional criticism is *not* mystical but is simply *labor*—the intellectual's need to keep up the racket—renders intellectual work the same as any other manual or mental labor, which is undertaken, after all, for financial gain. Blair's disdain for the modernist aesthetic could be read as concerned primarily with the ethics of false advertising: the critics laud modernists because readers will need to turn to the critics to understand what they are reading. Modernism is a "racket," and

172 CHAPTER FOUR

as a good consumer advocate Blair must expose that manipulation. Reading and friendship performed through the exchange of books cut through critical chatter to become "a voice answering a voice." Blair's discussion of *Orlando* works to empower her readers to pick up the novel, to interpret it on their own (because if there is no critical consensus, by extension, there must not be a "right" or a "wrong" answer to the meaning of the text), or to choose not to read it if it, like any of the other books Blair has discussed, does not seem like the *type* of text she would be interested in. And what is Blair's (metaphorical) offering of West and Woolf, after engaging and dismissing the critical chatter, if not a recapitulation of Orlando's observation? Her desire to discuss West with Keyes seems a desire to be a voice answering a voice—and her column enacts and enfolds her readers into this conversation, this relationship more suited to "the thing itself."

The women's friendship continued long beyond this exchange of a hamper of books, with Blair praising Keyes's novels in her columns and requesting advance copies in order to do so ("Will you be good enough to ask your publishers to send [proofs] to me? I hesitate to ask them because they have not been very liberal with review copies lately although I have boosted their books whenever I could"[58]). In May 1931, near the end of her time at *Good Housekeeping*, Blair writes to Keyes to praise her most recent novel, to mention her praise for it in *Good Housekeeping*, and to promise another "article" about it as soon as possible. She adds, "Did I tell you that Mr. Bigelow sent me a check for that month in which the article did not appear in the magazine? I think it was very fine of him"—thus explaining the absence of an April 1931 column, evidence of which I have not found. It is with the close of this letter, however, that I want to close this chapter: "I always come away from a visit with you encouraged and invigorated but I thought the last visit we had was especially helpful. I enjoyed the delightful luncheon and add that to the many lovely things for which I already owe you."[59] Simultaneously registering and failing to record a conversation that buoyed Blair for the future, this also promises the conversation will continue, in private and in the pages of middlebrow periodicals.

CHAPTER FIVE

The Contagion of Reading

After the depth of the family bond shown by
Andromache's good-by to Hector when he goes to fight
Achilles, the motives of the characters of a book like
'The Great Gatsby' seem weak and silly.
—Emily Newell Blair, *Good Housekeeping,*
November 1927[1]

F. Scott Fitzgerald's name appears throughout 1929 in *Good Housekeeping* magazine as one of three judges empaneled to identify the "Twelve Most Beautiful Women using Woodbury's Facial Soap,"[2] but Emily Newell Blair mentions his work only twice in ninety-one columns. Because her tenure as the magazine's books advisor coincided with the long gap between the publication of *The Great Gatsby* (1925) and *Tender as the Night* (1934), this is not necessarily surprising. Fitzgerald's collection of short fiction, *All the Sad Young Men,* did appear in February of 1926 just as Blair was launching her column, and in the regular places it was both generally well-received and more widely reviewed than many of his other short story volumes or even *Gatsby* itself.[3] It is tempting to speculate that Fitzgerald's close association with the *Saturday Evening Post* in the mid-1920s[4] had something to do with Blair's silence—the *Post* was not a direct competitor to *Good Housekeeping* itself but certainly was a major rival to fellow Hearst properties *Hearst's International* and *Cosmopolitan* (the two would merge in 1926). But, of the nine stories in *All the Sad Young Men,* only one had previously appeared in the *Post,* and two had been in *Hearst's.* Since Blair only writes about the most *current* publications in her columns, aside from the rare instances when she references an author's back catalog in the service of reviewing a new title (see chapter 2), unless she were writing about *All the Sad Young Men,* it would make little sense for Blair to mention Fitzgerald or any of his works. *Gatsby's* sales had been disappointing—only around twenty-one thousand copies[5]—so it would not have rated as one of the "books being

173

generally read and discussed today" like Anita Loos's *Gentlemen Prefer Blondes*, which had merited a reference a year after its publication.[6] It was, famously, dismissed by more popular reviewers, many of whom simply ignored it, and even H. L. Mencken panned the novel; only the likes of Gilbert Seldes, T. S. Eliot, and Gertrude Stein had embraced it. Wearing her "reviewer hat" and describing a weekly mail dump very like Blair's, twenty-first-century critic Maureen Corrigan writes that she might not have decided to review *Gatsby* either:

> I get upwards of two hundred books a week delivered to my front porch, sent by reviewers hoping for a review on *Fresh Air*. If I take a mental time capsule back and imagine a roughly equivalent situation in 1925 (when a lot fewer books were published each year), I honestly think that my first reaction upon ripping open the Scribner's mailer and seeing a slim novel called *The Great Gatsby* might have been: *Oh, another Fitzgerald*. Like most other reviewers, I would have had Fitzgerald pegged as a "topical" Jazz Age writer, and I think I would have been a little weary of his "flappers and philosophers." I might well have passed on novel number three. *After all*, I could have reasoned, *it looks a little thin, and the title is kind of blah*.[7]

It would have been unusual for Blair to reach all the way back into the spring lists from 1925 to comment on a book that had sold so few copies, and one imagines her echoing Corrigan's imagined 1925 self in regard to Fitzgerald's follow-up story collection.

And yet, in 1927, Blair refers to *The Great Gatsby* twice—first in February and again in November. In the February 1927 column, *Gatsby* is the counterexample that demonstrates the superiority of Margaret Leech's *Tin Wedding*. While the latter, presumably like *Gatsby*, tells a story that is potentially off-putting, "there is nothing offensive in the telling," because it is narrated through the eyes of "a well-bred and innately fine woman," again, apparently, in contrast to the jejune Nick Carraway. And Leech's book is a more accurate portrait of this social world than Fitzgerald's: "The people who make up the background of the book are a Long Island society set more authentic and convincing to me than Fitzgerald shows in 'The Great Gatsby,' though equally silly and superficial; as gay an irresponsible, but less coarse and vulgar."[8] Blair goes on to pardon Leech for writing a novel of "revolt" (not Blair's favorite genre); *Tin Wedding* is different because Leech is "adroitly" pointing out the "double standard" regarding monogamy promoted, by "such apostles of the new society as Heywood Broun." It is done so subtly that these hipster critics "give her book not only a serious consideration but high praise"[9]—Blair's lack of allegiance to avant-garde cliques allows her to see what Leech is doing, and to pass along that hint to her readers.

The Contagion of Reading

Then, in the middle of her annual children's books column, Blair refers to *The Great Gatsby* again, in the passage I have chosen as this chapter's epigraph. This time, *Gatsby* is representative of the bad books against which good parental book selection will "inoculate" young readers. Why choose this novel as the example of the "poor taste" that might be the fate of adults who, as children, did not have parents who properly monitored and cultivated their reading options? And why offer as a palliative the *Iliad* scene of the parting of Hector and Andromache, which classical scholars in the beginning of the twentieth century (many of whose books Blair has recommended in previous columns) found "a supreme poetic absurdity"[10] because it takes place five days before the fight with Achilles, and Hector spends three of those nights back at home with his wife? Why offer any adult book for particular disparagement in the midst of a column entitled "Exposing All Children to the Best Books—so That They Will Be Immune to the Effects of Bad Ones"? The first book Blair recommends in her inaugural children's book column begins to suggest an answer to those questions.

Julia Wise and the *Winnetka Graded Book List*

Blair published a column on children's literature every November. This was timed to coincide with Children's Book Week, which was inaugurated in 1919 as a promotional campaign to launch the holiday book buying season.

> The week was a collaborative project by three influential people with a professional interest in children's books: Franklyn Mathiews, librarian of the Boy Scouts; Frederic Melcher, publisher and editor of *Publisher's Weekly*; and librarian Anne Carroll Moore. To Mathiews, Children's Book Week was part of a moral crusade against dime novels and "cheap reading"; to Melcher it was an opportunity for children's book publishers to give their products maximum visibility for holiday sales. To Moore, it supported librarians' ongoing campaign to encourage children's library use and to heighten public awareness of the variety and value of good literature for young readers.[11]

Blair writes that this designated week made her think about the questions she is frequently asked by her friend Julia Wise, a young mother who occasionally "drops into my pink stucco house between music lessons and dancing lessons and school.[12] This Julia may well be the Julia of previous columns, to whom, for example, Blair recommended *The Professor's House* in February 1926. But this time, rather than portraying Julia as a representative reader for whose individual tastes Blair will shape a set of recommendations, Blair offers here a representative mother, a paragon of sophisticated, dedicated

176 CHAPTER FIVE

maternity and, of course, of chic modern womanhood: "Julia Wise, in looks the slim, boyish, dashing, red-haired debutante, is by profession the mistress of a large stone house in the country and by vocation the mother of four children, a vocation she makes entertaining to her friends, interesting to her self, and beneficial to her children. Julia devotes herself to her children. Her days are given as methodically and as certainly to their development as their father's are to his business of banking. Their clothes, their manners, their lessons, their music, their exercise—these occupy her thoughts" (51).

Julia is devoted and attentive but by no means overbearing or compulsive— she is like a skillful gardener, who "retains perspective" and does not allow the plants—the children—to "dominate." And her queries to Blair about her children's reading are a part of this careful "cultivation" of her kindergarten. The aptly named Mrs. Wise understands how important it is to encourage a love of good reading in her children and fears the long-term damage that might be done by the introduction of the wrong kind of book—one too advanced, or too juvenile, or too "trashy"—at a sensitive moment. She turns to Blair with a rapid-fire series of questions about which books might be appropriate for each of her children, and then finally, "Would you buy a set of books for the children?" She needs the assistance of an expert.

Fortunately, Blair replies, scientific principles have been put to the task of helping the Julia Wises of the world in their child-book-buying work, just as they have been deployed in the rest of the magazine to help rationalize and perfect other areas of housework. Since the logic of the test kitchen was scientific housekeeping, science should also be the underpinning of reading advice for children. And so, in a column flanked in the margins by the mail-in form for Good Housekeeping Institute Bulletins on "labor-saving and time-saving methods of housekeeping," we find that the very first recommendation Blair makes in her inaugural children's book column in November 1926 is *not* a book for children to read but is a heavily quantitative, "scientific" guide titled *What Children Like to Read: Winnetka Graded Book List* (*WGBL*). Although Blair will eventually mention juvenile titles in this column, she begins with a lengthy and detailed description of the methods by which Carleton Washburne, the Winnetka, Illinois, superintendent of schools, and Mabel Vogel, his research assistant, arrived at a book recommendation list that would take into account the interests of children while eliminating "the trashy books, no matter how well-liked" (230).

While the logic of the *WGBL* seems consistent with Blair's approach to adult book recommendations, this last caveat is significant. Blair's columns

The Contagion of Reading 177

rarely caution readers *against* particular books, and from her silence on a book a reader might infer not that it is a "trashy book," just that it is not right for a given readerly type. In the case of the *WGBL*, the ostensibly neutral polling method gives way to explicit curation when the list is compiled. Washburne and Vogel polled 36,750 children about whether they "liked" or "disliked" the books they read during the 1924–25 academic year, and the resulting list purported to be a scientific guide to matching children with books that were "liked" by others of the same age, reading level, gender, or interests. But this ostensible "guidance" model is ultimately usurped by the impulse to prescription, and it is this turn that results in a public controversy over the *WGBL* in the pages of the *Library Journal* magazine. Children's reading becomes the site of a proxy battle over whether tastes should be molded or respected and guided. For the librarians, it is a moment of contestation over an educator model versus a concierge model of youth services librarianship, and for Blair, it is the moment where her rela- tively ecumenical approach to reading advice meets its limits. In her children's books columns, we see Blair torn between insisting that children should not be forced to read particular books, for fear that they might never enjoy reading, and prescribing books or reading programs lest they become attached to bad books along the way. Ultimately, Blair points to parents, explaining that it is their responsibility to curate the books that fall into their children's hands. This oblique suasion might take place in a library, where the children's room "bears the odor of research, of scholarship. And there, too, is expert help" (236), but Blair prefers it happen through the purchase of appropriate and well-written books that are *also* sturdy and attractive commodities. Either way, a combina- tion of guidance and seeming nonchalance is the only way to proceed to make sure that children cultivate "taste." Blair's celebration of the *WGBL*'s impulse to selectivity, and of the importance of identifying specific trashy children's books, extends from her 1926 column through all of her subsequent November col- umns. This also, it seems, gives her the opportunity to express negative opin- ions of specific adult titles, like *Gatsby*, that she might otherwise have chosen not to call out by name.

The Winnetka Study Method

The growing Progressive Era professionalism of youth services librarianship sparked a flourishing of survey-based research on children's reading practices and the uses of the children's room. The study that produced the *WGBL* dif- fered from most of its predecessors because it relied on a unique collaboration

178   CHAPTER FIVE

between librarians and educators, two groups that were frequently at odds about children's reading.[13] It was initiated by educators and administered by teachers, and teachers aided with the "detail work" of the list. But it was funded by the Carnegie Corporation through the American Library Association, and a stable of children's librarians made the final decisions about which books should be included in the published guide, "evaluating the books from the standpoint of literary quality and . . . checking the accuracy of the children's comments."[14] The *WGBL* was used in libraries but was primarily marketed to parents and teachers; it ultimately functioned to facilitate librarian outreach beyond the children's room, closing the loop between the increased production of literature targeted specifically to children in the first three decades of the twentieth century and the resulting increase in personnel and real estate devoted to children's literature in libraries.[15]

Children from across the United States participated in the study, filling out a common ballot for every book they read and submitting the completed ballots to their sponsoring teacher. They were asked for each book's bibliographic information but also for personally identifying information: their name, age, gender (boy or girl), school, grade, and teacher. There is a spot on the ballot for teachers to indicate the child's "reading grade" as determined by the Stanford Silent Reading Test, "which in every case was given and scored by the child's teacher. . . . After a good many preliminary studies this reading grade was found to be the most desirable and practical means of grading the books. After all, it is the children's reading ability which counts rather than the room that they happen to be sitting in." Immediately the authors acknowledge that "their age counts, too, of course" (*WGBL* 6–7). All of these metrics would ultimately factor into each book's listing in the *WGBL*.

Next, the children were asked to evaluate the book. First, they could check a box indicating how much they "liked" it ("One of the best books I ever read"; "A good book, I like it"; "Not so very interesting"; "I don't like it"). Another column of check boxes registered the relative ease or difficulty the child encountered while reading the book ("Too easy"; "Just about right"; "A little hard"; "Too hard"). And, finally, children were invited to "write on the other side of this slip what you like best about this book, or why you like it" (*WGBL* 6). After accumulating and tabulating the roughly 100,000 ballots that were returned to them (one-third of the number distributed), the compilers of the *WGBL* ended up with a list of books separated by grade and offered in descending order of "the simple product of the number of cities in which a book was read and the number of children who read and liked it," a number that they term the "index of popularity" (*WGBL* 33). This "index" then determined the order in which the books appeared in lists grouped by grade and lists grouped by age, although, as we will see, it became a key point of critique for the librarians who would register their objections to the *WGBL* project.

In her November 1926 column, Blair celebrates the Winnetka project's goal of determining "what books the children liked" (230), because "it is obviously that you can not make children like books, enjoy reading, unless you give them books they will enjoy" (51). She describes the next stage of the process as equally essential and commonsensical: "Having discovered what books the children liked, the next step was to determine and grade the literary merits of these books. They wished to eliminate the trashy books no matter how well-liked. They wished to star those of high literary value" (230). The resulting curated list, presented in full by grade level and then cross-indexed to the children's chronological age, was thus a product of objective and subjective responses from the children and of subjective evaluation by a panel of librarians selected for the project by the American Library Association. Each entry consisted of both a welter of numbers and a representative comment chosen by the compilers from all of those written on the backs of the ballots.

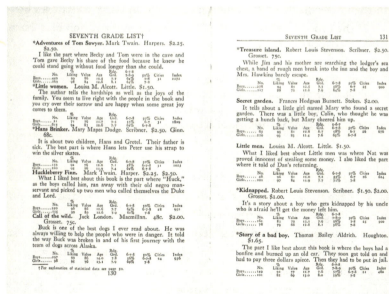

FIGURE 6. The first two pages of the seventh-grade list, *What Children Like to Read: The Winnetka Graded Book List* (New York: Rand McNally & Company, 1926), 130–31. Credit: American Library Association.

180 CHAPTER FIVE

In an excerpt from the seventh-grade portion of the list we can get a taste of the information that someone consulting the *WGBL* would have at their fingertips when trying to recommend a book to a child. Of these books, the top ten seventh-grade titles by "index of popularity," six are starred, indicating that the majority of librarians judged them to be "of high literary value": *Adventures of Tom Sawyer, Little Women, Hans Brinker, Treasure Island, Kidnapped,* and *Story of a Bad Boy.* The *WGBL* preface describes the librarian's deliberations, while also suggesting that the openness of the criteria for whether a book was literary or trashy led to significant disagreements: "The question as to the literary merit of the books was a serious one. When is a book trashy? When is it of high literary value? We knew of no way to answer these questions scientifically. Our only recourse seemed to be the opinion of experts. The American Library Association very kindly gave us the names of a number of expert children's librarians whose judgments could be relied upon in such matters" (*WGBL* 8).

That this "expertise" was not defined by any set criteria remains unremarked by Washburne and Vogel; the ALA merely recommended sixteen of its members for the panel, of whom thirteen agreed to perform the task. The *WGBL* introduction does, however, reveal the guidance that had been given to the librarians to assist in their judgments, and here we can see how this part of the process, at least, is utterly subject to confirmation bias. Each librarian was to grade each book as

> of unquestionable literary merit
> valuable for the list, although not of high literary quality
> not recommended—because of low literary value
> not recommended—because of subject content (*WGBL* 42)

The librarians also had the option to flag a title with a question mark if they did not know it well enough to pass judgment, although one imagines that having been named an "expert" by their professional organization might dissuade the judges from admitting a lack of familiarity with too many titles. And then the surveyors offered not a set of criteria for each category but a list of titles for extrapolating and/or calibrating the criteria for oneself. Category 1 would include works like *Heidi, Tom Sawyer, Little Women, Kidnapped,* and *Little Black Sambo;* category 2, *Anne of Green Gables, Puritan Twins, The Virginian,* and *Little Lord Fauntleroy.* Into category 3 went *Bobbsey Twins, Honey Bunch, Mystery at Number Six, Shifting for Himself,* and *Adventures of Reddy*

Fox—in other words, syndicate books. And condemned from the start to category 4, with inappropriate content, are *The Harvester, The Circular Staircase, The Hound of the Baskervilles, and When a Man's a Man.* Given that these titles are being offered as the model titles for each category, it is utterly logical that the books listed here in the instructions were judged accordingly by the librarians. There are no explicit criteria given for inclusion in any category; it seems that Vogel and Washburne assumed that the panel, and the adults reading the methodology essay in 1926, would presumably know the reasons.

Even so, Washburne and Vogel blithely note, "As was to be expected the librarians did not agree with each other." The problem? "There apparently is no single standard of literary value" (*WGBL* 8): thus the preface, which we might presume was penned by either Washburne or Vogel but not both. The introduction, on which one guesses the other investigator took the writing lead, notes the three-fourths supermajority requirement for either starring or jettisoning a title and explains that even though there are 119 starred books in the final list, "only 35 of these were rated 1 unanimously." Anticipating rancor, the introduction continues, "There are therefore doubtless many books not starred which some experts will feel should be, and there are doubtless many books included in the list which some experts will feel should be excluded. There being at present no objective way of determining literary value of books, it is clearly impossible to prepare a list which will be satisfactory to everyone" (*WGBL* 43).

It is possible to hear, around the edges of this statement, the weariness of a researcher who has had to mediate some lively disagreements over the relative "literary merit" or trashiness of several books, perhaps including arguments over a number of criteria being proposed as objective, universal markers of "literary value." That this was a tedious process seems even clearer from the subsequent discussion of the books that were left off the *WGBL*: "The data gathered on these books are of so much value that we hesitate to exclude any. The 110 which were excluded . . . have been mimeographed with the corresponding data and are available in the research office of the Winnetka Public Schools for anyone who wishes them" (*WGBL* 43). This researcher, quite plainly, loathes to lose such a trove of information on books that many children will have read, and will have enjoyed reading; requesting that list is not therefore morbid or prurient interest but is scientific curiosity.

We will turn in a moment to the "trashy" books list, but first it seems important to note that there is no one list in the *WGBL* that simply includes all the

182 CHAPTER FIVE

books that received the "high literary value" seal of approval. The asterisk is the only mark of librarian approval in the *WGBL*, unless you want to count the tacit approval of the book appearing at all (instead of being relegated to the trashy list). But again, the asterisk is not a determining factor in the order of the books' appearance in their grade-level lists; the "index" trumps all other considerations, and the top of the grade lists are not always so stacked with starred titles. The librarian "on the ground," using the *WGBL* to help a child or a parent in the selection of a book, will not necessarily be using an "expert librarian's" opinion of "literary merit" as the preeminent metric for selection; children's rankings, and then their comments, may well be more influential. Many, like the seventh-grade list, *are* filled with starred titles, and the *WGBL* cites this fact both to reinforce their reliance on child recommendation and to validate their "index." Might the study ultimately indicate that popularity follows from literary merit? Let's first look closely at the entries for the two highest-indexed books in the seventh-grade list: *Tom Sawyer* and *Little Women*.

Always Read the Comments Section

How were the children's back-of-the-ballot comments winnowed and a representative comment chosen for inclusion in the *WGBL*? Since each book was only mentioned once in the whole volume, and it was placed in the "grade level list" that most closely approximated the median grade range of the readers who "liked" it, each book only had *one* representative comment to "advertise" it to the children, parents, and librarians consulting the list. The compilers describe their method of selection and their aims for the comments in their introduction: "We wanted each comment to be something like an advance scene that is flashed on a movie screen. We wanted a child to be able to tell by looking at the comment whether or not he would probably like to read the book. Where a particular incident was mentioned by several children as the reason they liked the book, we have chosen a comment that mentions this incident" (*WGBL* 45). The focus on "incidents" and "scenes" in the search for comments might be thought to predispose the selections toward adventure stories, or it might reflect a presupposition that the child readers are attracted by incidents rather than moods or more general approbation. Washburne and Vogel offer an analysis that keys the kinds of comments children offer to the relative "quality" of the books: "May there not be some significance to the fact that certain books stimulate children to interesting, worthwhile comments while others result in such vague remarks as 'It is about how to keep from getting sick, and so forth'?" (*WGBL* 45). On the other hand, perhaps the responses produced for each book had more to do with the children's awareness of the expectation of particular types of responses about particular books. Kate McDowell's caveat about children's responses to professional queries seems particularly copacetic here—we might postulate that the books that were considered "valuable" by the librarians tended to elicit the kinds of comments that the librarians considered "valuable." The children knew what they were supposed to do with certain books, and they performed accordingly. McDowell contends that "even these heavily mediated records, collected by professionals who had a vested interest in educating children and directing their reading, demonstrate that children were capable of agency."[16] The questionnaire responses that are cited in the book are fascinating documents of reception but of course are heavily mediated by the adults who were compiling the materials. At the same time, because the original completed ballots seem to be lost to posterity,[17] all that remains for us is a curated set of these mediated records. Moreover, it is probably safe to assume that the comments that are offered in each book's official entry are either fully aligned with, or at least not at odds with, the librarians' and researchers' ideas about what a child should find compelling about each book. Still, there are two instances of fleeting evidence of the children's deviation from—if not active resistance to—the compilers' expectations. The first is in the comments rejected as "amusing" that the compilers cite in their introduction for giggles; the second is in their lamentations about the children's unfortunate, but enthusiastic, embrace of books that the librarians determined to be trashy.

The plan to include an enticing representative comment with each book seems to have posed some challenges to the list's compilers. The children, it seems, did not cooperate by writing the kinds of comments that the compilers wanted to include: "Children as a whole . . . did not give particularly stimulating comments" (*WGBL* 45). The editors describe the comments they received as "sometimes very helpful, sometimes vague and general, and sometimes quite amusing" (*WGBL* 7), and they reproduce some of the latter for the entertainment of their adult readers:

> An eleven year old boy from Mason City, Iowa, says of *Texan star*: 'I like this book because it suits my taste. I have a wild taste.' . . . *Adventures of Tom Sawyer* gets this comment from a 13 year old boy in Omaha: 'I like

184   CHAPTER FIVE

this book but yet I think it is one of the worst books for boys in their mature age. This book is so unlike real life that some small boys might get confused with his former way of living. But yet it is very interesting for it is a humorous story.' An eleven year old boy from Flint, Michigan, also comments on *Tom Sawyer*. He says: 'I awallwes [*sic*] put a check in the square that says one of the best books I ever read because I haven't had a bad book yet out of the library and I am in the 5a. I think this book is a dandy. (*WGBL* 7–8)

What accounts for these comments being singled out as particularly "amusing"? The answer to this question with regard to the little boy from Mason City with "wild taste" almost goes without saying—here is a child who describes himself probably more accurately than he himself knows and whose reaction to a text that is acceptable but that does not hold "high literary value" is charmingly apropos. *Texan Star*, a juvenile historical novel about Santa Ana's rebellion, appears, unstarred, in the lower half of the eighth-grade list; read by forty-nine boys, 98 percent of whom liked it, but only three girls (two of whom liked it). It follows the adventures of a young boy who functions as a Zelig-like figure and who "voluntarily went to Mexico to share the imprisonment of Stephen F. Austin in 1834 and . . . escaped to warn Texas" about the impending threat from Mexico.[18] The boy with "wild taste" is probably a bit too young for this book, and it shows; he registers none of the historical resonances, just enjoys the Western rough-riding adventure. He reads it, in other words, like he might read a dime novel, despite its not being "trashy." The reader of the introduction would know, presumably without having to look, that *Texan Star* falls in the "acceptable" category and would know that it should not be read for the "wildness" it might offer. The narrative framing of these children's responses is similar to that discussed by McDowell in her overview of librarians' surveys of children's reading habits, "Children's Voices in Librarian's Words," in which she notes instances where the author presumes, for example, her audience's shared assumption that "no children's librarian would encourage a child to read as many as 'three to five books a week' lest they detract from the child's schoolwork," or describes as "mournful" the child who responds that he gets no help in selecting his books.[19]

The two boys who offer amusing comments on *Tom Sawyer*, on the other hand, are responding to a book that is a star of the juvenile division. The official list entry for *Tom Sawyer* indicates that 449 boys and 269 girls from thirty-two cities read the book and that 99 percent of the boys and 98 percent of the girls reported "liking" it. This resulted in a phenomenally high index of popularity (2272), the highest such score in the volume. The median age of the readers was 12.5, so the "mature" thirteen-year-old who offered the first "amusing" response was actually safely in the range of potential readers, despite the suggestion that his advanced years and heightened understanding allow him to see its irreality and its unsuitability for younger readers. Of course, if one reads Tom as a Quixote, and his adventures as a comment on his Quixotism, one is at least in part suggesting that a reader of a "mature age" is a more likely ideal reader for the novel than a child who would want to go out and unironically pursue Tom's over-the-top lifestyle. As James Machor and Beverly Lyon Clark have both noted, *Tom Sawyer* and *Huckleberry Finn* were both still paired in discussions as Twain's masterpieces—presumably adult facing at least as much as child facing—until the late 1920s, and many saw the former as more than just a "boy's book." Machor writes, "For instance, two common readers, A. H. Kiernan and Edmund Blunden, who were both soldiers in the British army during World War I, mentioned *Tom Sawyer* (but not *Huck Finn*) as the novel they were carrying around and reading during down times. Blunden, in fact, called the novel 'my principle book and bible.' Others privileged *Tom Sawyer* because they read it more as an autobiography than a novel and thus treasured it because it brought them closest to Twain himself."[20] The boy from Omaha is perhaps onto something and will appreciate the novel more once he is fully initiated into the space of satire.

Indeed, the little boy in fifth grade who says that he likes every book and that *Tom Sawyer* is "a dandy" proves very well his thirteen-year-old colleague's point. He takes the book as an adventure story and is not worried about the "reality" or "irreality" of the plots because such considerations are not a part of the adventure reading experience. At the same time, he is singled out among these respondents as a faulty speller and clearly has a propensity to misread the text. He is probably too immature for *Tom Sawyer*. At the same time, being too young for *Tom Sawyer* was apparently one of the conditions for a heightened enjoyment of the book. *Tom Sawyer* was in fact termed more "enjoyable" by younger readers than by older ones. While the book appears in the sections of the list keyed toward adolescent readers (seventh grade—typically twelve-to-thirteen-year-olds), this list marks a transition from purely juvenile texts to more "adult"—or even proto-"young adult"—texts (for comparison, the sixth-grade list is topped by *Heidi* and the eighth-grade list is topped by Booth Tarkington's *Penrod*). But the book was given a higher "interest value" by younger readers—boys in third, fourth, and fifth grade—than those in its

186 CHAPTER FIVE

"reading grade." Without coming right out and saying it, the compilers admit that this is a function of the novel's generic complexity; comparing it to *The Dutch Twins*, which is enjoyed by second- through fifth-grade readers and not at all by older readers, "The drop in *Tom Sawyer's* interest value in the ninth and tenth grades is perhaps consistent with the type of book, and is in interesting contrast with *Huckleberry Finn* which is practically as well liked by the most mature readers as by any" (*WGBL* 36–37). In this case, the librarians' shared assumptions seem to be that these children offer "amusing" responses because they misread their books and that they did so because they were mismatched with the books. Their comments may have been unintentionally accurate, or the misreadings may have offered charming insight into their author's personality. But the humor lies in the gap between the child's comment and an unarticulated, but shared, assumption about how the book *should* have been meaningful to a child saying they enjoyed it.

To further parse the "joke" in these amusing comments, we might turn to the endorsed comment that accompanies *Tom Sawyer's* entry in the list. "I like the part where Becky and Tom were in the cave and Tom gave Becky his share of the food because he knew he could stand going without food longer than she could" (*WGBL* 130). This comment gives no hint that *Tom Sawyer* centers on the shenanigans of two young boys (Becky, not Huck, is the sidekick here); certainly it is not an antebellum tale, or one that even mildly satirizes its eponymous "hero" as an antihero. This comment, rather, singles out Tom's gentlemanly self-sacrifice in the cave and suggests that the novel should be read as a chivalric romance, and unironically so. Out of, potentially, 718 comments on the novel, how and why was this comment chosen for the *WGBL*? The introduction details this process: first, the compilers looked for "comments which cite incidents that illustrate the type of story which was read"—this suggests that they wanted comments that spoke to the *genre* of the story. Then, within those comments, they asked, "First, how stimulating is the comment? second, is it typical? and third, is it well-expressed?" Sometimes, they had to use "the least poor of the typical" comments. Finally, "after the five or six best comments on each book were chosen in the research office, they were balloted on by seven teachers in the Winnetka schools. The comment receiving a plurality of votes was selected for publication" (*WGBL* 45).

This is a process governed at each stage by subjective opinions and group dynamics and that relies on adults' ideas about what would be "stimulating" for children and modifies that further by demanding "typicality" and felicity

The Contagion of Reading   187

of expression. There is no telling whether the chosen *Tom Sawyer* comment was "typical" of a majority of the 718 or whether it was just the most well-written, or if it was *atypical* but served the guiding principles of the librarian panel. In the absence of the original ballots, one might even question whether it was, in fact, written by a child. I find it difficult to believe that this was the scene most frequently referenced by the 718 commenters on *Tom Sawyer*—as opposed to Tom finding Joe in the cave, or the discovery of his death at the conclusion, or Huck and Tom witnessing Joe's crime, or the boys faking their death and showing up at their funeral, or even the whitewashing-the-fence episode. This is not even necessarily the most chivalric moment in the text; for that one might turn to Tom's taking Becky's whipping for her and note that Judge Thatcher's reaction when he hears about it extends Twain's satire of chivalry to the adults who embrace it: "The Judge said with a fine outburst that it was a noble, a generous, a magnanimous lie—a lie that was worthy to hold up its head and march down through history breast to breast with George Washington's lauded Truth about the hatchet!"[21] It could be argued, however, that Tom's sacrifice of his share of the food (their "wedding cake") is a rare moment where the text applauds the vestigial merit that remains behind the chivalric theater. Tom does keep hunting for a way out of the cave in order to save himself and Becky, and, true to form, he embellishes dramatically upon that part of the story when he recounts it to his adult listeners from Judge Thatcher's sofa. But this sacrifice of food is a substantial moment of nobility and self-denial, and Tom does not seem to exploit it in his narrative. It demonstrates virtues that would certainly be celebrated by the Progressive Era educators and librarians who, McDowell reminds us, "needed to prove both that their institutionalized social amelioration efforts were necessary and that they had positive effects."[22] It also sees both Tom and Becky turning the corner from childhood into early adolescence—one could imagine true depth of feeling in their relationship going forward to an adult "marriage," as opposed to a schoolroom "wedding"—although Twain shuts that down as quickly as possible in his conclusion. In the end, the research office and the Winnetka teachers chose a comment that focused the users of the list on the romantic aspect of *Tom Sawyer* rather than on the adventure tale or any number of satirical jabs at chivalry, river-town societies, or young boys and older men who take their adventure-book reading too literally.

The representative comment for the second book on the seventh-grade list, *Little Women*, seems to have a similar filtering function. Alcott's novel was also starred for its "unquestionable literary merit," and its index of popularity was quite high (1829) because of the wide geographic distribution of the novel across thirty-one cities. The readership is even more gender skewed than that of Twain's work; it was read by 613 girls and liked by 94 percent of them, but only by twenty-one boys and liked only by 71 percent of those. As a result of— and/or in acquiescence to—that imbalance, the representative comment is a model of sentimental reading modes: "The author tells the hardships as well as the joys of the family. You seem to live right with the people in the book and you cry over their sorrow and are happy when some great joy comes to them" (*WGBL* 130). There are no specific incidents noted in this comment, obviously, and it is a comment that seems directed to an adult rather than to a fellow seventh grader. Any number of highly exciting events—Amy and Jo's fight and the burning of the manuscript; Amy's fall through the ice, the Marches' many theatrical performances, their various "romps" with Laurie, Amy's limes and her punishment at school—are ignored in favor of a frankly generic description that avoids singling out any one March sister for praise, blame, or identification. While the reader is highly identified with "the people in the book," this comment protects the centrality of the family unit. If we imagine the *WGBL* being used in a book-choosing situation, in a library, classroom, or home, this vagueness is clearly beneficial because it avoids priming the reader to gravitate toward any one March sister. It is also consistent with the book's reputation in the 1920s, by which time it had "become an icon of sentiment" and "an icon of domesticity."[23] Beverly Lyon Clark argues that the spinoffs of the novel in the opening decades of the twentieth century show that "when Alcott's academic reputation was declining, her reputation among more common people was, in contrast, cresting."[24] The comment in the *WGBL* is consistent with this contemporaneous reputation, so one imagines that the compilers would have been unsurprised, or even relieved, if it had been in fact the most "typical" comment offered by a child reader.

The comment about *Huckleberry Finn*, fourth in the seventh-grade list, by contrast, places the novel firmly in the category of adventure story: "What I liked best about this book is the part where 'Huck,' as the boys called him, ran away with their old negro manservant and picked up two men who called themselves the Duke and Lord" (*WGBL* 130). *Huckleberry Finn* is clearly being presented here as a "boy's book" in ways that we might have expected for *Tom Sawyer*, and it has not been starred as a book of "unquestionable literary merit." The difference between the two seems to be a difference in genre:

The Twain novel that can be reconciled with romance has "unquestionable literary merit" and a universal appeal; the book that is most "likely" to be read as a rollicking adventure story does not. But there is an added twist: not only was *Huckleberry Finn* not chosen as meritorious, but two librarians voted to exclude it from the list either because of "low literary value" or because of its inappropriate "subject content," and one considered it "trashy."[25] This fact, freely admitted in the methodological introduction to the list, ultimately leads Blair to temper her recommendation of the *WGBL*: "With some of their findings I, and many other parents, would not agree. For instance, one of the judging librarians rated 'Huckleberry Finn' among the trashy. But why expect a single standard of excellence for children's books when there is none for adult books?" (230). The question of "merit," and whether it is the function of the list to guide or to dictate tastes to librarians, parents, and children, undergirds the curating of the "representative comments" and exposes an ideological dispute within contemporaneous library studies: should libraries condemn and refuse to circulate books that might not be "good for" children?

Trashy Books and Competing Priorities

Washburne and Vogel admit that many of the books that the librarians considered trashy had high indices of popularity. "One series of books which was read and liked by 900 children was unanimously voted trashy by the librarians. The children rating these books gave them a high value; 98% of the children enjoyed them." They then go on to ask, rhetorically, "What is it that makes children enjoy these books which are considered trashy by children's librarians?" (*WGBL* 8–9). While they don't answer this question, they do find some comfort in the fact that the children's apparent delight in trashy books seems to be offset by their approbation of many books that were classified as "high value" or were at the very least not considered trashy: "On the other hand, of the ten most popular books, not one was rated trashy by the judging librarians (although one librarian so considered *Huckleberry Finn*!). For the most part the children's taste does not appear to be very far wrong" (*WGBL* 44). Perhaps—but once again we must consider the likelihood that the children were commenting as they thought they were supposed to be commenting, celebrating books they knew the adult researchers wanted them to like. Their preferences might not have been "very far wrong" because they were good at reading their audience of librarians and teachers.

190   CHAPTER FIVE

Even so, this compliance apparently had its limits; while the librarians all rated *The Rose and the Ring, Don Quixote,* and *Peacock Pie* high on their list of suitable books, more than half of the children rating those books did not like them. There may also have been some conflict between the librarians and the educators, as we can hear frustration just around the edges of the lament that "the schools apparently were not able to get the children to read *The Wind in the Willows, The Iliad for Boys and Girls, Roosevelt's Letters to His Children,* and a number of other highly recommended books, although in the very few cases where they were read there were always some children who liked them" (*WGBL* 9). The conflict among the teachers' assignment of books, the librarians' recommendations, and the children's preferences is at its most intense here, and we can discern most clearly the axis along which the educators and the librarians are disagreeing about their roles: are they to *instruct* children which books to read and how to read or enjoy them, or to *guide* them to the books they might enjoy based on their individual predilections and peer recommendations? The *WGBL* seems to be primarily driven by the latter model, except for the presence of the list of "excluded books," which was available by request and was ultimately printed in the February and March 1927 issues of the *Elementary English Review.*

These 112 titles were all determined to have "low literary value" or "undesirable subject matter" by three-fourths of the committee of children's librarians, but they are given the same attention here as the titles in the main *WGBL,* down to the representative comment for each title. While *Huckleberry Finn* escaped relegation, Twain's *Tom Sawyer Abroad* was considered trashy (presumably because of literary value, an assessment with which the few reviewers who read it would agree[26]) alongside a large number of Zane Grey, Carolyn Wells, Bobbsey Twins, Little Colonel, Tom Swift, and Augusta Seaman books. Much of Gene Stratton Porter's oeuvre—*Girl of the Limberlost, Laddie, Michael O'Halloran, Her Father's Daughter,* and *Freckles*—is on the list, as are Eleanor Porter's *Pollyanna* and *Just David.* All of these very popular books also inspired rather wholesome comments: "In this story I like Pollyanna's 'glad game' so much that my little sister and I are going to try and play it (on a small scale)." "It's about a boy who lives a plain life and is very contented. And it also shows that a boy ten years old isn't as helpless as you would think him to be."[27] A brief essay accompanying the list in the *Elementary English Review* makes these texts' exclusion a bit more legible. After bemoaning the prevalence of "running away" stories on the list, and the stylistics of the Bobbsey Twins and Freddy and Flossie books ("the flatness and monotony of a mediocre English theme"), Bertha Hatch and Annie Spencer Cutter, both librarians, write,

> An analysis of the children's own notes brings out the following elements of appeal:
>
> Excitement and superfluous action
> Mystery
> Sentimentality
> Mischief and Practical Jokes
> Accomplishment of the impossible by young people
> Happy and illogical ending
> Running away (mentioned five times)
>
> Summed up these represent the wish fulfilment of day-dreaming. Which of these are legitimate appeals?[28]

Kate McDowell notes that Progressive Era librarians came to embrace an ideal of leading children to "select books that required the work of good, careful reading" as opposed to skipping or quick reading.[29] This ideal would clearly lead librarians to reject texts that seemed to provide formulaic pleasures like those listed above. The "sentimentality" criticized here is presumably different from that praised in *Little Women* as "wholesome sentiment and real idealism"; one assumes the obverse of these constitutes the major flaw in both Porters' books. An editorial in the same volume of the *Elementary English Review* encourages teachers to study the children's comments because "teachers are usually shocked when they learn what their children are reading after school" and this list will help them understand the pull of trashy books so they might work to counter it. "What children really enjoy in reading affects their taste more deeply than what they are told to enjoy in school," this unsigned editorial contends. Moreover, "The more deeply a child is interested in trashy books, the more resentful he will feel at random thrusts from his teacher at books he likes."[30] Teachers need to know what these trashy books are so they might identify their children who are attracted to them, avoid fomenting resentment, and redirect their students to more quality books by presenting them more compellingly and more subtly. Teachers must "acquaint [themselves] with these books and their relation to child psychology," because "no teacher can gain the real confidence of his children in reading matters, who is not well informed and sympathetic toward the reading which his children are doing outside of school."[31] In order to circumvent the appeal of bad books, teachers must become conversant with them.

There were many who felt that the *WGBL* erred too far on the side of "enjoyment" and did not require enough input from librarians on the book selection of and for children. The *Library Journal* had published a generally positive review of the *WGBL* in January of 1926, concluding by citing Washburne and Vogel's assertion that the list "should help children to find books for themselves in the library and more particularly it should help parents, librarians and teachers in recommending books which are reasonably sure to be interesting and suitable for children of various ages and degrees of reading ability."[32] But in April, the magazine published a lengthy rejection of the list written by nine "prominent librarians," which enumerates seven major objections to the Winnetka research group's methodology and conclusions. While the compilers specified that "experts in the field of education and statistics have given their advice in making the handling of the data scientific" (*WGBL* 6), the objectors gave the book to "two specialists in statistical and scientific survey," who objected to the notion that the survey actually reflected any true measure of "popularity" or "liking" by the children surveyed. "The fact that the study showed such a high percentage of liking on the children's part, should have made the investigators question their data. The study is really and almost solely a study of the books available to certain children and in no sense tests the child's capacity for appreciation."[33] The objectors note that the children probably didn't feel free to express dislike of the books they were offered ("children are rarely spontaneous or exact when writing such comments for adults"[34]), and find the index of popularity a "weak foundation" for the choice to publish the book list as a buying guide for youth services librarians and parents. The idea that popularity might be a basis for recommending a book, rather than its status as a "masterpiece," was also problematic, as was the notion that librarians would rely on "medians, averages, and quartiles and more especially on the basis of the 'index of popularity'" rather than their own personal knowledge of the books and the library patrons. "It would be most unfortunate," the nine objectors lament, "if we should go back to the old lock step in children's reading and try to standardize in a book list what children should read. Individual taste will always elude statistics and grading and we are no more able to fit one little girl with a book because her twin sister likes it than we are able to make every adult like parsnips."[35] But the most concerning thing to this group seems to be the assumption that children can recommend books to each other: "The general conclusions of the Winnetka investigators seem to be that what the child, with a very limited range of books available, appears to want is what children generally should

The Contagion of Reading   193

have. They are concerned with the immediate and not with the potential. They must then assume that the child is born with a self-propelling power with a discrimination in reading which they would scarcely grant him in the arts, in ethics or in food selection."[36] In the case of this study, children were not given the opportunity to claim a "taste" for certain worthy books, and the objectors fear that readers of the study will take the list as a "scientific" last word on the books that are suitable for children and, by omission, those that are not.

Washburn and Vogel published a rebuttal to this critique in the very next issue of the *Library Journal*, doubling down on the range of titles (emphasizing that even small towns have extensive library collections), and appealing to the *WGBL*'s commercial success as an indicator of its quality: "No publication of the American Library Association has sold so widely during the first three months of its existence as has the Winnetka Graded Book List."[37] One marker of the *WGBL*'s reach—and potential contributor to its popularity— was Blair's recommendation of the volume to the concerned mothers among her *Good Housekeeping* readers.

The Julia Wises of the World

We can return, now, to the November 1926 edition of *Good Housekeeping*, in which Blair initially extols the virtues of the *WGBL* for several column inches. She offers the American Library Association's contact information so that her readers can send away for a copy of the *WGBL* just as they could and presumably regularly did send away for the Good Housekeeping Institute pamphlets advertised in an adjacent column. Eventually, however, like the *Library Journal* critics, Blair cautions her readers to use the list the same way she has told them to use her recommendations for adults: as a *guide*, not a prescription. Not only is the list incomplete, with some very excellent books read by too few children to merit inclusion, there are children who like different things. "Then, too, Julia's children may have a more cultivated taste than the average child. She must not make the mistake of standardizing her children's tastes. She must help them to make their own findings by discovering their tastes and developing them individually. To do this she must supplement these Winnetka Lists and even abridge them. For myself, I think they contain too many 'juveniles'—by which are meant children's books written specially for children, and alas, too often written 'down' to children" (232).

194   CHAPTER FIVE

The Winnetka list is helpful so far as it goes, but it is not an aspirational list. If the Julia Wises of the world rely on its recommendations, they are not acknowledging their own children's ability to do better than these average children—are not nudging their children forward to more sophisticated literature. Blair suggests that Julia's children are *already* "more cultivated" than average children, and what mother would not like to think so? While the encomium to "help them make their own findings" seems like an embrace of individual, possibly eclectic, taste, it directly follows a caution against "averages" and "standardization" that implies that *some* tastes are actually not very good. What if Julia Wise's child "enjoys" the "juveniles" that Blair thinks are too prevalent in the *WGBL*, and are "written 'down' to children"? Should Julia then help her child "discover" and "develop" that taste? It is clear that she should not—she should instead work toward ensuring, somehow, that her child's taste develops in some better direction.

The remainder of Blair's column describes how Julia might help her children "make their own findings" by carefully cultivating their immediate reading environment—in other words, by only allowing them to stumble across the right kinds of books in their purportedly independent investigations. This is how Blair says her own mother did it; her stated policy was "to let us browse where we would. This does not mean that she would have let us read anything and everything. But there were no books that were denied the children" (232). Somehow, paradoxically, Blair's mother was both a gatekeeper *and* radically permissive. The cognitive dissonance is profound—but necessary. Blair's ethic of individual tastes has met its limit when it comes to children's reading and maternal obligations, and such contradictions abound throughout this column. Blair attributes her good taste in adult books—and resistance to the grown-up equivalents to trashy childhood offerings—to her mother's progressive tendency to give her free reign in the "adult" library. "By the time a schoolmate lent me 'Dora Thorne,' my adolescent craving for romance had been satisfied by Bulwer Lytton's 'My Novel,' 'The Wandering Jew,' and most of Scott. Or perhaps we did not think Dora Thorne worth the necessary scheming and plotting when 'Pride and Prejudice' could be had without it, and so preferred Jane Austen on the library sofa to Bertha [M. Clay] on the old bed in the attic" (232).

One can never prevent a child's exposure to bad books, but by "inoculating" them against such exposure one can blunt their power, protect the child from their contagion. Blair and her siblings would not have come across *Dora*

Thorne in their home bookshelves, so they would never run the risk of falling under that novel's sway. While Blair's mother did not explicitly *prescribe* particular books to her children, she did in fact carefully *curate* their home library. So by the time Blair got to school and was exposed to *Dora Thorne,* she had built up a sturdy immune response. The savvy mother, like Blair's mother, should take care to obscure the degree to which she hopes to channel or influence her children's interests.

Indeed, this apparently laissez-faire attitude is the only way to produce the desired results. Blair observes, "You can give books to children, but you can't make them like them. The book must do that." This is why the Julia Wises of the world should in fact judge a book, or at least an *edition* of a standard text, by its cover. The *WGBL* falls short of her standards on this score: "I prefer better editions than many of those listed. I do not question the wisdom of noting in such a book the cheapest editions available. A cheap one is probably better than none, but, foolish as it may sound, I would rather my children had fewer books and better ones as to binding, illustrations, paper, for ownership of books is one thing and companionship is entirely another" (234).

Ostensibly, this is an argument about sturdiness, about attracting the child to the volume, but Blair's later exclamation—"All those ugly cheap reprints of the masterpieces!"—evinces her distaste and the presumptive attitudes of *Good Housekeeping* readers, who should consider the externals of the books they give their children in the same way they assess the toys they buy for them. And the best possible things would lead to the best possible future. As Susan J. Matt explains, "Children's social futures and fates rested on the crucial consumer decisions that their parents made in the present. . . . They had best make wise consumer decisions if they wanted their children to grow up to be the social, economic, and intellectual equals of their peers."[38] Books are *things,* and they should ideally be owned, and they should ideally be beautiful, sturdy, and expensive.

Blair's mother does seem to have had a significant influence; Blair will use the "inoculation" trope repeatedly in her children's literature columns but will also do so in reference to her own reading. In June 1926, she talks about her habit of setting books aside during the spring to "provide my inoculation against the boredom and physical discomfort of our long, hot summer, for I live in one of the Inferno states, meaning one of those states where temperature is delivered direct each morning from the heat-factory described by Dante."[39] Blair mentions that her friends "often express their surprise at finding books about my house or on my table with pages uncut—and yet I owe my acquaintance with books largely to my custom of buying the books I should like to read" (236). Blair might never make it to the library, she says, but having a book lying around the house is frequently the nudge she needs to open it, to read it, in a spare moment.

The most famous collector of books with uncut pages in twentieth-century literature is of course Jay Gatsby. His books are "Absolutely real—have pages and everything . . . bona-fide piece[s] of printed matter."[40] But presumably, at least if we are to believe the owl-eyed man's assessment, he never intends to read them. Is Blair's defensiveness about her own uncut books a reaction to this library? Do her friends' comments imply that she is simply a "Belasco" like Gatsby? One doubts this, but as we will see her *readers* come to doubt her claims to having read so many books every month. Gatsby's pretense to literariness is perhaps as galling as the other "weak and silly" motives of the characters in the novel. Is she referring to Gatsby or some other contemporaneous work when she also insists that a childhood familiarity with Shakespeare enables one of her sisters to endure in the face of "[today's] neurotic literature in which the abnormal is posed as the real, the unsound as the natural," and she feels that "she misses her center of gravity. By her Shakespeare she has learned to discover what is wrong. Alas that some of those authors were not exposed to Shakespeare when they were young!" (207). If not Fitzgerald, perhaps this references Anderson—the coded language of "neurosis" and "unsoundness" are, at any rate, common in contemporaneous condemnations of avant-garde literary productions.

The stakes are high. In her 1930 Children's Book Month column, Blair expands on the need for children's fiction, in particular, to be chosen carefully by parents—to choose a book rashly is tantamount to leaving your child with an "unknown nurse"—or a scheming and deceptive one:

> Fiction appeals to our emotions; we take it in by way of the imagination, and what enters into a man in that way retires deep into his subconscious and stays, sometimes to wreak sad disaster. To take a simple case, many a child has lived in terror for years because of tales that scared him in childhood. Men have gone all through their lives prejudiced against a race or nation because of some story read while young. Others have set up wrong ideals for themselves to follow because a hero in a book acted a certain way successfully. Some have been led to believe that certain causes bring sure results, and when life taught them they do not, have developed into unhappy cynics. Men and women here, there, everywhere have all unconsciously patterned

their lives after characters, some good, some bad, they lived with in a printed page. Some have gone fearing their neighbors, some unduly trusting them. And some have even learned to take as virtues vices.[41]

The mother herself must become a taster and tester of books. Like Blair, she must curate and guide, without seeming to dictate or to condemn. Because it does in fact matter what books children read, and, as this passage signifies, it does in fact matter what kinds of books *adults* read. Blair's concierge model, like the *WGBL*, is less liberal than its presentation would suggest.

EPILOGUE

Trouble, Antidotes

It is not always books about which I am enthusiastic,
but the reading of the books.

—Emily Newell Blair, February 1927[1]

The approach Blair inaugurated in February 1926 seems to have been appealing and successful, given that her columns continued to appear regularly through late 1933. But as her tenure at the magazine grew longer, and her national profile grew larger, Blair's writing began to evince a growing impatience with questions that had never particularly troubled her before. *Good Housekeeping* never explains either Blair's nine-month hiatus between November 1933 and August 1934 or her departure after her final column. Blair herself gives no indication that she will no longer be writing about books in the magazine, and she does not explain the end of her *Good Housekeeping* position in her autobiography.

The troubles seem to begin in 1931, as the United States sank deeper into the Depression and Blair, in between political seasons, had spent a relatively fallow four years staying close to home in Joplin. She found herself frustrated with what she terms, in *Bridging Two Eras*, her editors' "order-and-collaboration method of dealing with writers." Elaborating, Blair describes a journalistic process that, while hardly unusual, set limitations on her authorial freedoms that clearly rankled. "The editor had the idea. He wanted someone to write it. He gave the order. You wrote the article. He corrected and changed it. Sometimes the author had to do it over several times." No correspondence in Blair's archives suggests that her relationship with the editors at *Good Housekeeping* followed this pattern, but her autobiography only exonerates *Century* magazine from this behavior. Moreover, it was getting difficult to "get enough material away from the centers": "Editors told me it was almost impossible for a writer to live away from New York, that only two or three writers in the country managed to do it." It was not just editorial snubbing that was bothering Blair, however; she

Trouble, Antidotes

had begun to feel the lack of local colleagues, isolated as she was in Joplin, Missouri. "I believed I needed the stimulus of being with people who were doing the same thing I was, who talked my trade. It took a great deal of energy and time to live two lives simultaneously."[2]

"When Do You Read?" asks the title of Blair's January 1931 column. Reading this title in the table of contents,[3] a reader might well assume that the question is directed at her. It is not in quotation marks, so it couldn't be a citation of some question asked to Blair, could it? It must be a voice internal to the magazine—Blair herself, or the benevolent omniscient voice of *Good Housekeeping*, that "voiceover narrator" that seems to speak all of the callouts in the magazine. One might predict the full header will be a setup-and-response like, "When Do You Read? Emily Newell Blair Tells How to Find That Extra Fifteen Minutes a Day." This was *not*, however, the angle of the column; the question might be voiced by *Good Housekeeping*'s omniscient narrator, but it is posed to the magazine's own agent. "Emily Newell Blair Answers That Question by Listing the Books She Read on a Lecture Tour." This is not a column oriented toward the audience's practices but one that will reveal Blair's practices. In the column opener, Blair reproduces a barrage of harshly phrased, frankly impertinent questions that might well prompt an involuntary defensive response:

> "Do you really read all the books you write about? My husband says it is impossible. He says you could not possibly find time."
> "Do you read a book clear through? Or do you simply skim it over?"
> "How can you read so many books a month and remember all that is in them? I should think your mind would be a potpourri, and when you were through you would not be able to keep separate one book from another."
> "How do you get all these books in when you are flying about on these lecture trips? When do you get time to read?"[4]

Blair's readers, and their spouses, cannot imagine how Blair reads dozens of books every month with her grueling schedule. And this goes to Blair's credibility—maybe she doesn't actually read books all the way through, or maybe she doesn't really remember them properly when she is writing about them. The intervention of the skeptical husband in the first question is particularly interesting. Male rationality has spoken to judge this female reading adviser as full of bunk. Blair's notoriety has, as notoriety often will, brought her to the attention of skeptics as well as uncritical fans. She has become an object of curiosity that overshadows the books themselves.

In the next month's column, February 1931, Blair leads with a similarly suspicious question: "You are usually so enthusiastic over the books you tell us about. . . . Surely you must read some that do not appeal to you. It would help me tremendously in making my own decisions and in writing reviews for my club if you would tell us about some of them sometime—why you do not care for them, how you evaluate them."[5] This reader is trying to model her own practice on Blair's and is having difficulty because she only has an example of a positive review. It is an understandable question given Blair's practice of offering models for readership. It only follows that many of her readers will take not just her targeted friends as models (Herma or Charlotte), but also Blair herself, and just as they might want to know how to respond positively to a book, and why, they might want to emulate her methods of disapproval. As we have already seen, however, and this reader surely should have remembered, Blair is *not* just a cheerleader; she frequently discusses books, and authors, that disappoint her. In her June 1928 column, delightfully titled "Books That Count: By a Woman Who Uses Her Own Wide Experience and Splendid Critical Judgement to Arrive at Her Sum Total," Blair again takes on the task of advising her friend Minnie Fisher Cunningham, this time about books she might want to read in between stops during her US Senate campaign. "Everything I read must count," Minnie tells Blair. Blair knows that her friend is asking, on the one hand, "Whether she might 'miss some vital aspect of the political situation of her day' if she 'left this book until after the election,'" but, on the other, that "honest and clear-minded, [Minnie] knows that it is not only knowledge of facts that increases value, but also understanding and sympathy, so that a book which increases her stock of one or exercise of the other may be said, in her definition of it, to 'count.'"[6] In figuring out this calculus, Blair discusses a number of political histories, biographies, and autobiographies, both fiction and non-, many of which are flawed. In summing up Frederick Hazlitt Brennan's *God Got One Vote*, for example, she writes, "Given just a bit of the gift of the gods to reproduce by words, or of imagination to create by vision, this might have been a great book. . . . It is a pity that, being so good, the book is not better."[7] The book might "fit in" to Minnie's list, but it is hardly a rousing recommendation. Blair is even more querulous when she turns her attention to Fannie Hurst's genre-bending fictional political quasi-biography, *A President Is Born* (1928). "Politicians are tricksy bodies to evoke out of the void," she writes, transitioning from Brennan's work, "Perhaps that is why Fannie Hurst took such a

Trouble, Antidotes

queer way of introducing President David Schuyler to us." Hurst, Blair suspects, is having some fun with her audience, or maybe at the expense thereof:

> Just what his becoming President has to do with it we never quite understand, unless it is to justify a misleading title. ... This David might be on his way to becoming a bond salesman or a farmer or a lawyer or a movie magnate. I doubt not this brilliant author—for she is brilliant in spite of our repeated disappointments over her failures—has her own whimsical reason for this title. Perhaps she means to say, "Men are not born presidents—they become so." Or perhaps she means to say, "Presidents are just like anybody else." Or, "Here's a possibility—who knows?" Or even, "Every mother thinks her son is born to be president." Or perhaps she is just having her little joke with Americans. Or it may be her splendid gift for headlines.[8]

As in the *Orlando* review, when Blair multiplied potential interpretive angles for Woolf's novel, she seems to be reveling in proposing multiple equally insipid "reasons" for Hurst's title. (And perhaps Blair's *Good Housekeeping* page designer or copywriter took umbrage, or wanted to join in on the fun, by parrying "splendid gift for headlines" in the column's headline with "splendid critical judgement"?)

Significantly, Blair does *not* take issue with Hurst's nonstandard diction, offering instead a defense of experimentation that H. L. Mencken, and many twentieth-century academic acolytes of high modernism, surely would not have expected in the pages of *Good Housekeeping*. Her lively meditation merits another extended citation:

> There may be objections to her style. In that, too, she fumbles. But again to a purpose. Unless we believe that the final word has been said on sentence structure, punctuation, and use of words to express thought, which surely no person can affirm who knows the history of human expression, we must realize that custom in this matter, also, must change to meet our altered conditions of life, our mental habits. The use of periods to suggest words, the dropping of verbs unnecessary to the meaning, the substitution of reiteration for an array of adjectives for emphasis, are efforts, perhaps not yet successful, to get effects with a saving of time to both writer and reader, necessary in this day of weekly magazines and many books, and their competition with the screen and the radio for our attention. Of course, they are annoying to those who learned their grammar in the Victorian school. But I doubt not that when words first came to take the place of pictures in the literature of primitive man, there were those who charged these words with being meaningless and scorned the innovation.[9]

A full year before encouraging her readers to ignore the critical "racket" that would make *Orlando* seem too cerebral for them to simply enjoy, Blair explains that, actually, linguistic experimentation could be considered not just a new way of writing that more accurately captures the spirit of modern life, but a *time-saving* device, or an "innovation" on the part of authors to adapt their work to the busy schedules of modern audiences. She is offering a reverse angle on the formal argument by privileging the reader's experience of the text, but does so matter-of-factly: of course authors like Hurst have in mind their readers' convenience and satisfaction when they attempt experiments like these. And that imputed good "purpose" excuses Hurst's "fumble."

And yet! After all this, Blair recalls that she was making recommendations for her friend Minnie's particular, and peculiar, circumstances. The column breaks, with the subject header "As a Release from Strain," and Blair figuratively takes *A President Is Born* out of Minnie's hands and puts it back on the bookstore display table. "In the midst of a campaign, however, is no time to adjust oneself to the strange and effortful. Minnie will want books that reach her without a strain upon her habits of reading or processes of understanding."[10] It is not just the reader herself who matters; it is the reader's need at a given moment. The reader is not obligated to adjust her "habits," or her expectations, or her desires, to any given book; she should instead choose a book that fits her needs, her mood, her energy level. This also implies that, when not campaigning, Minnie might well appreciate *A President Is Born.* Minnie, herself, is not just one type of reader—no one is. Blair isn't either. She sometimes "find[s] it hard to read" (June 1930).[11] She can "read to learn" one month (January 1929)[12] then turn around a few months later looking for "some rattling good stories" (June 1929).[13] It would make no sense for Blair to excoriate the "rattling good story" just because she is in the mood to learn—so, when she presents either one, she reads *as if* she is a particular type of reader, a reader who will enjoy a given book.

Blair has even already addressed, at some length, the question of her "enthusiasm." She opens her February 1927 column with a query that is nearly identical to that of the book club reader whose skepticism request opened her February 1931 column and the third paragraph of this epilogue. "'How can you like every book you read?' asked one of the strangers who came up to greet me after my lecture on the season's books before the women's club at Liberty, Missouri." When Blair protests, "But I don't. . . . Why do you say that?" the stranger replies, "Because you're always so enthusiastic about all these books you write and talk about. Aren't you?"[14] In these early days, only one year into her tenure at *Good Housekeeping*, Blair seems a bit more patient. This question has not come from an anonymous reader, but a fellow Missourian, a "stranger," but a women's club member, who has approached a Blair who is speaking on a local, not a national, stage. Blair does not snap back an answer but takes some time, she says, to think about why someone might get the impression that she is undifferentiatedly enthusiastic. It becomes, to a certain degree, the implication that Blair is *uncritical* that bothers her in this early column. Exploring the notion of "enthusiasm" and "pleasure," and asking where either resides when it comes to reading and writing about books, Blair needs to assert that "some I do not like at all. Some bore me, and some tire me, two different things. Some offend me. Some, I confess, shock me. Some insult me. And some annoy me."[15] But Blair's pleasure, and her consequent enthusiasm, come from the anticipation she feels when she opens a book, wondering which reaction she will have *this* time. "For in the quest is pleasure, the pleasure of the search. Even when a book turns out a bore, one has the satisfaction of recognizing it for a bore, which is a great fillip to one's pride. By finding it tiresome, one flatters one's imagination. When it offends us, we recognize our good taste. Even when it annoys us, we enjoy discovering the reason."[16] Blair is, indeed, offended, annoyed, and bored by some of the titles she mentions in this column—and she writes, enthusiastically, about each experience in turn. Her consistent use of the first-person plural throughout this column includes and engages the *Good Housekeeping* reader in her "quest," thus the apparent lack of concern that her reviewing might actually be depriving others of "pleasure of the search."

The apparent need to repeat herself might explain Blair's somewhat salty response in 1931. "Since the object of my articles has been to bring to the attention of my readers the books that I thought they would enjoy, I have naturally taken pains to pick out the books that gave me the greatest pleasure or reward. Hence the enthusiasm." Disingenuous? Perhaps, but a good gambit for a column; Blair will now show her readers what it would look like if she did just write about every book as came across her desk, in sequence, whether or not she would have recommended them in a typical month. She does so, she writes, "with the hope that many of my readers will tell me whether they like best the enthusiasm or the report."[17] Her exasperation is evident, and Blair returns periodically to this tone while discussing eleven books about which, actually, she is relatively "enthusiastic." The dilemma Blair faces here, after five years at *Good Housekeeping*, prefigures the well-documented difficulties that celebrities and social media influencers have faced in the era of online fandom. The authenticity she was able to perform through the selective revelation of personal information has also opened her up to suspicions of inauthenticity.[18] In light of what seems to be increasing readerly incredulity, Blair clearly feels she must spend some time addressing her critics. Blair seems a bit weary of the grind.

The demands of the column certainly may have been growing too onerous by 1931, particularly with all of Blair's other writing and speaking obligations. In her autobiography, Blair describes the years between 1929 and 1932 as uneventful, but this is only true relative to Blair's standard state of activity and her typically demanding travel schedule. She spent one summer in New York, during which she wrote a lifestyle monograph, *The Creation of a Home*, and became a member of a writerly group around John and Margaret Farrar, but otherwise Blair was largely stationed in Joplin. She was thwarted, repeatedly, in attempts to travel to Europe: "Harry and I had tickets three times, but something always interfered, so we finally decided to wait until the following year. Then came the depression."[19] Blair was in fact pursuing a frantic work agenda even without considering her *Good Housekeeping* responsibilities, lecturing frequently to women's clubs as well as freelancing as a political correspondent for various news syndicates. Her schedule was particularly unwieldy in the summer of 1932, when she undertook a strenuous cross-country speaking schedule in support of Franklin Delano Roosevelt's presidential campaign. After requesting one three-day break in her schedule to write her *Good Housekeeping* column, "for I kept up my reading, doing a book in my berth or hotel at night, or in a railroad station between trains," she gets waylaid by an urgent invitation to speak in Columbia, Missouri. Feeling that the speech was an unmitigated "failure," Blair talked over possible revisions with her husband "as we drove the two hundred miles home that night"[20] (not an easy trip in the days before the interstate system). After spending the last two days of her "break" writing a new speech, Blair is off again on tour with a deadline looming: "By plane to El Dorado, Kansas. A speech in the afternoon; a fifty-mile drive and an evening speech in Winfield; another drive and a luncheon in Anthony; another drive and a speech in Hutchinson. The train there and a luncheon speech in Denver; a radio speech and the train again for Salt Lake. It was Sunday, and I spent it in my rooms doing the *Good*

Housekeeping article and got it off at two o'clock Monday morning. At six I took a plane for Pasco, Washington."

Blair was fifty-five years old in 1932, which makes the sandwiched-in all-nighter to write her *Good Housekeeping* article nearly as harrowing as the extreme travel narrative (she flew to Pasco in a biplane with an open cockpit). But this is only about one-quarter of her itinerary for the summer. In total this trip would comprise "fifteen days, twenty-five hundred miles, and twenty-eight speeches, not to mention the conferences, the organization talks, the dinners, teas, and luncheons." Little wonder that, in between Kansas City and Warrensburg, Missouri, Blair also lists (without fanfare or pause) "a cold, a doctor, and an osteopath."[21] Along the way, she was almost certainly reading for her next column; she filed one every month in 1932, but none of them mentions exhaustion or illness.

In May 1933, however, Blair leverages a bout of influenza to craft a column titled "Books as Trouble Antidotes." She herself has just recovered from the flu, which had confined her to her bed when she had been hoping to "have a good time" in Washington, DC. Ill on vacation, Blair nevertheless was able to enjoy reading while feverish, and this spurs her to observe, "How popular books should be today when nearly every one finds some trouble or other perches upon his bedpost every morning!" It is easy to understand how Blair might, at this stage, appreciate some forced convalescence, but the analogy could also land as a bit inappropriate to a reader who might not have the resources to take to her bed when ill or the time to sit and read when perfectly well. The rest of this issue of *Good Housekeeping* was intensively concerned with the financial crisis, endeavoring to guide its audience in the proper comportment of the marginally better-off middle-class woman. It opens with a full-page editorial entitled "The Wages of Labor," in which Editor-in-Chief William F. Bigelow challenges the consumers of America to eschew cheaply produced goods in favor of items manufactured by laborers who would receive a fair wage for their work: "We are not criticizing those who are buying the best they can afford. Millions are out of work. But millions more are working, and a fast multitude of them have been driving the wage scale downward, and making it harder for business to get on its feet again, by buying low-quality products or deliberately waiting until merchants have been forced to sacrifice their legitimate profits and, to forestall a complete loss, sell their goods for whatever they will bring."[22]

This editorial exemplifies the ideological construction of the middle class in the 1930s as a group that needed literally to buy into the economic and social reforms of the New Deal.[23] The *Good Housekeeping* reader was responsible for making a significant and patriotic contribution to the national economic recovery. She was one of the consumers who could "assure the worker of his wage—and his buying power—by spending wisely now,"[24] and she had an obligation to the national economy to stop economizing, at least when it comes to paying a little more for goods produced in the United States.

Blair's offer of literature as an anodyne, either a palliative or an antidote to quotidian concerns, seems to run counter to the bracing tone of Bigelow's editorial and, frankly, to what one might expect in May 1933, at the pivot point of the Great Depression.[25] Is Blair recommending escapism in this column, in a moment marked by the "political radicalization of literary culture," when it was presumably no longer possible to ignore the precarity of the working class or the mutual interdependence of all members of a civil society?[26] Actually, that is precisely what she is doing. At this moment of crisis, Blair's literal and metaphorical, and uncharacteristic, retreat to her bed reveals the mutual interdependence of a progressive middlebrow orientation and a middle-class identity. We see in her recommendation of escape the degree to which class, as Wai Chee Dimock and Michael Gilmore put it in their introduction to *Rethinking Class*, "can be understood as a mediate relation between the economic and the noneconomic, as a mode of structuration, a set of constitutive relays linking economic identities with social identities."[27] In a moment of systemic financial collapse, social identifications might not fluctuate as rapidly as personal finances; when they do not, as in the 1930s, it becomes apparent that "middle class" is more of an ideological position than a financial one. Middlebrow cultural modes thus serve to define and express a "middleclassness" that primarily signifies one is *not* financially precarious. Historian Burton Bledstein writes that the question "What did people mean when they represented themselves as middle class?" is one of the most important in American history; that he does so in the language of representation underscores the degree to which class is a set of social constructions that are linked to, but are not dependent on, economic conditions.[28]

In their return to Muncie, Indiana, in 1935, Robert S. Lynd and Helen Merrill Lynd found local newspapers and businessmen expounding the notion that "depressions are merely 'psychological'": "This whole depression business is largely mental. . . . If tomorrow morning everybody should wake up with a resolve to unwind the red yarn that is wound about his old leather purse, and then would carry his resolve into effect, by August first, at the latest,

Trouble, Antidotes 207

the whole country could join in singing, 'Happy Days are Here Again.'"[29] Business owners—as opposed to the working people of Muncie—escaped from the Depression largely unscathed; to them, the Lynds observed, "'good times' mean 'profits'; to the latter, 'a steady job.'"[30] While articles such as these could clearly be read as symptoms of the civic booster's stubborn reluctance to admit the underlying structural weaknesses of unregulated capitalism, we might also grant that prosperity was both culturally relative and a function of individual psychology. Indeed, in the 1930s, middle-classness was less a function of finances and more, as Jennifer Parchesky argues, an identity interpolated by middlebrow cultural products which "positione[ed] their audiences in particular relationships to the cultural formations they represented; that is, they shaped the way their audiences perceived and interpreted their experiences of everyday life."[31] Robert Seguin describes the middle class as "not so much . . . thing or idea, but more as a social-semantic structure capable of a range of investments, and supporting a range of practices and beliefs."[32] As Jaime Harker puts it, "The very notion of 'middle America' was a creation of middlebrow culture during the interwar period."[33]

If Blair's "Trouble Antidotes" column effectively shores up her readers' middle-*class* identities by encouraging them to lean into middle*brow* tastes, it also functions to reinforce the message of Bigelow's column and, consequently, to prime the *Good Housekeeping* reader to consume. Observing that "it is the patient one prescribes for, not the trouble,"[34] Blair suggests several novels, some that do indeed offer their readers vicarious escapes to different geographies or to historical settings. But even novels treating contemporaneous, local subjects will treat economy-induced malaise if they are the type to offer "a sense of proportion" rather than an indictment of the social system:

> I would prescribe fiction—but fiction of a special kind. Not "Ann Vickers," with its arraignment of a criminal system under the guise of a novel, and its distorted characters; nor even Fannie Hurst's "Imitation of Life," sound and sane though it may be as a study of the self-made woman pushed into success through economic need and paying the price for her success without whining. Rather I would select a novel about simple people going their daily round and meeting their daily problems with a nobility which makes one proud to be human, with no realization themselves that they are noble, and no insistence on the author's part that they are.[35]

This paean to the "nobility" of "simple people going about their daily round" romanticizes the workers whose livelihoods Bigelow asks *Good Housekeeping* readers to support with their consumer choices, and in doing so it bolsters that project by encouraging the reader to see those workers through a sentimental filter. Blair does not suggest, in this column, incisive political science or economics treatises or histories like those she recommended to Minnie Fisher Cunningham, nor does she offer heady philosophic and sociological works like those she sent to Frances Parkinson Keyes on her cruise. Instead, Blair recommends books that she says are "as free from mawkish sentiment as from maudlin cynicism" that will help "restor[e] the reader's sense of proportion" and "give a new connotation to that threadbare adjective, 'wholesome.' Perhaps they are the vanguard of a new type which, though it can treat the simple annals of the poor realistically, reveals also the dignity and beauty that lies in meeting bravely the conditions of life, whatever the estate to which one is called."[36] Blair's readers must not be drawn into sentimental identifications that would lead them to mistakenly imagine themselves precarious, just as they must not become too cynical to buy American.

The two books she particularly cautions her readers against are Sinclair Lewis's *Ann Vickers* and Fannie Hurst's *Imitation of Life*. Blair's explicit recommendation against *Vickers* suggests that it was a "book everyone is talking about"; in fact, it was both the "fifth leading seller among novels" in 1933 and "critically respected in some quarters too." It provides the kind of social analysis that Keyes might have appreciated; Gordon Hutner, for example, reads the book as a hallmark of "the era's reexamining of the relation between the public and private spheres" in the wake of the Crash, which "led novelists to wonder what effects its disillusioning aftermath would have on how Americans conducted intimate life, a concern ultimately dominating middle-class writing for the rest of the decade."[37] No audience hoping to look at the world, for a time, through a rose-colored lens (and not, as with *Dusty Answer*, a smashed one), would be well-served by Lewis's book, which portrays "distorted" characters and only masquerades as novel.

If Lewis's book is the one suffering from "maudlin cynicism," Hurst's would presumably be the one guilty of "mawkish sentiment," making it yet another disappointment from Fannie Hurst. In this, Blair would have good company, even among Hurst's contemporary defenders. A *Bookman* headline dubbed Hurst the "Sob-Sister of American Fiction," but the profile that follows suggests that any unironic, or perhaps insufficiently "smart," reading of that title is misleading. "As a story-teller her chief problem has been to make the reader shed the tears from which she has forced herself to refrain. She is the sob-sister of American fiction in the sublimated sense of that vulgar phrase. I use that phrase not as a literal characterization, but only for the most human connotations that are to be extracted from it."[38] The problem seems to be audience susceptibility to sobbing, perhaps mixed somewhat with Hurst's willingness to indulge such sentimentality. Hurst, in other words, tended to be misread, by both her allies and her harshest critics. The only way Blair might consider any of Hurst's *Imitation* characters a "success" would be to call Bea Pullman a "self-made woman," but doing so requires disregarding the degree to which her success relies on exploiting Delilah at every step. In fact, this seems to be exactly what white critics in 1933 did with the novel, celebrating it as an indictment of the pursuit of fame and fortune rather than a parody of racial stereotyping and a condemnation of racial and cultural appropriation. "As the *New York Times* reviewer understood it, . . . Miss Hurst wishes to point out that fame does not constitute real living, and that one who lives only in an objective sense finds life empty and bitter indeed.'"[39] Delilah in this case is read as a "true" character, not an imitation, by white audiences who could not recognize, would not fathom, a critique of white privilege. Bea, whose character arc ends with her "paying the price," is not noble, not tragic—Hurst is *manipulating* readers' sympathies, and this violates the progressive middlebrow sensibility.

Nine Months Later: Or, a Confusion in Lieu of a Conclusion

For her final column, which appears in the last issue in 1934, Blair goes back into the archives for books that should not be "overlooked by the very readers who would most enjoy them."[40] These are not books that have won awards, although Blair claims that she was inspired to write this column by the conferral of the Pulitzer Prize on a dark horse novel *Lamb in His Bosom* by Caroline Miller. "Why, I asked myself, should only prize novels be recalled to the attention of readers? Why not also a few others which should not be missed?" And so, Blair offers *Mandoa-Mandoa*, by Winifred Holtby, for "any one seeking to revalue his own concepts of civilization." On the other hand, "If it is smiles you wish, then another spring book should be read, *The Flowering Thorn* by Margery Sharp. It is that rare thing, a light novel altogether wholesome, which appeals to your intelligence rather than your emotions and has, besides, importance."[41]

Blair's final book recommendation is Zora Neale Hurston's first novel, *Jonah's Gourd Vine*, and this choice could be seen as an example both of the expansion of the middlebrow mode of reading and the ways that a middle-brow identification could be exclusionary. Blair tells her readers, "It is a novel about Negroes by a Negro, which reveals them as members of their own race with its own characteristics, and members of the human family with the characteristics common to it. This is a social document which one who wishes to be 'up' on fiction or sociology will find valuable."[42] This moment recalls Mary Church Terrell's complaint, cited by Jamie Harker, that she could not be published in an "average magazine" (read: one with a primarily white audience) because "nobody wants to know a colored woman's opinions about her own status or that of her group. When she dares express it, no matter how mild or tactful it may be, it is called 'Propaganda,' or is labeled 'controversial.'"[43] Terrell was writing about the publishing environment of the late 1880s; by 1934, the presumption seems to have shifted. Now, the work of a Black writer about Black subjects is presumed to be sociology, and the Black subjects represented therein have become metonymy for the race. This qualified embrace of Hurston's work is arguably more thoroughly othering than the simple exclusion encountered by Terrell or, in Harker's example, the Black middlebrow writer Jesse Fauset. Hurston's work, particularly when couched in these terms, could rest easy with an audience that "tended to see the African-American community as uniform: primitive, sensual, funny, musical, rhythmic, and simple."[44] This inclination might explain Blair's regular advocacy of DuBose Heyward's *Porgy*, set, like Hurston's novel, in the Deep South and centered on the life of a Black man. In May 1926, Blair recommended *Porgy* in terms similar to those she uses in 1934 to recommend *Jonah's Gourd Vine*: it is a book that one must read if one wants to keep up with the literary times: "Since so many people say it is *the* book of the year, the girls should have an opportunity to read that. College-bred girls, teachers like mine, who are essentially interested in the trend of literature, hate to get out of it as you hate to get away from a daily newspaper. You feel something must be happening."[45] Blair must diverge from her standard operating procedure of book summary when it comes to *Porgy*, however; she insists that it must be read to be understood, that "it would be sacrilege as well as idiocy for me to paraphrase, because it is the way Heyward tells the story that makes you accept Porgy as a great tragic character and so all that happens to him as of significance."[46] In other words, the reader needs to experience these characters through reading their words in (purportedly) Gullah dialect, needing specifically to read slowly through Heyward's narrative of a hurricane.

Trouble, Antidotes 211

If it seems like the generic characteristics of "literature" and "sociology" are becoming blurry here, well, they are. And when I add a third novel to the mix, one that Blair did *not* review, attempts to discern Blair's basis for distinguishing them (is it the race of the author? The quality of the dialect? How would she know about the latter, since she is a white woman from Missouri?)—well, they get frustrating. That third novel is Julia Peterkin's *Black April* (1927). Susan Millar Williams, Peterkin biographer and scholar, notes the "echoes" of *Black April* in Hurston's novel, locating these echoes in "both theme and style."[47] What is the difference for Blair? Is it that she has perceived a shift in middle-brow tastes and thinks her readers might be ready for something in 1934 that they would not have appreciated (or against which they might have rebelled) in 1927? Is the difference that Peterkin's novel, *not* "by a Negro," cannot therefore be read as sociology? And why would that be problematic? Blair insisted that the (purportedly accurate) presence of transcribed Gullah in *Porgy* was necessary to the production of certain effects in "college-bred" women readers, and contemporaneous anthropologists considered Peterkin's representations in *Black April* to be even more reliable than Heyward's.[48] The problem for Blair, then, is presumably not that a white author cannot write "sociologically" about Southern Black subjects. Maybe, though, they can only do so if the resultant portrait of a philandering Black man is legible as "tragic." This would suggest that Blair reads John Buddy's fate as tragic, and the fate of Peterkin's April as . . . something else. This would have been a departure from her professional critical compatriots' assessments of *Black April*; it was considered "tragic" in the *Saturday Review of Literature* (March 19, 1927)[49] and *Time* (April 4, 1927)[50]; the *New York Times*[51] and *The Independent*[52] come close with "heroic." How can a sociological work be properly considered "tragic"?[53]

In such a case, Occam's razor is a useful critical tool. In my introduction, I discussed Peterkin's sole contribution to *Good Housekeeping*, her June 1930 story "The Diamond Ring." I did not, however, mention *Good Housekeeping*'s promotion of the story in the previous issue. "Our Own Four Walls: A Meeting Place for Good Housekeeping's Friends," claims to be a "behind-the-scenes" preview of forthcoming content; the May 1930 iteration includes an excerpt from the illustration that will accompany the story, an image of the young boy who is the central character, with the caption "Julia Peterkin's negro characters are famous. Here's another of them." The brief item about the story mentions *Black April* but focuses not on that novel's plot or the prevalence of incest and gangrene therein, but on Peterkin's Julliard School piano professor, who claims to be the person who encouraged her to publish her stories. It closes by referencing the accompanying image, and promising that "her story next month is about a little black boy who walks right out of the pages with his basket of 'wash' into the thick of your sympathies."[54] One piece of the puzzle: "The Diamond Ring" can be seen as consistent with the rest of the magazine's representations of Black characters; it sounds here like a slightly different take on Black children along the lines of "Lonch for Two" (see chapter 1). It is thus a progressive middlebrow text, not a "grotesque" like *Black April*, which even bona-fide professional critic Herschel Brickell—Southerner born-and-bred, general editor for Henry Holt and Company, literary editor of the *Post*, the only critic whom Willa Cather thought properly understood *The Professor's House* (see chapters 2 and 3)—confessed, in the pages of *The Bookman*, "leaves me a little nauseated, and frightfully mixed as to the complications of naïve but nevertheless incestuous relationships."[55]

Blair's May 1930 column begins on page 84 of this issue, fewer than twenty pages before "Our Own Four Walls." Its title? "Pleasant Books Are Books Worth Reading When Recommended by Emily Newell Blair." Beneath a photograph of a smiling Blair reading a book (which is repurposed from the May 1926 column, in which Blair recommended *The Private Life of Helen of Troy* and *Porgy*), a caption cites a line from this month's column: "Given two books of equal literary merit and equal truth to life, I should always choose the one that dealt with pleasant people pleasantly."[56] Blair's column is a meditation on the kinds of books that qualify as having "literary merit" and showing "truth to life," but she also reiterates that she "can not speak for reviewers. My task is not to review books . . . but to indicate to my readers, as well as I can, what books of the many published will meet their needs and tastes."[57] Perhaps, then, the *Porgy–Black April–Jonah's Gourd Vine* dilemma is resolvable only through recourse to this metric: their inclusion or exclusion is based on their potential to be "enjoyed" by Blair's *Good Housekeeping* readers, middlebrows who need not try to read like anyone but themselves.

Franklin Delano Roosevelt sought to reward Blair for her work on his campaign with a government post, but she declined any sinecure for herself. Instead, she sought a position for her husband, Harry, who she knew "would leave Missouri only if he were offered a job."[58] And so he was appointed assistant attorney general in charge of the Lands Division, and he and Blair moved to Washington, DC, in 1933. She did accept an unsalaried position on the Consumer's Board of the National Recovery Act, which she held from

August 1933 until she was one of the six board members chosen by Roosevelt to liquidate the NRA after the Supreme Court deemed it unconstitutional in 1935. These dates almost explain the end of Blair's reading advice column for *Good Housekeeping*—but not precisely. Blair wraps up her narrative in *Bridging Two Eras* in the mid-1930s, not with chronological precision but by explaining that she realized around this time that she and the other progressive idealists of her generation had been naïve to think that their accomplishments in the late 1920s had solved poverty, inequality, intolerance, and cruelty. "Liberty was a possession. One simply decided how and when to use it. This was our prewar idea, and so fixed were we in it that we took the idea for the fact."[59] Perhaps the end of Blair's time at *Good Housekeeping* can be seen as a symptom of the death of a progressive middlebrow ethos, or if not its death, the diminution of its market value. This would explain the magazine's choice not to replace her with another taster and tester of books.

Notes

PREFACE

1 Emily Newell Blair, "When Do You Read?" *Good Housekeeping*, January 1931, 138.
2 Blair, January 1931, 96.
3 Elizabeth Kastor, "Giving Them Elle, after a Fashion," *Washington Post*, August 23, 1985, https://www.washingtonpost.com/archive/lifestyle/1985/08/23/giving-them-elle-after-a-fashion/ec5f2fe2-cb32-4e2d-98bd-bb2ccbd0f28e/.
4 Lauren Strach and Malcolm Russell, "The Good Housekeeping Seal of Approval: From Innovative Consumer Protection to Popular Badge of Quality," *Essays in Economic and Business History* 21 (2003): 159. The latter study, undertaken in an effort to determine whether consumer protections instituted in the 1970s had any impact on consumer understanding of what exactly the seal promised (a refund from *Good Housekeeping?* Adherence to governmental safety regulations?), found increased skepticism on the part of college-educated respondents but also found that such skepticism did not have an appreciable impact on whether they purchased products bearing the seal or not. While the high school–educated group tended to seek out the seal more frequently than the college-educated group, subjects in both groups bought seal-bearing products at roughly the same rate. Michael V. Laric and Dan Sarel, "Consumer (Mis) Perceptions and Usage of Third Party Certification Marks, 1972 and 1980: Did Public Policy Have an Impact?" *Journal of Marketing* 45 (Summer 1981): 135–42. As I will discuss in my introduction, education levels are not reliably determinant of "brow level," but it seems here that the more likely a subject was to have a middlebrow sensibility, the more likely they were to put great stock in the seal, at least through 1980.
5 Katharine Q. Seelye, "Polishing the Good Housekeeping Seal," *New York Times*, November 20, 2006, https://www.nytimes.com/2006/11/20/business/media/20house keeping.html.
6 https://www.goodhousekeeping.com/search/?q=books.
7 https://www.goodhousekeeping.com/life/entertainment/a34686888/gh-book-club/.
8 Emily Newell Blair, "Choose for Yourself," *Good Housekeeping*, January 1928) 141.

INTRODUCTION: CHOOSE FOR YOURSELF

1 Virginia Woolf, "Middlebrow," in *The Death of the Moth* (New York: Harcourt, Brace, 1942), 179. Originally written in 1932 as a letter to *The New Statesman*, the letter remained unsent, and this essay remained unpublished until collected posthumously in *The Death of the Moth*.
2 *Good Housekeeping* featured a color Jessie Willcox Smith illustration on every cover from December 1917 through April 1933, "one of the longest single runs of published covers in the history of pictorial illustration." Accounting for the lack of an issue in January 1920 (because of a strike) and a one-off cover in May 1934, Smith illustrated 184 covers for the

216 NOTES TO PAGES xii–5

magazine and became utterly identified with it during the 1920s and early 1930s. Edward D. Nudelman, *Jessie Willcox Smith: A Bibliography* (Gretna, LA: Pelican, 1989), 19.

3 Mary Ellen Zuckerman, *A History of Popular Women's Magazine in the United States, 1792–1995* (Westport, CT: Greenwood Press, 1998), 3.

4 "The History of the Good Housekeeping Seal," *Good Housekeeping*, May 1985, 354; Zuckerman, *A History*, 63. The history of the seal and the institutes will be discussed at greater length in chapter 1.

5 Swinnerton was a fixture in *Good Housekeeping* magazine and across the Hearst publications. His *Kiddies of the Canyon Country* comic had been a regular feature in the magazine from May 1922 through December 1926, and his series *Near to Nature Babies* ran from July 1927 through the end of 1929. After illustrating a number of articles for *Good Housekeeping* during the early 1930s, Swinnerton revived the now-renamed *Canyon Kiddies* series from August 1933 through September 1938. Harold G. Davidson, *Jimmy Swinnerton: The Artist and His Work* (New York: Hearst Books, 1985), 86–87, 92, 99, 110.

6 The Cornwell painting accompanied the second installment of a series of twelve articles by Bruce Barton, the author of *The Man Nobody Knows*, in which "the Man of Galilee will be made more real to you." Bruce Barton, "The Woman at the Well," *Good Housekeeping*, January 1928, 48. I will discuss Barton's work and his connection to *Good Housekeeping* at greater length in chapter 1.

7 Emily Newell Blair, "Choose for Yourself," *Good Housekeeping*, January 1928, 51. Blair's column titles are sometimes difficult to codify. Some feature long preambles or "kickers," which result in a title resembling those from the eighteenth century: "Few People Agree about Books[;] Emily Newell Blair Gives You a Clever Summary of the Newest Ones so that You may With Confidence Choose for Yourself." The table of contents for this issue lists Blair's article with the title "Choose Your Own Books" ("Contents," *Good Housekeeping*, January 1928, 2). Here, and in subsequent citations, I typically work from the article title page and cite discernable titles and subtitles, jettisoning to kickers.

8 "Contents," *Good Housekeeping*, January 1928, 2.

9 T. J. Jackson Lears, *Fables of Abundance: A Cultural History of Advertising in America* (New York: Basic Books, 1994), 196.

10 By the end of 1928, Blair's column would migrate further back in the book, appearing amid the "Departments," although it was still listed in the table of contents as a "Special Article."

11 Mabie's columns are at the center of my *Reading Up: Middle-Class Readers and the Culture of Success in the Early Twentieth-Century United States* (Philadelphia: Temple University Press, 2012). Beginning in March 1926, *McCalls* ran a compendium feature titled "What's Going on in the World," in which a "Book of the Month" feature written by Laurence Stallings ran alongside reviews of the "Film of the Month," the "Play of the Month," and, eventually, the "World Event of the Month" (*McCalls*, March 1926, 18–19), but this is nowhere near as extensive a feature as Blair's monthly column. The UK version of *Good Housekeeping* ran its own books column, authored by Clemence Dane, from 1923 through 1933, when Winifred Holtby assumed the post. Dane's columns have, unlike Blair's, attracted considerable scholarly attention, and they have a distinctive tone that is quite different from Blair's; see Stella Deen, "Clemence Dane's Literary Criticism for *Good Housekeeping*: Cultivating a 'Small, Comical, Lovable, Eternal Public' of Book Lovers," in *Women's Periodicals and Print Culture in Britain, 1818–1939: The Interwar Period*, ed. Catherine Clay, Maria DiCenzo, Barbara Green, Fiona Hackney (Edinburgh: Edinburgh

NOTES TO PAGES 5–8   217

University Press, 2017), 58–71; and Deen, "Cultivating Citizen Readers: Clemence Dane's Historical Essays in *Good Housekeeping*," *Journal of Modern Periodical Studies* 10, nos. 1–2 (2019): 98–128. While a Blair-Dane comparative analysis is outside the scope of this study, it would definitely be a valuable addition to the scholarship of transatlantic periodicals, women's periodicals, and popular modernism.

12 Emily Newell Blair, "A Road Log of New Books, by a Woman Who Knows the Country of Which She Writes," *Good Housekeeping*, July 1926, 220.

13 Woolf, "Middlebrow," 179.

14 Russell Lynes, "Highbrow, Lowbrow, Middlebrow," *Harper's*, February 1949, 19–28.

15 Melissa Sullivan and Sophie Blanch, "Introduction: The Middlebrow—within or without Modernism," *Modernist Cultures* 6, no. 1 (2011): 1.

16 Woolf, "Middlebrow," 186.

17 Nicola Humble, "Sitting Forward or Sitting Back: Highbrow v. Middlebrow Reading," *Modernist Cultures* 6, no. 1 (2011): 44–46.

18 Aaron Jaffe, *Modernism and the Culture of Celebrity* (Cambridge: Cambridge University Press, 2005), 9.

19 Mark McGurl, *The Novel Art: Elevations of American Fiction after Henry James* (Princeton, NJ: Princeton University Press, 2001), 2.

20 Raymond Williams, "When Was Modernism?," in *Culture and Politics*, ed. Phil O'Brien (London: Verso, 2022), 207. I am here referencing the new transcription made from a recording of Williams's lecture, not the previously published Inglis reconstruction in *Politics of Modernism* (London: Verso, 1989).

21 Andreas Huyssen, *After the Great Divide: Modernism, Mass Culture, Postmodernism* (Bloomington: Indiana University Press, 1986), viii, vii.

22 Williams, "When Was Modernism?," 217.

23 "New modernist studies" as a departure from "old modernist studies" is, as K. Merinda Simmons and James A. Crank note, generally given a point of origin in the 1990s, with the beginning of publication of the journal *Modernism/modernity* and the formation of the Modernist Studies Association. The publications of Douglas Mao and Rebecca L. Walkowitz's *Bad Modernisms* (Durham, NC: Duke University Press, 2006), and the editors' follow-up "The New Modernist Studies," *PMLA* 123, no. 3 (May 2008): 737–48, are also credited with codifying the notion that "modernism" should be pluralized and decapitalized; see K. Merinda Simmons and James A. Crank, *Race and New Modernisms* (London: Bloomsbury Academic, 2019), 7–8.

24 Lawrence Rainey, "Modernism and Popular Culture," in *The Bloomsbury Companion to Modernist Literature*, ed. Ulrike Maude and Mark Nixon (London: Bloomsbury Academic, 2018), 188. This essay has a more polemical tone than Rainey's foundational *Institutions of Modernism: Literary Elites and Public Culture* (New Haven, CT: Yale University Press, 1998), which argues that modernism "did indeed entail a certain retreat from the domain of public culture, but one that also continued to overlap and intersect with the public realm in a variety of contradictory ways" (3). This is no doubt a mark of Rainey's frustration with the persistence of the "Great Divide theory" and its attainment of shorthand status. Rainey, "Modernism and Popular Culture," 172.

25 Scott McCracken, "Anything but a Clean Relationship: Modernism and the Everyday," in *The Bloomsbury Companion to Modernist Literature* ed. Ulrike Maude and Mark Nixon (London: Bloomsbury Academic, 2018), 31.

218 NOTES TO PAGES 8–11

26 McCracken, "Anything But," 39.

27 Bryony Randall offers an extensive taxonomy of work from the 1990s through the 2000s in "Modernist Literature and the Everyday," *Literature Compass* 7, no. 9 (2010): 824–35.

28 Catherine Turner, *Marketing Modernism between the Two World Wars* (Amherst: University of Massachusetts Press, 2003), 1–3.

29 John Guillory, *Professing Criticism: Essays on the Organization of Literary Study* (Chicago: University of Chicago Press, 2022), 329 (emphasis in original).

30 Mark Morrisson, "Beyond Little Magazines: American Modernism and the Turn to Big Magazines," *Journal of Modern Periodical Studies* 11, no. 1 (2020): 2, 3. See also Greg Barnhisel, "Small Magazines," in *American Literature in Transition: 1920–1930*, ed. Ichiro Takayoshi (New York: Cambridge University Press, 2018), 417–33.

31 Sean Latham and Robert Scholes published "The Rise of Periodical Studies" in *PMLA* 121, no. 2 (2006): 517–31, in which they noted that digitization was ushering in both greater accessibility and new difficulties for scholars for whom the "cultural turn" had rendered periodical studies increasingly compelling. But even before this point, there were already a number of significant studies that looked at wider-circulation periodicals as conversant with and contributing to US "modernist" culture. Christopher P. Wilson, "The Rhetoric of Consumption: Mass-Market Magazines and the Demise of the Gentle Reader, 1880–1920," in *The Culture of Consumption*, ed. Richard Wrightman Fox and T. J. Jackson Lears (New York: Pantheon Books, 1983), 40–64; George H. Douglas, *The Smart Magazines* (Hamden, CT: Archon Books, 1991); Joan Shelley Rubin, *The Making of Middlebrow Culture* (Chapel Hill: University of North Carolina Press, 1992); Daniel Morris, "Ernest Hemingway and *Life*: Consuming Revolutions," *American Periodicals* 3 (1993): 62–74; Helen Damon Moore, *Magazines for the Millions: Gender and Commerce in the "Ladies' Home Journal" and the "Saturday Evening Post,"* 1880–1910 (Albany: State University of New York Press, 1994); Jennifer Scanlon, *Inarticulate Longings: The "Ladies' Home Journal," Gender, and the Promises of Consumer Culture* (New York: Routledge, 1995); and Helen Gruber Garvey, *The Adman in the Parlor: Magazines and the Gendering of Consumer Culture, 1880s to 1910s* (New York: Oxford University Press, 1996).

32 Andrew Thacker, "General Introduction: 'Magazines, Magazines, Magazines!'" in *The Oxford Critical and Cultural History of Modernist Magazines: Volume II: North America 1894–1960*, ed. Peter Brooker and Andrew Thacker (Oxford: Oxford University Press, 2012), 21. Thacker's notion of the "periodical field" follows Bourdieu's articulation of the cultural field, which has "its own laws of functioning independent of those of politics and the economy . . . it is a veritable social universe where, in accordance with its particular laws, there accumulates a particular form of capital and where relations of force of a particular type are exerted." Pierre Bourdieu, *The Field of Cultural Production: Essays on Art and Literature*, ed. Randal Johnson (Cambridge: Polity Press, 1993), 162, 164.

33 Robert Scholes, "Afterword," in *Little Magazines & Modernism: New Approaches*, ed. Suzanne W. Churchill and Adam McKible (Hampshire, UK: Ashgate Publishing, 2001), 217–18.

34 These are the specific titles discussed at length by Donal Harris in *On Company Time: American Modernism in the Big Magazines* (New York: Columbia University Press, 2016). Work on *Vanity Fair*, *Vogue*, and other "smart magazines" is extensive; some examples, in addition to Douglas, *The Smart Magazines*, are Faye Hammill, *Women, Celebrity, and Literary Culture between the Wars* (Austin: University of Texas Press, 2007); Catherine

NOTES TO PAGES 11–15

Keyser, *Playing Smart: New York Women Writers and Modern Magazine Culture* (New Brunswick, NJ: Rutgers University Press, 2010); and Natalie Kalich, "'How Fatally Outmoded Is Your Point of View?' *Vanity Fair's* Articulation of Modernist Culture to the Modern Reader," *Reception: Texts, Readers, Audiences, History* 6 (2014): 19–37.

35 For *Ladies' Home Journal* see n28 above; for the UK *Good Housekeeping*, see n9 above as well as Fiona Hackney, "'Women Are News': British Women's Magazines 1919–1939," in *Transatlantic Print Culture, 1880–1940: Emerging Media, Emerging Modernisms*, ed. Ann Ardis and Patrick Collier (New York: Palgrave Macmillian, 2008), 114–33; Alice Wood, "Housekeeping, Citizenship, and Nationhood in *Good Housekeeping* and *Modern Home*," in *Women's Periodicals and Print Culture in Britain, 1918–1939: The Interwar Period*, ed. Catherine Clay, Maria DiCenzo, Barbara Green, and Fiona Hackley (Edinburgh: Edinburgh University Press, 2018), 210–24; and Alice Wood, *Modernism and Modernity in British Women's Magazines* (New York: Routledge, 2020), 42–51.

36 I depart here from the notion that, by the 1920s and 1930s, "middlebrow culture" still "names a set of processes within mass culture directed toward a particular 'common interest': identifying and teaching high culture." Daniel Tracy, "Investing in 'Modernism': Smart Magazines, Parody, and Middlebrow Professional Judgement," *Journal of Modern Periodical Studies* 1, no. 1 (2010): 40. This is absolutely the stock in trade of the "smart" magazines, but, as I will argue, Blair works to separate herself and her readers from such aspirations, and she accomplishes this by explicitly disdaining, dismissing, or just performing indifference toward figures and texts that smack of "smartness."

37 Blair, January 1928, 51.

38 Emily Newell Blair, "Which Books Shall Live?," *Good Housekeeping*, January 1927, 51.

39 Blair, January 1927, 51.

40 Rubin, *Middlebrow Culture*, 25.

41 Rubin, *Middlebrow Culture*, 27.

42 Rubin, *Middlebrow Culture*, 93–110; Janice Radway, *A Feeling for Books: The Book-of-the-Month Club, Literary Taste, and Middle-Class Desire* (Chapel Hill: University of North Carolina Press, 1997), 193–94.

43 See Rubin, *Middlebrow Culture*, 27–29; Radway, *A Feeling for Books*, 145–47; Amy L. Blair, *Reading Up*, 195–97.

44 Jaime Harker, "Progressive Middlebrow: Dorothy Canfield, Women's Magazines, and Popular Feminism in the Twenties," in *Middlebrow Moderns*, ed. Lisa Botshon and Margaret Goldsmith (Boston: Northeastern University Press, 2003), 119, 120.

45 Blair, January 1927, 51.

46 The literature on nineteenth-century domesticity and women's reading is vast, but I am particularly thinking here about Deidre Shauna Lynch's *Loving Literature: A Cultural History* (Chicago: University of Chicago Press, 2015), which you should go read now before returning to this note. Valuable work on celebrity book clubs is (at the time of writing) forthcoming from Tamara Bhalla ("To Understand the Other, You Have to Be a Mother: Jenna Bush Hager's #ReadWithJenna Book Club and the Politics of Race, Empathy, and Motherhood," *Reception: Texts, Readers, Audiences, History* 16 [2024]) and Kristin Matthews ("#WellReadBlackGirl: Connection, Community, and Creation in a Virtual Age," *Reception: Texts, Readers, Audiences, History*, 16 [2024]). The literature on twenty-first-century notions of "self-care" and the long history of similar ideas grows daily, exponentially, and appears in every possible outlet. A quick search unearths an article in the "Art of Medicine" section of the *Lancet* (Mandip Aujla and Manjulaa Narasimhan, "The Cycling

NOTES TO PAGES 15–18

of Self-Care through History," *Lancet* 402, no. 10417 [December 2, 2023]: 2066–67); an article from one of the most progressive periodicals currently in circulation, *Teen Vogue*, on the concept's connection to the Black Panther movement (Leonora E. Houseworth, "The Radical History of Self-Care," *Teen Vogue*, January 14, 2021, https://www.teenvogue.com /story/the-radical-history-of-self-care.); and an intriguingly scholarly (though alas, devoid of citations) blog post on the homepage of Silk and Sonder, a lifestyle brand, clearly targeted to women, and centered around self-care journals to help "bring your . . . goals to life—one page, one habit at a time in just 5 minutes a day" (Olivia Groves, "The Powerful History of Self-Care and How to Honor it Today," https://www.silkandsonder.com/blogs /news/the-origin-of-self-care-the-fascinating-history-and-3-huge-ways-it-can-help-you -right-now.). The last title attests to the long rhetorical echo extending from the Harvard Classic's Five-Foot Shelf of Books . . . although the digital age seems to have whittled Eliot's "fifteen minutes a day" down to five.

47 Blair, January 1927, 121.

48 Blair, January 1927, 125.

49 Blair, January 1927, 125. Blair's description of *The Story of Philosophy* shares the initial dismissiveness characteristic of many of her mentions of the "outline" volumes whose vogue was, per Joan Shelley Rubin, "the interwar period's most important nonfiction publishing trend." Rubin, *Middlebrow Culture*, 209. Blair immediately moderates her dismissiveness, however admitting that "for those who once studied philosophy in pursuit of a college degree, and for those who have not yet learned that philosophy is 'a search for reality,' it is entertaining reading. For the former it may be review; for the latter, discovery; for both it is stimulating." Blair, January 1927, 125. Key for my purposes here is Blair's identifying Durant as essential for the reader who wants to keep up, not necessarily with trends in philosophy but with trends in contemporaneous reading; for a thorough discussion of Durant's work and the reception and impact of *The Story of Philosophy* in particular, see Rubin, *Middlebrow Culture*, 209–65.

50 Gordon Hutner, *What America Read: Taste, Class, and the Novel, 1920–1960* (Chapel Hill: University of North Carolina Press, 2009), 54.

51 Hutner builds this argument with extensive evidence from contemporary reviews, particularly in pp. 44–63 of his study, although Blair's columns are not a part of his archive.

52 Harker, "Progressive Middlebrow"; Radway, *A Feeling for Books*, 179.

53 Siân Round, "Southern Stories for Northern Readers: Julia Peterkin's Short Stories in *The Reviewer* and the Disruption of Dialect," *Journal of Modern Periodical Studies* 14, no. 1 (2023): 47–69.

54 Peterkin appears again, fully domesticated, alongside fellow middlebrow celebrities Dorothy Canfield Fisher, Edna St. Vincent Millay, Ellen Glasgow, Grace Noll Crowell, Dorothy Dix, Katherine Newlin Burt, Lenora Mattingly Weber, and Bess Streeter Aldrich in "Springtime Pilgrimage to the Gardens of Nine Women who Wield a Spade as Well as a Pen," *Good Housekeeping*, May 1938, 50–53, 154, 156, 158–63.

55 Blair does *not* review all of *Good Housekeeping's* fiction contributors in her columns. There seems to be no cross-promotional quid pro quo at work, but she does mention a work's *Good Housekeeping* ties if there are any. In the June 1930 issue that features Peterkin, for example, Blair reviews Ruth Suckow's *The Kramer Girls* and notes that it had been serialized in *Good Housekeeping*.

56 Paula Rabinowitz, *American Pulp: How Paperbacks Brought Modernism to Main Street* (Princeton, NJ: Princeton University Press, 2014), 32.

NOTES TO PAGES 18–27

57 Rabinowitz, *American Pulp*, 22.

58 Advertisement, *Good Housekeeping*, November 1927, 292.

59 Barnhisel, "Small Magazines," 418.

60 Rubin, *Middlebrow Culture*, 87.

61 May Lamberton Becker, "The Reader's Guide," *Saturday Review of Literature*, December 10, 1927, 445.

62 Blair, January 1927, 51.

63 Blair, January 1928, 51.

64 Blair, January 1928, 138.

65 Humble, "Sitting Forward or Sitting Back," 46–47.

66 Blair, January 1928, 141.

CHAPTER ONE

1 Advertisement, *Good Housekeeping*, February 1926, 246.

2 For "horizon of expectations," see Wolfgang Iser, *The Act of Reading: A Theory of Aesthetic Response* (Baltimore: Johns Hopkins University Press, 1978).

3 Here I follow a methodology proposed by Margaret Beetham, "Open and Closed: The Periodical as a Publishing Genre," *Victorian Periodicals Review* 22, no. 3 (1989): 96–100, and urged repeatedly by Ann Ardis in the modernist context (e.g., in the MLA 2013 special session "What Is a Journal?": Ann Ardis, "Towards a Theory of Periodical Studies," https://jvc.oup.com/2012/12/24/what-is-a-journal-mla2013/.) The paired special issues of the *Journal of Modern Periodical Studies* 6, no. 2 (2015), and *English Studies in Canada* 41, no. 1 (March 2015), have also influenced my approach.

4 Correspondence with Nicole Saporita, senior editor of *Good Housekeeping* (May 22, 2019), and Jane Francisco, editorial director of Hearst Lifestyle Group (June 25, 2019), confirmed that the *Good Housekeeping* archives are not open to the public. Saporita also indicated that the in-house archives consist exclusively of back issues and not of any editorial documents from the Bigelow period or any other. Katy Conover, manager of the Hearst UK Library and Archive, also confirmed no equivalent entity at Hearst US, and the absence of materials from the US editorial side in her collection (October 23, 2023).

5 Janet Mabie, "Editor of Good Housekeeping Maintains Common Touch," *Christian Science Monitor*, June 24, 1932, 3.

6 Mary Ellen Zuckerman, *A History of Popular Women's Magazine in the United States, 1792–1995* (Westport, CT: Greenwood Press, 1998), 108, 63–65.

7 Katharine Fisher, "Housekeeping Emerges from the Eighties," *Good Housekeeping*, May 1935, 225–26.

8 Sarah A. Leavitt, *From Catharine Beecher to Martha Stewart: A Cultural History of Domestic Advice* (Chapel Hill: University of North Carolina Press, 2002), 41.

9 "Good Housekeeping Brings You Leisure," *Good Housekeeping*, October 1928, 5.

10 Zuckerman, *A History*, 129; "An Analysis of the Subscription Circulation of Forty-Four Magazines in Metropolitan Cincinnati, 1923," 33. J. Walter Thompson Company, New York Office, Research Department Records, 1923–1986 and Undated. Box 3. David M. Rubenstein Rare Book and Manuscript Library, Duke University, Durham, NC.

11 Meeting Notes, Representatives' Meeting, August 22, 1928, 6. J. Walter Thompson Company, Staff Meeting Minutes. Box 1. David M. Rubenstein Rare Book and Manuscript Library.

NOTES TO PAGES 27–30

12 Zuckerman, *A History*, 131.

13 "An Analysis," 34.

14 Robert S. Lynd and Helen Merrell Lynd, *Middletown: A Study in Modern American Culture* (New York: Harcourt Brace, 1957), 158.

15 Amy Sopcak-Joseph has shown that subscription strategies for even one of the earliest women's periodicals, *Godey's Lady's Book*, tried to curtail this practice by encouraging borrowers to become subscribers in the name of respectability. Amy Sopcak-Joseph, "Reconstructing and Gendering the Distribution Networks of *Godey's Lady's Book* in the Nineteenth Century," *Book History* 22 (2019): 161–95.

16 Meeting Notes, Representatives' Meeting, February 7, 1928, 3. J. Walter Thompson Company, Staff Meeting Minutes. Box 1.

17 "An Analysis," 21.

18 "An Analysis," 234.

19 "An Analysis," 30.

20 "Magazine Survey among Women in Rochester, N. Y.," n.p. [6, 3], J. Walter Thompson Company 16mm Microfilm Investigations, 1913–1950 and Undated. David M. Rubenstein Rare Book and Manuscript Library.

21 "Magazine Survey," n.p. [7]. The survey also notes that *The American Magazine* was popular "especially among Class C women," who the survey describes living in "homes of those with little education and taste, but with incomes about the same or a little smaller than Class B. These are usually homes of skilled mechanics, mill operators, petty trades people, etc. They have no servants." "Magazine Survey," n.p. [3]. In 1931, *Good Housekeeping* published *Women and Magazines: A Study of Magazine Consciousness and Magazine Preference* (New York: International Magazine Company, 1931), which purported to offer a synthesis of such surveys conducted by forty-five advertising agencies (one of which is in fact the J. Walter Thompson Company). The results as printed in this publication are consistent with those I have discussed here, but they do not reproduce any individual survey answers; it is a bit more of a blunt instrument that demonstrates, with 185 pages of maps printed on heavy paper, that *Good Housekeeping* is apparently the magazine most housewives would prefer to subscribe to.

22 Meeting Notes, August 22, 1928, 2–5.

23 "Limited investigation of Women's Attitude toward the Ladies' Home Journal," October, 1934, n.p., J. Walter Thompson Company 16 mm Microfilm Investigations, 1913–1950 and Undated.

24 *Good Housekeeping: The Shortest Route to the National Market* (New York: International Magazine Company, 1928), 7.

25 *The Shortest Route*, 8.

26 *The Shortest Route*, 8.

27 The 1923 Cincinnati survey found that 77.9 percent of the *Good Housekeeping* subscribers were married, and 20 percent were unmarried. This is a slightly lower ratio than some of the other Big Six magazines: *Delineator's* audience was 90.7 percent married, and *Butterick's* 90.3 percent. *McCalls* and *Pictorial Review* had married audiences in the 80 percent range. This may account for the relative predominance of stories about unmarried women in the *Good Housekeeping* fiction mix, as we will see below. "An Analysis," 33, 216–17.

28 Mabie, "Editor of Good Housekeeping," 3.

29 Daniel Henderson, "Good Housekeeping's Story," *The Quill*, October 1936, 9. We can assume that "normal" also meant "white." None of the J. Walter Thompson surveys broke

NOTES TO PAGES 31–43

down their respondents by race, which suggests that the presumption was that all of the readers were white. As discussed above, *The Shortest Route* does identify "literate native white families" as their target audience. This of course does not mean that women of color never read *Good Housekeeping*, but as we will see, they would almost exclusively find themselves represented in a marginal, subservient, or demeaning fashion.

30 Edward D. Nudleman, *Jessie Willcox Smith: American Illustrator* (Gretna, LA: Pelican Publishing, 1990), 39.

31 "The Secret Was about Covers," *Good Housekeeping*, November 1917, 32.

32 Frank Luther Mott, *A History of American Magazines 1905–1930*, vol. 5 (Boston: Harvard University Press, 1968), 136.

33 Scanlon, *Inarticulate Longings*, 211–12; "History of Woodbury's Soap and Preparations 1901 to 1929, Inclusive," Account Files, Jergens, J. Walter Thompson Company Archives, David M. Rubenstein Rare Book and Manuscript Library; "Revised Schedule of Insertions: Magazine" April 23, 1929, Account Files, Jergens, J. Walter Thompson Company Archives; "Revised Schedule of Insertions: Magazine" July 2, 1929, Account Files, Jergens, J. Walter Thompson Company Archives.

34 Scanlon, *Inarticulate Longings* 199; 201.

35 "What Is False Advertising?" *Business Week*, December 23, 1939, 24.

36 Mott, *A History*, 140–41.

37 "Seal of Disapproval," *Business Week*, August 26, 1939, 20.

38 Scanlon, *Inarticulate Longings*, 68.

39 Advertisement for Old Dutch Cleanser, *Good Housekeeping*, February 1926, inside cover. All subsequent references to materials in this issue of the magazine will be made parenthetically in the text.

40 See Suellen Hoy, *Chasing Dirt: The American Pursuit of Cleanliness* (New York: Oxford University Press, 1995).

41 Leavitt, *From Beecher to Stewart* 5; 207n5. Roland Marchand, *Advertising the American Dream: Making Way for Modernity, 1920–1940* (Berkeley: University of California Press, 1985), xvii.

42 As Scanlon points out, "This type of advertisement, an illustrated feature story, was a popular approach among copywriters." Scanlon, *Inarticulate Longings*, 201.

43 The March 1926 Nujol ad, which is more of a "story ad" than the February installment, is similarly alarmist: "You Threaten Their Whole Lives with Failure" (267)—the problem being that constipated Peggy can no longer study, and her grades are suffering terribly. "Especially important is it to future health that girls of the adolescent age should cultivate the habit of internal cleanliness—that is, complete freedom from constipation." As with the home, so is the "habit of cleanliness" essential for the intestines.

44 For a discussion of this history as well as an extensive reading of the frequently dangerous women's health advice offered in *Good Housekeeping*, see Kim Chuppa-Cornell, "Filling a Vacuum: Women's Health Information in *Good Housekeeping*'s Articles and Advertisements, 1920–1965," *The Historian* 67, no. 3 (Fall 2005): 454–73.

45 Leavitt, *From Beecher to Stewart*, 205.

46 An engaging account of Wiley's tenure in the Department of Agriculture and his work to establish the Board of Food and Drug Inspection (USDA) may be found in Deborah Blum, *The Poison Squad: One Chemist's Single-Minded Crusade for Food Safety at the Turn of the Twentieth Century* (New York: Penguin, 2018). *Good Housekeeping*'s enticing offer is detailed on 261.

224 NOTES TO PAGES 44–65

47 William F. Bigelow, "Dr. Harvey W. Wiley," *Good Housekeeping*, September, 1930, 4.

48 Harvey W. Wiley, *An Autobiography* (New York: Bobbs-Merrill, 1930), 302.

49 Wiley, *An Autobiography*, 303.

50 Wiley, *An Autobiography*, 304.

51 Erin Smith, *What Would Jesus Read? Popular Religious Books and Everyday Life in Twentieth-Century America* (Chapel Hill: University of North Carolina Press, 2015), 27.

52 Smith, *What Would Jesus Read?*, 35. All summary outside this direct quotation is also derived from Smith, whose account of the novel's reception is valuable additional context for the impact Sheldon's presence would have had in the magazine.

53 A full account of Sheldon's remarkable relationship with modern print culture is beyond the scope of this study; for this valuable context, see Smith, *What Would Jesus Read?*

54 Smith, *What Would Jesus Read?*, 107.

55 The phrase is Kenneth Burke's, and is evoked by Erin Smith in her discussion of *The Man Nobody Knows*. See Smith, *What Would Jesus Read?*, 108; Kenneth Burke, "Literature as Equipment for Living," in *The Philosophy of Literary Form* (Berkeley: University of California Press, 1973), 293–304.

56 Barbara Ryan, "Teasing Out Clues, Not Kooks: *The Man Nobody Knows* and Ben-Hur," *Reception: Texts, Readers, Audiences, History* 5 (2013): 12.

57 Simone Weil Davis, *Living Up to the Ads: Gender Fictions of the 1920s* (Durham, NC: Duke University Press, 2000), 2.

58 Eventually, Bigelow would collect marital advice from the magazine into the *Good Housekeeping Marriage Book*, initially published in 1938 and still in print in 2020.

59 Leavitt, *From Beecher to Stewart*, 5.

60 Henderson, "Good Housekeeping's Story," 9.

61 Henderson, "Good Housekeeping's Story," 9. A 1937 profile of Bigelow in *The Writer* (which borrows very heavily from *The Quill's* profile) emphasizes the fiction content of the magazine as the main reason that "men read it too," although this runs contrary to Bigelow's representation of his target market here. John Drewry, "Good Housekeeping— Men Read It Too," *The Writer*, October 1937, 321, 319.

62 When published in novel form, *The Blue Window* would sell enough copies to make it one of the top ten best-selling novels of 1926 according to Alice Payne Hackett, *Fifty Years of Best Sellers 1895–1945* (New York: R. R. Bowker, 1945), 53.

63 Temple Bailey, "The Blue Window," *Good Housekeeping*, March 1926, 83.

64 Bailey, "The Blue Window," 271.

65 Bailey, "The Blue Window," 272.

66 William J. Locke, "Perella," *Good Housekeeping*, August 1926, 52.

67 Locke, "Perella," 200.

68 Maureen Honey, "Introduction," *Breaking the Ties That Bind: Popular Stories of the New Woman, 1915–1930* (Norman: University of Oklahoma Press, 1998).

69 Robin Bernstein, *Racial Innocence: Performing American Childhood from Slavery to Civil Rights* (Durham: Duke University Press, 2011), 33.

70 Bernstein, *Racial Innocence*, 55. A full discussion of the comic representations of Topsy may be found in Bernstein *Racial Innocence*, 47–55.

71 For more on the ways that representations of children of color related to representations of and concerns for white children in Progressive Era publications, see Lara Saguisag, *Incorrigibles and Innocents: Constructing Childhood and Citizenship in Progressive-Era Comics* (Camden, NJ: Rutgers University Press, 2019), 56.

NOTES TO PAGES 65-78

72 See 216, n5, for the timeline of Swinnerton's contributions to *Good Housekeeping*.

73 Saguisag, *Incorrigibles and Innocents*, 55.

74 Rob Wilson's *Script Magazine*, February 17, 1940.

75 Harold G. Davidson, *Jimmy Swinnerton: The Artist and His Work* (New York: Hearst Books, 1985), 92. Swinnerton is apparently still a draw in contemporary collectors' circles; eBay and used bookstore listings of the magazine frequently tout that a given issue includes his work intact, and individual leaves command exorbitant prices.

76 Joan Shelley Rubin, *The Making of Middlebrow Culture* (Chapel Hill: University of North Carolina Press, 1992), 28.

CHAPTER TWO

1 Emily Newell Blair, "Tasting and Testing Books: A New Service for the Readers of Good Housekeeping by Emily Newell Blair," *Good Housekeeping*, February 1926, 43. Subsequent references indicated parenthetically in text.

2 Denise Gigante, *Taste: A Literary History* (New Haven, CT: Yale University Press, 2003), 15.

3 The term "reading formation" is Tony Bennett's and describes the whole social network within which readers interpret texts, particularly popular texts. (Bennett, "Texts, Readers, Reading Formations." *Midwest Modern Language Association*. 16, no. 1 [Spring 1983]: 3–17.) Stanley Fish argues that readers do not approach books individually, but as readers of an "interpretive community": "Indeed, it is interpretive communities, rather than either the text or reader, that produce meanings." Stanley Fish, *Is There a Text in This Class?* (Cambridge: Harvard University Press, 1980), 14.

4 Emily Newell Blair, *Bridging Two Eras: The Autobiography of Emily Newell Blair, 1877–1951*, ed. Virginia Leans Laas (Columbia: University of Missouri Press, 1999), 140.

5 Blair, *Bridging Two Eras*, 141.

6 Emily Newell Blair, "Letters of a Contented Wife," *The American Magazine*, December 1910, 135.

7 Blair, "Contented Wife," 138.

8 Blair, *Bridging Two Eras*, 231.

9 Blair, *Bridging Two Eras*, 231.

10 Eleanore Bailey Johnson to Speakers Bureau, October 17, 1932, Emily Newell Blair Family Papers, Western Reserve Historical Society, Cleveland, OH. Also cited in Virginia Laas, "Reward for Party Service: Emily Newell Blair and Political Patronage in the New Deal," in *The Southern Elite and Social Change*, ed. Randy Finley and Thomas A. DeBlack (Fayetteville: The University of Arkansas Press, 2002), 123.

11 Blair, *Bridging Two Eras*, 307.

12 Blair, *Bridging Two Eras*, 308.

13 Blair, *Bridging Two Eras*, 308.

14 Blair, *Bridging Two Eras*, 309.

15 Blair, *Bridging Two Eras*, 308.

16 For more on this parallel, see the epilogue.

17 Emily Newell Blair, "When You Select Books for Men, Get a Man to Help You," *Good Housekeeping*, July 1930, 110.

18 Jessica Burstein, "A Few Words about Dubuque: Modernism, Sentimentalism, and the Blasé," *American Literary History* 14, no. 2 (2002): 239.

NOTES TO PAGES 78–87

19 "The New Yorker," *Time*, March 2, 1925, 18.

20 Emily Newell Blair, "Treasure-Trove," *Good Housekeeping*, June 1927, 92.

21 Blair, "Books That Count," *Good Housekeeping*, June 1928, 57.

22 Emily Newell Blair, "If You Are Looking for Friends," *Good Housekeeping*, September 1927, 51.

23 Emily Newell Blair, "Books for the Business Woman, From the Novel to the Newest Philosophy," *Good Housekeeping*, July 1929, 104.

24 Emily Newell Blair, "The Books Men Like," *Good Housekeeping*, March 1927, 51.

25 Emily Newell Blair, "Books to Buy and Keep," *Good Housekeeping*, April 1926, 51.

26 Emily Newell Blair, "From a Flood of Books, Emily Newell Blair Selects a Desirable Dozen," *Good Housekeeping*, August 1928, 59.

27 Similar to "haul" videos are "unboxing" videos focused on the appeal of toy and technology unboxing. See, e.g., Sharif Mowlabocus, "'Let's Get This Thing Open': The Pleasures of Unboxing Videos," *European Journal of Cultural Studies* 23, no. 4 (2020): 564–79.

28 Kate Kennedy, host, "Deep Dive: Mormon Mommy Blog Empires," Be There in Five (podcast), August 7 2019, https://www.bethereinfive.com/podcast/2019/8/7/70-deep-dive -mormon-mommy-blog-empires; Rob Fishman, quoted in Bianca Bosker, "Instamom: The Enviable, Highly Profitable Life of Amber Fillerup Clark, Perfect Mother and Social-Media Influencer," *Atlantic Monthly*, March 2017, https://www.theatlantic.com/magazine /archive/2017/03/instamom/513827/.

29 For the early history of the *New Yorker*, which was launched in 1925, see Mary F. Corey, *The World through a Monocle: "The New Yorker" at Midcentury* (Cambridge, MA: Harvard University Press, 1999), 5–6.

30 Anne Parrish, *The Perennial Bachelor* (New York: Harper and Brothers, 1925), 57.

31 Parrish, *Perennial Bachelor*, 228–29.

32 Parrish, *Perennial Bachelor*, 277.

33 Parrish, *Perennial Bachelor*, 281.

34 Parrish, *Perennial Bachelor*, 333.

35 Henry Longan Stuart, "Family Decadence and Tragedy the Theme of a Prize Novel," *New York Times*, September 6, 1925, BR9.

36 "Books," *New Yorker*, October 10, 1925, 18.

37 "Wins Harper Prize," *Chicago Daily News*, August 26, 1925, 18. A search of the Midwest and Western US databases in the Readex *America's Historical Newspapers* database reveals that versions of this article also appeared in the *Seattle Post-Intelligencer*, August 16, 1925, 19 (6M); *Milwaukee Journal*, August 21, 1925, 10; *Kansas City Star*, August 22, 1925, 6; *Dallas Morning News*, August 23, 1925, 27; *Sacramento Bee*, August 29, 1925, 37; *San Francisco Chronicle*, August 30, 1925, 42, and *Detroit News*, September 20, 1925, 30 (12M). These almost certainly were not the only papers to take advantage of this preproduced material, and many of them did also follow with original reviews of the novel, even sometimes in the same article as the press release language.

38 "Books," *New Yorker* October 10, 1925, 18.

39 "Another Study in Frustration of Human Hopes," *Sacramento Bee* August 29, 1925, 37 (5B).

40 "A Prize Deserved," *Times-Picayune* (New Orleans) October 4, 1925, 36 (B6).

41 H. A. Small, "Anne Parrish Flashes a Bright Mirror on Many Bygone Years," *San Francisco Chronicle*, August 30, 1925, 42 (4D).

42 Anne Cleeland, "A Parcel of Books," *Forum* 75, no. 5 (May 1926), 799.

NOTES TO PAGES 88–98

43 Cleeland. "A Parcel," 799.

44 These Westerns, and the degree to which they depart from the Western "formula," are discussed at length by Norris Yates in *Gender and Genre: An Introduction to Women Writers of Formula Westerns, 1900–1950* (Albuquerque: University of New Mexico Press, 1995).

45 See *Dallas Morning News*, November 15, 1925, 8.

46 "Winning of Oregon in a New Novel by Mrs. Morrow," *New York Times* October 25, 1925, BR8.

47 I am not alone in thinking that this is a stretch—Nina Baym directly contrasts Morrow's Whitman with another novel's "New Woman" heroine in *Women Writers of the American West, 1833–1927* (Urbana: University of Illinois Press, 2011), 54.

48 Baym, *Women Writers*, 55.

49 The *Kansas City Star*, which is one of the few reviews that mentioned Morrow's previous work by title, was also one of the few reviews to frame the text as a romance, its history "interwoven with the theme of a husband's fight to gain his wife's love." "Winning of Oregon, Bohemian Marriage, a Fight for Bread," *Kansas City Star*, November 7, 1925, 16.

50 "'We Must March' Is Chronicle of Oregon Heroine," *Chicago Daily Tribune*, December 5, 1925, 13.

51 See Amy L. Blair, *Reading Up: Middle-Class Readers and the Culture of Success in the Early Twentieth-Century United States* (Philadelphia, PA: Temple University Press, 2012).

52 Amusingly, but perhaps not surprisingly, Byron's makeover becomes the subject of a number of articles in contemporaneous periodicals, not all of which are tongue-in-cheek, the discuss the possibilities of such a plan for weight loss. See, e.g., Antoinette Donnelly, "Even 'Glorious Apollo' Occasionally Took Measures to Reduce," *Chicago Daily Tribune*, August 27, 1925, 18.

53 E. Barrington, *Glorious Apollo* (New York: Dodd, Mead and Company, 1925), 12.

54 Barrington, *Glorious Apollo*, 14.

55 E.g., Radway observes that her readers "do not apply the principles of organization of the fantasy world to their own nor do they learn how to get more from their own relationships through romance reading." Janice Radway, *Reading the Romance* (Chapel Hill: University of North Carolina Press, 1984), 186.

56 "The Editor Recommends: Lady Byron Rendered Divine—or Almost," *The Bookman* September 1925, 62.

57 Rachel Hope Cleves, "What Could Happen to Michael Jackson's Legacy? A Famed Writer's Fall Could Offer Clues." *TheConversation.com*, March 14, 2019. https://the conversation.com/what-will-happen-to-michael-jacksons-legacy-a-famed-writers-fall-could-offer-clues-113327. Evelyn Waugh, *Brideshead Revisited: The Sacred and Profane Memories of Captain Charles Ryder* (London: Chapman and Hall, 1949), 20. Graham Greene, "Norman Douglas," *Collected Essays* (New York: Viking, 1969), 363.

58 Dorothy G. Van Doren, "South Wind," *Forum*, June 1925, 927.

59 Van Doren, "South Wind," 927.

60 Advertisement, Modern Library, *New Yorker*, February 13, 1926, 2.

61 Elinor Wylie, *The Venetian Glass Nephew* (New York: George H. Doran Company, 1925), 92.

62 Wylie, *Venetian Glass Nephew*, 181.

63 "'Little Opera' Withdrawn: 'The Venetian Glass Nephew' Closes suddenly at the Vanderbilt." *New York Times* March 3, 1931, 41; Internet Broadway Database, "The Venetian Glass Nephew." https://www.ibdb.com/broadway-production/the-venetian-glass-nephew-11327.

NOTES TO PAGES 98–108

64 Advertisement, Reader's Club, *New York Times* July 15, 1945, 74.

65 Joseph Wood Krutch, "A Dream of Venice," *The Nation*, October 21, 1925, 465.

66 "Books," *New Yorker*, September 12, 1925, 23.

67 Harry Hansen, "Fippany Enters New York," *Chicago Daily News*, August 26, 1925, 18.

68 Grace Norman Tuttle, "Books and Writers," *Miami Herald*, September 20, 1925, 8H.

69 "Realism and Fancy," *The Bookman: A Review of Books and Life*, 42, no. 2 (October 1925), 206.

70 Barry Benefield, *The Chicken-Wagon Family* (New York: Century, 1925), 177.

71 Nicholas Syrett, *American Child Bride: A History of Minors and Marriage in the United States* (Chapel Hill: University of North Carolina Press, 2016), 170.

72 Melanie Dawson, *Edith Wharton and the Modern Privileges of Age* (Gainesville: University Press of Florida, 2020), 153.

73 The review of the *Chicken-Wagon Family* in the *Dallas Morning News* takes special notice of the Klan rally scene, commenting that "not a few Texas readers will be reminded of events of recent years in the recital of what the reporter saw on a certain evening in the Trinity River bottoms west of Dallas." "Pleasing Story has Some of Its Scenes in Dallas," *Dallas Morning News*, September 6, 1925.

74 Published in 1928, Edith Wharton's *The Children* also features a flirtation between an older man and a "child-woman," fifteen-year-old Judith Wheater. Despite the fact that *The Children* was a very popular novel, written by a Pulitzer Prize–winning author and a Book-of-the-Month Club selection, Blair never mentions it.

75 "A. E. Newton Dies; Book Collector, 76," *New York Times*, September 30, 1940, 23.

76 Florence Finch Kelly, "Bibles and Hymnals Also Lure the Collector," *New York Times*, September 20, 1925, BR5.

77 "Latest Works of Fiction," *New York Times*, April 29, 1923, BR 14.

78 Brian Bruce, "Thomas Boyd: Jazz Age Author and Editor," *Minnesota History* (Spring 1998): 2–17.

79 John Farrar, "Three Novels," *The Bookman* 60 (November 1924): 342.

80 *New York Times Book Review*, August 30, 1925, BR8.

81 For Fitzgerald's contempt for the novel of farm life, and his dramatic falling out with Boyd over *Samuel Drummond* and Boyd's reaction to *The Great Gatsby*, see Brian Bruce, *Thomas Boyd: Lost Author of the "Lost Generation"* (Akron, OH: University of Akron Press, 2006), 81–89.

82 Thomas Boyd, *Samuel Drummond* (New York: Charles Scribner's Sons, 1925), 19.

83 Herbert S. Gorman, "Peccadilloes of Samuel Pepys in a New Biography," *New York Times* (October 11, 1925), BR2.

84 *Richmond Palladium and Sun-Telegram*, October 24, 1925, 5.

85 "In Brief Review," *The Bookman; A Review of Books and Life* 62, no. 4 (December 1925), 510.

86 There was considerable concern that women on campus would distract men from their studies, but sexual licentiousness was not an element of these warnings, at least through the middle of the century. See, e.g., Lynn Dorothy Gordon, *Gender and Higher Education in the Progressive Era* (New Haven, CT: Yale University Press, 1990); Helen Lefkowitz Horowitz, *Campus Life: Undergraduate Cultures from the End of the Eighteenth Century to the Present* (Chicago: University of Chicago Press, 1987); Christine D. Myers, *University Coeducation in the Victorian Era: Inclusion in the United States and the United Kingdom* (New York: Palgrave Macmillan, 2010).

NOTES TO PAGES 108–117   229

87 J. Lucas-Dubreton, *Samuel Pepys: A Portrait in Miniature*, trans. H. F. Stenning (London: A. M. Philpot, Ltd.), 1925, 280.

88 Nicola Humble, *The Feminine Middlebrow Novel, 1920s to 1950s: Class, Domesticity, and Bohemianism* (New York: Oxford University Press, 2001), 13.

89 Humble, *Feminine Middlebrow Novel*, 11.

CHAPTER THREE

1 Emily Newell Blair, "Some Books Worth While, Selected for Good Housekeeping by a Woman Who Can Read between the Lines," *Good Housekeeping*, October 1926, 51.

2 Catherine Turner, *Marketing Modernism between the Two World Wars* (Amherst: University of Massachussetts Press, 2003), 13–14.

3 Seguin, *Around Quitting Time: Work and Middle-Class Fantasy in American Fiction* (Durham, NC: Duke University Press, 2001). 77; Raymond Williams, "When Was Modernism?," in *Culture and Politics*, ed. Phil O'Brien (London: Verso, 2022), 207.

4 Jessica Burstein, "A Few Words about Dubuque: Modernism, Sentimentalism, and the Blasé," *American Literary History* 14, no. 2 (2002): 239.

5 Emily Newell Blair to Frances Parkinson Keyes, February 25, 1925. Emily Newell Blair Family Papers, Western Reserve Historical Society, Cleveland, OH.

6 "Tell Me a Book to Read," *New Yorker*, November 7, 1925, 35.

7 Herschel Brickell, "An Armful of Fiction," *The Bookman* 57, no. 3 (November 1925): 337–40.

8 "Among the New Books," *Life*, September 24, 1925, 35.

9 "Sherwood Anderson Contemplates Life on the Levee," *New York Times Book Review*, September 20, 1925, 43.

10 "Anderson Contemplates," 4.

11 Turner, *Marketing Modernism*, 13–14.

12 "Sherwood Anderson Stumbles along the River, Still Groping," *Kansas City Star* (Kansas City, MO), October 25, 1925, 6.

13 "If You Ask Us," *Kansas City Star* (Kansas City, MO), October 3, 1925, 6.

14 "Sherwood Anderson Is Disappointing in His Much-Heralded New Novel," *Dallas Morning News*, September 27, 1925, 11.

15 "Sherwood Anderson Is Disappointing," 11.

16 "Literature—and Less," *Times-Picayune* (New Orleans), September 27, 1925, 97.

17 Walter B. Rideout, *Sherwood Anderson: A Writer in America, Volume 1* (Madison: University of Wisconsin Press, 2006), 540.

18 Rideout, *Sherwood Anderson*, 584–85.

19 Sherwood Anderson, *Dark Laughter* (New York: Liveright, 1970), 305. Subsequent references cited parenthetically in text as *DL* and page number.

20 Rose Wilder Lane did indeed tell a story like this to a large audience at a Parisian garden party Anderson attended in the early 1920s, but she was nonetheless distressed when it became one of the most infamous moments in Anderson's novel. See William Holz, "Sherwood Anderson and Rose Wilder Lane: Source and Method in 'Dark Laughter,'" *Journal of Modern Literature* 12, no. 1 (March 1985), 131–52; Caroline Frasier, *Prairie Fires: The American Dreams of Laura Ingalls Wilder* (New York: Picador, 2017), 307–8.

21 See, e.g., Julie Taylor's discussion of *Dark Laughter* and *Nigger Heaven* as modernist primitivism against which Toomer writes in *Cane*. "Animating *Cane*: Race, Affect, History and

230 NOTES TO PAGES 117–135

Jean Toomer," in *Modernism and Affect*, ed. Julie Taylor (Edinburgh: Edinburgh University Press, 2015), 131–47.

22 Emily Newell Blair, "Tasting and Testing Books," *Good Housekeeping*, May 1926, 260.

23 Jaime Harker, *America the Middlebrow: Women's Novels, Progressivism, and Middlebrow Authorship between the Wars* (Amherst: University of Massachusetts Press, 2007), 65.

24 Blair, May 1926, 259.

25 Janis P. Stout, "Dorothy Canfield, Willa Cather, and the Uncertainties of Middlebrow and Highbrow, *Studies in the Novel* 44, no. 1 (Spring 2012): 27–48.

26 Janis P. Stout, "Modernist by Association: Willa Cather's New York / New Mexico Circle," *American Literary Realism* 47, no. 2 (Winter 2015): 117–35.

27 Stout, "Dorothy Canfield," 29.

28 "Willa Cather's 'Professor's House' among new Novels," *New York Times* September 6, 1925, BR8.

29 Leonard Baird, "Life and Letters," *Life*, October 1, 1925, 22.

30 "Among the New Books," *Life*, September 24, 1925, 35.

31 Schuyler Ashley, "Willa Cather's Professor Is a Living Character," *Kansas City Star* (October 3, 1925), 6.

32 "Books," *New Yorker*, September 19, 1925, 21.

33 "Tell Me A Book to Read," *New Yorker*, November 7, 1925, 35.

34 Herschel Brickell, "An Armful of Fiction," *The Bookman* 57, no. 3 (November 1925), 339.

35 Jennifer L. Bradley, "To Entertain, To Educate, To Elevate: Cather and the Commodification of Manners at the *Home Monthly*," in *Willa Cather and Material Culture: Real-World Writing, Writing the Real World* (Tuscaloosa: University of Alabama Press, 2005), 37.

36 Peter Benson, "Willa Cather at 'Home Monthly,'" *Biography* 4, no. 3 (Summer 1981), 227–48.

37 Bradley, "To Entertain," 41.

38 Willa Cather, *The Professor's House*, ed. Frederick M. Link (Lincoln: University of Nebraska Press, 2002), 12. All subsequent references cited parenthetically as *PH* and page number.

39 Charles Johanningsmeier, "Determining How Readers Responded to Cather's Fiction: The Cultural Work of *The Professor's House* in *Collier's Weekly*," *American Periodicals* 20, no. 1 (2010): 70–71.

40 Johanningsmeier, "Determining," 71.

41 Blair, January 1929, 180.

42 Blair, January 1929, 180.

43 May Lamberton Becker, "The Reader's Guide," *Saturday Review of Literature*, December 10, 1927, 445.

44 Becker, December 10, 1927, 445.

45 Vera Connolly, "The Cry of a Broken People," *Good Housekeeping*, February 1929, 31.

46 Connolly, "The Cry," 31.

47 Connolly, "The Cry," 231.

48 Connolly, "The Cry," 234.

49 Vera Connolly, "'We Still Get Robbed,'" *Good Housekeeping*, March 1929, 34.

50 See Chap. 2, page <<tk>>.

51 Emily Newell Blair, "Treasure-Trove," *Good Housekeeping*, June 1927, 92.

52 Richard Lingeman, *Sinclair Lewis: Rebel from Main Street* (St. Paul, MN: Borealis Books, 2002), 300.

NOTES TO PAGES 135–147

53 Lingemann, *Sinclair Lewis*, 301.

54 Blair, June 1927, 240.

55 Blair, June 1927, 92.

56 The debates over Carol were indeed heated when the novel appeared in 1920–21. For more see Amy L. Blair, "Main Street reading *Main Street*," in *New Directions in American Reception Study*, ed. Philip Goldstein and James L. Machor (New York: Oxford University Press, 2008), 139–58.

57 Rubin, *The Making of Middlebrow Culture*, 74.

58 Blair, June 1927, 240.

59 Blair, June 1927, 241.

60 Blair, June 1927, 242–43.

61 Blair, June 1927, 244.

62 Blair, June 1927, 244.

63 Blair, October 1926, 51.

64 Blair, October 1926, 51.

65 Blair, October 1926, 156.

66 Emily Newell Blair, "Books of Escape," *Good Housekeeping*, February 1928, 51.

67 Emily Newell Blair, "Books That Extend Life," *Good Housekeeping*, July 1928, 102.

68 Blair, July 1928, 102.

69 "The Editor Recommends," *The Bookman*, February 1926, 62.

70 Charles R. Walker, "Dreiser Moves Upward," *The Independent*, February 6, 1926.

71 Blair, October 1926, 159.

72 Blair, October 1926, 160.

73 The secondary literature on sentimentality is vast; the most thorough and succinct overview remains June Howard, "What Is Sentimentality?" *American Literary History* 11, no. 1 (Spring 1999): 63–81.

74 Brigette Nicole Fielder, "Animal Humanism: Race, Species, and Affective Kinship in Nineteenth-Century Abolitionism," *American Quarterly* 65, no. 3 (September 2013): 487–514.

75 Blair, October 1926, 160.

76 Elizabeth A. Drew, *The Modern Novel: Some Aspects of Contemporary Fiction* (New York: Harcourt, Brace 1926), 146, 147.

77 Drew, *The Modern Novel*, 144, 147.

78 Drew, *The Modern Novel*, 143.

79 Douglas Mao, *Solid Objects: Modernism and the Test of Production* (Princeton, NJ: Princeton University Press, 1998), 4.

CHAPTER FOUR

1 Emily Newell Blair, "A Road Log of New Books, by a Woman Who Knows the Country of Which She Writes," July 1926, 220.

2 Emily Newell Blair, "Emily Newell Blair Chooses a Hamper of Books for Frances Parkinson Keyes—and Other Travelers Too," *Good Housekeeping*, May 1929, 98.

3 Emily Newell Blair (ENB) to Frances Parkinson Keyes (FPK), June 26, 1919, Frances Parkinson Keyes Collection, Silver Special Collections Library, University of Vermont, Burlington, VT (hereafter FPKC).

NOTES TO PAGES 148–161

4 W. F. Bigelow, "William Frederick Bigelow to FPK, March 18, 1920." *Omeka@CTL*, http://ctl.w3.uvm.edu/omeka/items/show/1338.

5 FPK to ENB, January 25, 1925, B4:F6, Emily Newell Blair Family Papers, Western Reserve Historical Society, Cleveland, OH. (All subsequent items from this box and collection designated "ENBFP.")

6 ENB to FPK, February 25, 1925, FBKC.

7 ENB to Harry Blair, February 2, 1925, ENBFP.

8 FPK to ENB, March 7, 1926, ENBFP. In Keyes's letter to Bigelow cited above, she did suggest that Blair replace "Miss Toombs," but Toombs had been a political correspondent in the early 1920s, *not* a reading advisor. This does not mean that Keyes's approach didn't shift as her conversations with Bigelow progressed, but there is no documentary evidence that it did.

9 ENB to FPK, April 9, 1926, ENBFP.

10 Frances Parkinson Keyes, "Homes of Outstanding American Women," *Better Homes and Gardens*, February 1928, 73.

11 FPK to ENB, November 18, 1927, ENBFP.

12 FPK to ENB, February 12, 1928, ENBFP.

13 ENB to FPK, February 16, 1928, ENBFP.

14 ENB to FPK, May 15, 1928, ENBFP.

15 Frances Parkinson Keyes, "Seven Successful Women Who Command Important Parts in Washington Political Life," *Delineator*, July 1928, 83.

16 ENB to FPK, July 26, 1928, FPKC.

17 ENB to FPK, April 9, 1926, ENBFP.

18 *Good Housekeeping: The Shortest Route to the National Market* (New York: International Magazine Company, 1928), 8.

19 ENB to FPK, November 9, 1928, FPKC. Sadly, this letter has the following written in pencil at the top: "Other Blair correspondence destroyed as unimportant." Blair's practice of making and retaining carbon copies of her correspondence, fortunately, seems to have mitigated a good portion of that loss.

20 FPK to ENB, November 17, 1928, ENBFP.

21 ENB to FPK, December 21, 1928, ENBFP.

22 Blair, May 1929, 175.

23 Blair, May 1929, 176.

24 ENB to FPK, June 4, 1929, ENBFP.

25 FPK to ENB, July 3, 1929, ENBFP.

26 FPK to ENB, July 3, 1929, ENBFP.

27 Blair, May 1929, 176.

28 Rebecca West, "The Strange Necessity," in *The Strange Necessity: Essays and Reviews* (London: Virago, 1987), 69. Subsequent references parenthetical in text as *SN* and page number.

29 Laura Heffernan, "Reading Modernism's Cultural Field: Rebecca West's *The Strange Necessity* and the Aesthetic 'System of Relations,'" *Tulsa Studies in Women's Literature* 27, no. 2 (Fall 2008): 317, 319.

30 Virginia Woolf, *A Room of One's Own* (New York: Harvest, 1981), 35.

31 Heffernan, "Reading Modernism's Cultural Field," 320.

32 Rebecca West to Richard Ellman, November 7, 1958, *Selected Letters of Rebecca West*, ed. Bonnie Kime Scott (New Haven, CT: Yale, 2000), 327.

33 Heffernan, "Reading Modernism's Cultural Field," 322.

NOTES TO PAGES 161–173

34 Blair, May 1929, 176.

35 Blair, May 1929, 176.

36 Blair, May 1929, 176.

37 Michel de Certeau, *The Practice of Everyday Life*, trans. Steven Rendall (Berkeley: University of California Press, 1984), 166.

38 Blair, May 1929, 178.

39 Jeanne Dubino, "Introduction," in *Virginia Woolf and the Literary Marketplace*, ed. Jeanne Dubino (New York: Palgrave MacMillan, 2010).

40 Blair, May 1929, 178.

41 Blair, May 1929, 178.

42 Janice Radway, *A Feeling for Books: The Book-of-the-Month Club, Literary Taste, and Middle-Class Desire* (Chapel Hill: University of North Carolina Press, 1997), 178.

43 Radway, *A Feeling for Books*, 261.

44 Emily Newell Blair, "From a Flood of Books . . . ," *Good Housekeeping*, August 1928, 181.

45 Blair, August 1928, 181–82.

46 Henry Seidel Canby, "Orlando, a Biography" [Review of Virginia Woolf's *Orlando*], *Saturday Review of Literature*, November 3, 1928, 314.

47 Rebecca West, "High Fountain of Genius," in *The Gender of Modernism: A Critical Anthology*, ed. Bonnie Kime Scott (Bloomington: Indiana University Press, 1990), 594. While the passage Blair cites is indeed a part of West's review, it does not necessarily summarize it; West is also concerned in this review with thinking about Woolf's stature as an author of the first rank, akin in contemporary terms to Keats or Shelley in their own time, and with asserting that Woolf's work is as formally resonant as poetry.

48 Blair, May 1929, 178.

49 Dubino, "Introduction," 9.

50 Quoted by Beth Rigel Daugherty, "Reading, Taking Notes, and Writing: Virginia Stephen's Reviewing Practice," in *Virginia Woolf and the Literary Marketplace*, ed. Jeanne Dubino (New York: Palgrave MacMillan, 2010).

51 J. B. Priestley, cited in Melba Cuddy-Keane, *Virginia Woolf, The Intellectual, and the Public Sphere* (New York: Cambridge University Press, 2003), 24.

52 Cuddy-Keane, *Virginia Woolf, the Intellectual*, 24–25.

53 Virginia Woolf, "Middlebrow," in *The Death of the Moth* (New York: Harcourt, Brace, 1942), 180.

54 Woolf, "Middlebrow," 184.

55 Canby, "Orlando, a Biography," 314.

56 Woolf, "Middlebrow," 185.

57 Virginia Woolf, *Orlando* (New York: Harcourt Brace, 2006), 66.

58 ENB to FPK, May 27, 1930, ENBFP.

59 ENB to FPK, May 29, 1931, ENBFP.

CHAPTER FIVE

1 Emily Newell Blair, "The Contagion of Books: Emily Newell Blair Suggests Exposing All Children to the Best Books—So That They Will Be Immune to the Effects of Bad Ones," *Good Housekeeping*, November 1927, 30.

2 The first advertisement is published in the February 1929 issue, explaining that Fitzgerald qualifies to be on this panel with John Barrymore and Cornelius Vanderbilt Jr., "because,

234   NOTES TO PAGES 173–183

as the most brilliant of America's younger novelists, he was the first to discover and portray an enchanting new type of American girl. Because, at the age of 23, he woke up to
find himself famous as the author of *This Side of Paradise*. Because no other man of his
time writes so sympathetically, skilfully, and fascinatingly about women." Advertisement,
Woodbury Soap, *Good Housekeeping*, February 1929, 103. Advertisements followed
monthly with the names of the "winners," from March through November 1929.

3   Bryant Mangum speculates that the generally poor reception of Fitzgerald's short story
collections by "contemporary critics" was due to their being compilations of stories that
previously appeared in in "slick popular magazines that had paid Fitzgerald handsomely
for his contributions . . . frequently damning individual stories as potboilers." He continues, "And though the contemporary reception of *All the Sad Young Men* was much more
favorable than that of any preceding Fitzgerald short story volume, the litany of such
phrases as 'uneven,' 'popular magazine fiction,' and 'money-making' continued to appear,"
even though "Fitzgerald had taken pains to exclude his most popular stories from the
volume." "The Short Stories of F. Scott Fitzgerald," in *The Cambridge Companion to F.
Scott Fitzgerald*, ed. Ruth Prigozy (Cambridge: Cambridge University Press, 2002), 58.

4   Mangum, "The Short Stories," 70.

5   James L. W. West, "Introduction," in F. Scott Fitzgerald, *All the Sad Young Men* (Cambridge: Cambridge University Press, 2007), xiv.

6   See the introduction.

7   Maureen Corrigan, *So We Read On: How "The Great Gatsby" Came to Be and Why It
Endures* (New York: Little, Brown and Company, 2014), 203.

8   Emily Newell Blair, "Why I Like Books and Some of the Books I Like," *Good Housekeeping*, February 1927, 188.

9   Blair, February 1927, 189.

10   See, e.g., John A. Scott, "The Parting of Hector and Andromache," *Classical Journal* 9, no.
6 (March 1914): 274.

11   Christine A. Jenkins, "The History of Youth Services Librarianship: A Review of the
Research Literature," *Libraries and Culture* 35, no. 1 (Winter 2000): 112.

12   Emily Newell Blair, "The Companionship of Books: Emily Newell Blair Recommends
Books That Will Be Worth-while Friends for Your Children," *Good Housekeeping*,
November 1926, 51. Subsequent references parenthetical in text.

13   Kate McDowell, "Which Truth, What Fiction? Librarians' Book Recommendations for
Children, 1876–1890," *Education and the Culture of Print in Modern America*, ed. John
L. Rudolph and Adam R. Nelson (Amherst: University of Massachusetts Press, 2010),
15–35.

14   Carleton Washburne and Mabel Vogel, *What Children Liked to Read: Winnetka Graded
Book List* (New York: Rand McNally & Company, 1926), 5–6. Subsequent references
parenthetical as *WGBL* and page in text.

15   "The time period from 1890 to 1930 in the United States saw major growth in the production of children's literature. Children's literature grew from a small part of many publisher's wares to a major market force. . . . In public libraries, this surge of publishing was met
with the establishment of collections, rooms, and then departments devoted specifically
to youth services." Kate McDowell, "Toward a History of Children as Readers, 1890–
1930," *Book History* 12 (2009): 242.

16   McDowell "Toward a History," 242.

17   Many thanks to Betty Carbol of the Winnetka Public Schools, who enthusiastically

NOTES TO PAGES 184–197

embraced the project (as a former elementary school student of Mabel Vogel's!) and searched fruitlessly for these ballots.

18 "Book Reviews and Notices," *Southwestern Historical Quarterly* 16 (1913): 437.

19 Kate McDowell, "Children's Voices in Librarian's Words, 1890–1930," *Libraries and the Cultural Record* 46, no. 1 (2011): 81.

20 James L. Machor, *The Mercurial Mark Twain(s): Reception History, Audience Engagement, and Iconic Authorship* (New York: Routledge, 2023), 116. Beverly Lyon Clark notes that in the early years of the twentieth century, *Tom Sawyer* and *Huckleberry Finn* were still "tenuously yoked" together as children's literature but that by the 1920s "most critics agreed to classify *Tom Sawyer* as children's literature in order to separate it from *Huckleberry Finn* and extol the true greatness of the latter." Beverly Lyon Clark, *Kiddie Lit: The Cultural Construction of Children's Literature in America* (Baltimore: Johns Hopkins University Press, 2003), 90. Machor traces the critical reception of both books through the 1920s, finding in that decade the beginning of the "hypercanonization" of *Huckleberry Finn*, its ascendence into the high school and university classroom, and the critical consensus that it is a particularly great, and particularly "American," novel. Machor, *Mercurial*, 19–130.

21 Mark Twain, *The Adventures of Tom Sawyer* (New York: Penguin, 2014), 212.

22 McDowell, "Toward a History," 250.

23 Beverly Lyon Clark, *The Afterlife of "Little Women"* (Baltimore: Johns Hopkins University Press, 2014), 96, 101.

24 Clark, *The Afterlife*, 101.

25 The introduction first explains that *Huckleberry Finn* was "rated 1 by eight librarians, 2 by two librarians, 3 by one librarian, and 4 by one" and then says that "one librarian" considered it "trashy." Both 3 and 4 were rankings that would have excluded the book had they been given by a majority of librarians (*WGBL* 44).

26 Machor, *Mercurial*, 63–65.

27 Carleton Washburn and Mabel Vogel, "Supplement to the Winnetka Graded Book List (Concluded)," *Elementary English Review* 4, no. 3 (March 1927): 69.

28 Bertha Hatch and Annie Spencer Cutter, "Notes on the Winnetka Supplement," *Elementary English Review* 4, no. 2 (February 1927): 53.

29 McDowel, "Which Truth?," 18.

30 "Editorial: Why Study the Winnetka Experiment?," *Elementary English Review* 4, no. 2 (February 1927): 55.

31 "Why Study The Winnetka Experiment?," 55.

32 Harriet A. Wood, "The Winnetka Book List," *Library Journal* 51, no. 2 (January 15, 1926): 83.

33 Louise P. Latimer et al., "The Winnetka Graded Book List," *Library Journal* 51, no. 7 (April 1, 1926): 315.

34 Latimer et al., "The Winnetka Graded Book List," 317.

35 Latimer et al., "The Winnetka Graded Book List," 317.

36 Latimer et al., "The Winnetka Graded Book List," 318.

37 "The Winnetka Graded Book List: The Compilers Reply to Its Critics," *Library Journal* 51, no. 8 (April 15, 1926): 378.

38 Susan J. Matt, *Keeping Up with the Joneses: Envy in Consumer Society, 1890–1930* (Philadelphia: University of Pennsylvania Press, 2003), 173.

39 Emily Newell Blair, "Books for Your Vacation," *Good Housekeeping*, June 1926, 31.

40 F. Scott Fitzgerald, *The Great Gatsby* (New York: Norton, 2022), 32–33.

236   NOTES TO PAGES 198–206

41 Emily Newell Blair, "Emily Newell Blair Suggests Book to Buy for the Children," *Good Housekeeping*, November 1930, 132.

EPILOGUE

1 Blair, February 1927, 186.
2 Emily Newell Blair, *Bridging Two Eras: The Autobiography of Emily Newell Blair, 1877–1951*, ed. Virginia Leans Laas (Columbia: University of Missouri Press, 1999), 331.
3 As I mention in 216, n7, *Good Housekeeping*'s Contents page never reproduced the lengthy subtitles of Blair's columns.
4 Emily Newell Blair, "When Do You Read?" *Good Housekeeping*, January 1931, 96.
5 Emily Newell Blair, "Books—and Books: Reviewed Just as They Came," *Good Housekeeping*, February 1931, 94.
6 Blair, June 1928, 57.
7 Blair, June 1928, 197.
8 Blair, June 1928, 197–98.
9 Blair, June 1928, 198.
10 Blair, June 1928, 198.
11 Blair, June 1930, 50; see the introduction, this volume.
12 Blair, January 1929, 43.
13 Blair, June 1929, 67.
14 Blair, February 1927, 51.
15 Blair, February 1927, 51.
16 Blair, February 1927, 186.
17 Blair, February 1931, 94.
18 See for example Brooke Erin Duffy, *(Not) Getting Paid to Do What You Love: Gender, Social Media, and Aspirational Work* (New Haven, CT: Yale University Press, 2017; Crystal Abadin, "#familygoals: Family Influencers, Calibrated Amateurism, and Justifying Young Digital Labor," *Social Media + Society* 3, no. 2 (April-June 2017): 1–15.
19 Blair, *Bridging Two Eras*, 329.
20 Blair, *Bridging Two Eras*, 346.
21 Blair, *Bridging Two Eras*, 346–47.
22 William Frederick Bigelow, "The Wages of Labor," *Good Housekeeping*, May 1933, 4.
23 Amy L. Blair, "The Middle Class," in *American Literature in Translation: 1930–1940*, ed. Ichiro Takayoshi (Cambridge: Cambridge University Press, 2018), 27.
24 A. Blair, "The Middle Class," 27.
25 Franklin Delano Roosevelt was inaugurated in March 1933; by May 1933 New Deal reforms such as the Emergency Banking Act and the establishment of the Civilian Conservation Corps were already in place. May would see the creation of the Federal Emergency Relief Administration and the Tennessee Valley Authority, as well as the passage of the National Industrial Recovery Act. If *Good Housekeeping*'s production schedule in 1933 remained consistent with the schedule in 1929, Blair and Bigelow were both probably writing their columns in early April.
26 Ichiro Takeyoshi, "Introduction," in *American Literature in Transition, 1930–1940*, ed. Ichiro Takeyoshi, 1–24 (Cambridge: Cambridge University Press, 2018), offers a poetic, concise, detailed, and complex overview of this profoundly "transitional" moment.

NOTES TO PAGES 207–211   237

27 Wai Chee Dimock and Michael Gilmore, "Introduction," in *Rethinking Class: Literary Studies and Social Formations* (New York: Columbia University Press, 1994), 3.

28 Burton J. Bledstein, "Introduction," in *The Middling Sorts: Explorations in the History of the American Working Class* (New York: Routledge, 2001), 3.

29 Robert S. Lynd and Helen Merrell Lynd, *Middletown in Transition* (New York: Harcourt Brace Jovanovich, 1937), 17.

30 Lynd and Lynd, *Middletown in Transition*, 16.

31 Jennifer Parchesky, "Melodramas of Everyday Life: 1920s Popular Fictions and the Making of Middle America." PhD diss., Duke University, Durham, NC, 5.

32 Robert Seguin, *Around Quitting Time: Work and Middle-Class Fantasy in American Fiction* (Durham, NC: Duke University Press, 2001), 3–4.

33 Harker, *America the Middlebrow: Women's Novels, Progressivism, and Middlebrow Authorship between the Wars* (Amherst: University of Massachusetts Press, 2007), 20.

34 Emily Newell Blair, "Emily Newell Blair Names Some Books as Trouble Antidotes," *Good Housekeeping*, May 1933, 96.

35 Blair, May 1933, 90.

36 Blair, May 1933, 90.

37 Gordon Hutner, *What America Read: Taste, Class, and the Novel, 1920–1960* (Chapel Hill: University of North Carolina Press, 2009), 135.

38 Harry Salpeter, "Fannie Hurst: Sob-Sister of American Fiction," *The Bookman* 73 (August 1931), 612, 613.

39 Lori Harrison-Kahan, *The White Negress: Literature, Minstrelsy, and the Black-Jewish Imaginary* (New Brunswick, NJ: Rutgers University Press, 2011), 123; citing "Business Woman," *New York Times Book Review*, February 5, 1933, 7. I am indebted to Harrison-Kahan's reading of *Imitation of Life*, as well as her detailed treatment of the various stages of its reception as novel, then as a 1934 film adaptation, as adapted in 1959 by Douglas Sirk, and finally the resurgence of academic interest in Hurst, both as an author and as an activist with close ties to Zora Neale Hurston.

40 Emily Newell Blair, "Emily Newell Blair Discusses Some Distinctive Books of 1933–1934," *Good Housekeeping*, August 1934, 96.

41 Blair, August 1934, 96.

42 Blair, August 1934, 181.

43 Harker, *America the Middlebrow*, 61.

44 Harker, *America the Middlebrow*, 65.

45 Blair, "Tasting and Testing Books," *Good Housekeeping*, May 1926, 259.

46 Blair, May 1926, 259.

47 Susan Millar Williams, "'Something to Feel About': Zora Neale Hurston and Julia Peterkin in Africa Town," *Mississippi Quarterly* 63, nos. 1–2 (Winter-Spring 2010): 291.

48 I am not qualified to weigh in on the accuracy or inaccuracy of these assumptions, but Melissa L. Cooper is, and in her *Making Gullah: A History of Sapelo Islander, Race, and the American Imagination* (Chapel Hill: University of North Carolina Press, 2017) she registers "shock" that William R. Bascom, eventual president of the American Folklore Society and the first American anthropologist to undertake fieldwork with the Yoruba, cites *Black April* as evidence in a 1941 essay, "Acculturation among the Gullah Negroes." *American Anthropologist* 43, no. 1 (1941): 43–50. That he does so is, for Cooper, "even more shocking" than his citation of Mary Granger's *empirically* inaccurate FWP-sponsored *Drums and Shadows*. Bascom's PhD advisor, Melville Herskovits, had declined to endorse *Drums and*

238   NOTES TO PAGES 211–213

Shadows less than three years earlier, in September 1938, so his citation of that work was bad enough, but in declining the endorsement Herskovits was specifically "troubled by the fact that [Granger] had allowed popular writers like Julia Peterkin . . . to stand in for the research that "real" anthropologists conducted on African culture. On this he wrote: 'I would suggest that your bibliography be radically excised of a great many of the popular and semi-popular works of which it is composed.'" Cooper 149, citing Herskovits to Granger, September 12, 1938, Series 35/6, box 8, folder 10, Melville J. Herskovits Library of African Studies, Northwestern University, Evanston, IL, Melville Herskovits Papers.

49 Charles McD. Puckette, "On a Carolina Plantation," *Saturday Review of Literature*, March 19, 1927, 660.

50 "Bumper Product," *Time Magazine*, April 4, 1927, 47.

51 John W. Crawford, "Hound-Dogs and Bible Shouting," *New York Times*, March 6, 1927, 38.

52 "New Books in Brief Review: *Black April* by Julia Peterkin," *The Independent*, May 21, 1927, 544.

53 For the full, complex reception history of Hurston's work as a whole and *Jonah's Gourd Vine* in particular, see M. Genevieve West, *Zora Neale Hurston and American Literary Culture* (Gainesville: University Press of Florida, 2005).

54 "Our Own Four Walls: A Meeting Place for Good Housekeeping's Friends," *Good Housekeeping* (May 1930), 101.

55 Herschel Brickell, "The Editor Recommends," *The Bookman: A Review of Books and Life* (May 1927), 337.

56 Emily Newell Blair, "Pleasant Books Are Books Worth Reading When Recommended by Emily Newell Blair," *Good Housekeeping*, May 1930, 84.

57 Blair, May 1930, 84.

58 Virginia Jeans Laas, "Introduction," in Blair, *Bridging Two Eras*, xvi.

59 Blair, *Bridging Two Eras*, 354.

Index

Note: *Page numbers in italics indicate figures.*

the academy, 167–68
Addison, Joseph, 170
advertised products
  Battle Creek Health Builder, 127, *127*
  Chambers Fireless Gas Range, 35
  Chambers Range, 67
  Nujol, 36, 40–41, 223n43
  Old Dutch Cleanser, 34–35, 67
  testing of, 33
  Woodbury soap, 32, 233–34n2
advertisers, monthly index of, 32–33
advertising content, 11, 14, 24, 26, 34, 66. *See also* advertised products
  in "Big Six" women's magazines, 32
  fearmongering and, 36, 40–41
  index of, in *Good Housekeeping*, 32–33
  market surveys and, 29–31
  stylistic overlap with editorial copy, 32
  trusting in, 31–36
advice, 32, 36, 37, 45–46
  cooking advice, 40–47
  domestic advice, 37, 41
  lifestyle advice, 47–48
  spiritual advice, 49–51
Alcott, Louisa May, *Little Women*, 84, 182, 187–89, 191
Aldrich, Bess Streeter, 220n53
American Construction Council, 37
American Library Association, 22
  "Reading with a Purpose" pamphlet series, 128
  Winnetka Graded Book List and, 178, 179, 180–81, 193
The American Magazine, 222n21
  circulation of, 28
  Blair in, 73–74
Anderson, Sherwood, 17, 99, 108, 109, 112, 142

Dark Laughter, 110, 111–33, 137, 143, 229n20
  literary modernism and, 117
  parody of Rose Wilder Lane, 116–17
  primitivism of, 117
  reviews of, 114–15
Ashley, Schuyler, 115, 119, 230n31
Atlantic Monthly, 146–7, 226n28
Austen, Jane, 84, 86, 194
autobiographical writing, 51–55. *See also specific authors*

Bailey, Temple, 1
  The Blue Window, 57–58, 60
Banister, Margaret, 78–79, 134–35, 137
Barrington, E., 112
  Glorious Apollo, 93–95, 107, 113
Barrymore, John, 32, 233–34n2
Barton, Bruce, 1, 66, 67, 216n6
  "Do Too Many People Marry?," 49–51
  The Man Nobody Knows, 49, 216n6
Bascom, William R., 237–38n48
Baym, Nina, 89
BBC Radio, 168
Becker, May Lamberton, 18, 129
Beckett, Samuel, 158
Beecher, Catherine, 41
Beer, Thomas, *The Road to Heaven*, 165
Benefield, Barry, *The Chicken-Wagon Family*, 99–100, 106, 108–9, 118, 228n73
Bennett, Arnold, 15, 91
  Literary Taste and How to Form It, 170
Bennett, Tony, 225n3
Better Homes and Gardens, xii–xiv, 150–1
Bibesco, Marthe, *Catherine-Paris*, 165
Bigelow, William Frederick, 25, 30–1, 47, 75, 112, 146-148, 152, 155–6, 172, 224n58, 232n8, 236n25

240 INDEX

editorial style, 30–1, 55–6, 75, 147, 156
perception of *GH* audience, 25, 30–1, 224n61
"The Wages of Labor," 205–8
"big magazines," 5, 10–1, 18
"Big Six" women's magazines, 1, 5, 11, 25, 26, 32, 56, 222n27. *See also specific titles*
biographical writing, 54–55. *See also specific authors*
Black subjects, representation of, 48–9, 210–12
Blair, Emily Newell, xv, 40, 46, 75, 195–96. *See also* Blair, Emily Newell, columns of; Blair, Emily Newell, works of
  as advice columnist, 71–72
  background of, 72–81
  compared to influencers, 81
  disagreement with critics, 18–19
  domesticity of, 12
  as editor of *Missouri Woman*, 146
  family of, 77
  FDR and, 72, 213
  growing impatience with questions, 198–200
  at her desk, 80, *80*
  "inoculation" trope and, 22, 175, 195–96
  in Joplin, Missouri, 69, 70, 71, 72, 79, 82, 162, 198–99, 204
  Keyes and, 51, 145–47, 148, 151, 152–56
  employment by *GH*, 5, 212–13
  lectures by, 75, 199, 202–4
  literary modernism and, 142, 143–72, 174
  middlebrow sensibilities and, 11, 18–21, 169
  midwesternness of, 11, 12, 78, 82, 110–42
  as national vice chairperson of the Democratic Party, 72, 199
  political activity and, 46, 72–76, 148, 150, 151, 154, 204–5, 212–13
  readers and, 4, 5, 9, 12, 18–21, 72–73, 82, 87, 162–63
  reading courses and, 126, 128
  recommendations of, 18–23, 70–72, 82, 83–109, 110, 111, 119, 120, 140, 156–67, 175–77, 201, 208–9 (*see also* Blair, Emily Newell, columns of; *specific authors*)
  relationship with *GH* editors, 75, 112, 146–56, 172, 198

similarity to her readers, 72–73, 77–78, 82
skepticism about prescription, 20–21
vicarious reading and, 139–40
women's study club and, 69–71, 72, 79, 81, 82
women's suffrage and, 74
Blair, Emily Newell, columns of, 2–5, 220n54
  absence of April 1931 column, 172
  April 1926, 80 *80*
  August 1928, 80–81, 165
  August 1930, 117
  August 1934, 198, 209–13
  children's literature columns, 175–77
  February 1926, 24, 69–72, 77, 81–109, 110–113, 118, 119, 173, 175, 198
  February 1927, 174, 198, 201–3
  February 1928, 139
  February 1931, 200, 203–4
  January 1927, 12, 14–15, 18
  January 1928, 2–3, *3*, 11, 19–21, 216n7
  January 1929, 126–30, 170, 202
  January 1931, xi, 199
  June 1926, 195–6
  June 1927, 78–9, 134–7
  June 1928, 200–2
  June 1929, 202
  June 1930, 77, 202
  July 1926, 5, 143
  July 1928, 139
  July 1929, 79
  July 1930, 77
  July 1931, 79
  March 1927, 79
  May 1926, 210–12
  May 1929, "A Hamper of Books," 79, 144–56, *153*
  May 1930, 212
  May 1931, 79
  May 1933, "Books as Trouble Antidotes," 205, 206, 207–9
  November 1926, 175–77, 193–97
  November 1927, 173, 175
  November 1930, 196–97
  October 1926, 110, 117, 137–142
  September 1927, 79
  Tasting and Testing Books title, 4
  use of representative biography in, 55

INDEX

Blair, Emily Newell, works of. *See also* Blair, Emily Newell, columns of
  Bridging Two Eras, 72–73, 75, 76–77, 82, 198, 213
  "Creative Reading" course, 128, 129
  The Creation of a Home, 204
  "Letters from a Contented Wife," 73–74
Blair, Harry, 76, 148, 204, 212–13
Blanch, Sophie, 6
Bledstein, Burton, 206
Bloomsbury Group, 162, 168–69
boarding schools, Native Americans at, 132
Bobbsey Twins, 190
book clubs, 164–65, 201–2
The Bookman, 82, 94–95, 100, 105–6, 112, 119, 140, 208–9, 212
Book-of-the-Month Club (BOMC), 5, 14, 16, 164–65
book publication, 5
book reviewers. *See* critics
book reviews, 5, 18, 88, 94–95, 97, 99–100, 103–4, 113–14, 118–19, 134–35, 140–41. *See also specific reviewers and authors*
  newspaper, 5
  training of readers through, 128
books. *See also specific authors*
  gift of, 154, 156
  of identification, 139–40
  overlooked, 209–10
Booth, Alice, 117
Botshon, Lisa, 6–7
Bourdieu, Pierre, 157, 161, 218n31
Boyd, Thomas
  The Dark Cloud, 105–6
  Samuel Drummond, 104–5, 106, 112–13
  Through the Wheat, 105
Bradley, Jennifer, 120–21
Brame, Charlotte Mary, *Dora Thorne*, 194–95
Brennan, Frederick Hazlitt, *God Got One Vote*, 200–201
Brickell, Herschel, 212
Bromfield, Louis, 16, 112
  Possession, 91–93
Burt, Katherine Newlin, 220n53
Butterick Company, 88
Byron, Lord [George Gordon], 93–95

Canby, Henry Seidel, 16, 164–68
Canfield, Dorothy, *see* Fisher, Dorothy Canfield
Carbol, Betty, 234n17
Carlyle, Thomas, 97, 170
Carnegie Corporation, 178
Carnegie libraries, 69
Cather, Willa, 16, 21–22, 32, 109, 112, 164
  Death Comes for the Archbishop, 129
  Home Monthly and, 120–1
  literary modernism and, 16, 110–2, 118, 142
  middlebrow literature and, 118
  in *Collier's* magazine, 120, 124–5
  The Professor's House, 104, 110–33, 143–4, 175, 212
  popular reception of, 104, 110
  critical reception of, 16, 21, 112–15, 118–19
  science and, 121–22
  tourism in the American West and, 120, 130, 133
  periodical culture and, 110, 118, 120–22
Certeau, Michel de, 161
Chandler, Raymond, 8
Chicago Daily News, 99
Chicago Daily Tribune, 90
child development, 42
child marriage, 101–3
children's clothing, 39
children's literature, 22, 42, 175–77, 235n20
  Children's Book Month, 196–97
  Children's Book Week, 175
  literary merit and, 179–82, 188–93
  popularity and, 189–93
  taste and, 192, 193, 194
Christian Science Monitor, 30
Clark, Beverly Lyon, 185, 188, 235n20
class, 43, 169–70, 207
Cleeland, Anne, 87
Cleeves, Rachel Hope, 95
Collier, P. F., 66
Collier's magazine, 118, 122–23
Collins, Frederick L., 1
Connolly, Vera, 132–33
Conover, Katy, 221n4
Conrad, Joseph, 95, 112
consumer advocacy and activism, 31, 37, 111, 160

242 INDEX

Coolidge, Calvin, 37, 44, 74
Cooper, Melissa L., 237–38n48
Cornwell, Dean, 1, 216n6
Corrigan, Maureen, 174
Cosgrave, Jessica, 1
Cosmopolitan magazine, 73, 173 *see also*
Hearst's International/Cosmopolitan
Crank, James A., 217n23
criticism. *See also* book reviews
as labor, 171
meditations on, 167–72
professionalization of, 9
critics, 19–20, 70, 71–72, 86–87, 90, 94, 110–11, 140–41, 167–68. *See also specific critics*
Blair's frustration with, 18–19, 143–44
consumer economy and, 145
literary modernism and, 143–44
Woolf's attitude toward, 167–68
Crowell, Grace Noll, 220n53
Crowell publishing company, 27
Cuddy-Keane, Melba, 168
Cunningham, Minnie Fisher, 78–79, 134, 137, 200, 201, 208
Cutter, Annie Spencer, 191

Dallas Morning News, 115, 228n73
Dane, Clemence, 216–17n11
Dawson, Melanie, 102
Delineator, 4, 25, 88, 151, 222n27
Delmar, Viña, 17–18
Democratic National Committee (DNC), 74
Democratic Party, 74, 148
Democratic Women's Club, 74, 151
Dimock, Wai Chee, 206
Dix, Dorothy, 220n53
domesticity, 15, 26, 31, 37, 41, 52–53
Dos Passos, John, 16, 105, 143
Douglas, Norman, *South Wind*, 95–97, 108–9
Dr. Eliot's Five Foot Shelf of Books, 62–68, 126–8
Dreiser, Theodore, 109, 110–11
An American Tragedy, 110, 111, 137–42, 143
reviews of, 140–41
Drew, Elizabeth, "The Modern Novel," 142
Dubino, Jeanne, 167–68

Durant, Will, *The Story of Philosophy*, 15, 220n48

Easton, Florence, 54–55
editorial content, 24, 28, 205–8
demographic studies and, 29–31
stylistic overlap with advertisements, 32
educators, 178, 187, 189, 190
Elementary English Review, 190, 191
Eliot, T. S., 7, 8, 16, 21, 91, 156, 160, 174
Erskine, John, *Adam and Eve*, 18
Esquire magazine, 11
experimental literature, 143, 163, 201. *See also* literary modernism

Farrar, John, 204
Farrar, Margaret, 204
fashion content, 37–40
fashion advice, 25, 40
fashion department, 40
Faulkner, William, 16, 143
Federal Trade Commission, 33–34
Ferber, Edna, 106, 117
Show Boat, 117
So Big, 106
fiction content, 24, 25, 49, 55–66, 211, 220n54. *See also specific authors*
happy endings and, 56–7
in magazines, 120
serialized novels, 56–57, 71, 110, 120, 122–23
short fiction, 71
success attributed to, 55
in women's magazines, 120
Fish, Stanley, 225n3
Fisher, Dorothy Canfield, 14, 15, 118, 220n53
The Brimming Cup, 13
Fisher, Katharine A., 4, 25
Fitzgerald, F. Scott, 17, 32, 105, 143, 173–75, 233–34n2
All the Sad Young Men, 173, 234n3
The Great Gatsby, 173–75, 177, 196
Tender as the Night, 173
This Side of Paradise, 233–34n2
Ford, Ford Madox, 15–16
Forum magazine, 87, 96, 113
Freddie and Flossie books, 190

INDEX

Frederick, Christine, 34
friendship, reading and, 172
furnishings content, 37–40

Galsworthy, John, 56, 164
Gelzer, Jay, "Emmy and the Door," 60–61
Gibbs, A. Hamilton, 15
Gigante, Denise, 70
Gilmore, Michael, 206
Glasgow, Ellen, 56, 106, 220n53
Godey's Lady's Book, 222n15
Goldsmith, Meredith, 6–7
Good Housekeeping Bureau of Food,
    Sanitation, and Health, 43–45
Good Housekeeping Institute, 25–26, 125
Bulletins of, 176
Good Housekeeping magazine, xi, xiii–xv,
    1–23. *See also specific contributors*
    advertising content, 11, 14, 24, 26, 29–36,
        40–41, 66, 152, 233–34n2 (*see also*
        advertised products)
    archives of, 221n4
    circulation of, 26–27, 30, 32
    competitors of (*see* "Big Six" women's
        magazines), 25, 28–29, 37, 56
    consumer advocacy and activism in,
        25–26, 31, 37, 45, 111
    cover illustrations, 31–32
    Dr. Wiley's Question Box, 42, 43–46, 66
    editorial content, 24, 28, 29–31, 32, 205–8
    editorial structure, 11, 198
    ethos of, 24, 71
    Experiment Station, 25
    fashion content, 25, 37–40
    Federal Trade Commission and, 33–34
    fiction content, 11, 24, 25, 49, 55–66, 71,
        110, 120, 122–23, 211, 220n54 (*see also*
        specific authors)
    history of, 11
    homemaking content, 11, 26, 37–40, 130
    inattention to women of color, 30
    Institute Forum, 42–43
    "money back guaranty" of, 21, 24, 32,
        33–34, 33, 71
    newsstand price, 32
    parenting content, 30, 42
    physical features of, 24, 31–32

readership of, 11, 25, 28–30, 125, 126
    series about Native Americans in, 132
    shopping services, 40
    subscribers to, 222–23n29, 222n15, 222n27
    subscription rates, 26–27
Good Housekeeping Pattern Service, 39
Good Housekeeping Research Institute,
    xiv, 1
Good Housekeeping Seal of Approval, 1, 26,
    33, 215n4
Good Housekeeping Studio, 38
Good Housekeeping UK, xiv
Great Depression, 31, 32, 198, 206–7
Grey, Zane, 9, 190
Guillory, John, 9

Hager, Jenna Bush, 72
Harcourt, Alfred, 134
Hardy, Thomas, 91
Harker, Jaime, 7, 14, 117, 207, 210
Harriman, Ethel, *Romantic, I Call It*, 15
Harrison-Kahan, Lori, 237n39
Harvard Classics, the, *see Dr. Eliot's Five-Foot
    Shelf of Books*
Hearst's International/Cosmopolitan, 17–18,
    173. *See also* Cosmopolitan
Hearst US, 17–18, 32, 173, 221n4
Heffernan, Virginia, 157–160
Hemingway, Ernest, 15–6, 105, 143
Henry Holt and Company, 212
Herskovits, Melville, 237–38n48
Heyward, DuBose, 15
    Porgy, 117, 210–11, 212
Hicks, Granville, 16
highbrow culture, 6, 22, 109, 161, 168–9
highbrow literature, 111–4, 120, 129, 168–9
    debates on, 113–14
higher education, women and, 107, 228n86
high modernism, 142, 166, 201
Holtby, Winifred, 216–17n11
    Mandoa-Mandoa, 209
homemaking content
    home decoration, 38, 40, 159
    household hints columns, 42–43
    household management, 150
    scientific housekeeping, 34–35
Home Monthly, 120–21

INDEX

Homer
   The Iliad, 173, 175
   Odyssey, 163
Humble, Nicola, 6, 20, 108
humor, racist, 63–66
Hurst, Fannie, 237n39
   Imitation of Life, 207, 208–9
   A President Is Born, 200–201
Hurston, Zora Neale, 23, 237n39
   Jonah's Gourd Vine, 210–2
Hutchinson, A. S. M., 115
Hutner, Gordon, 7, 16, 208
   What America Read, 113
Huxley, Aldous, 95
Huyssen, Andreas, 7–8

illustrations, 211, 215–16n2, 216n6. *See also specific illustrators*
The Independent, 140, 211
Indian boarding schools, 132
Indian Bureau, 132

Jaffe, Aaron, 7, 9
Jaillant, Lise, 7
James, Henry, 91
Johanningsmeier, Charles, 122–23
Johnson, Ben, 169, 170
Joyce, James, 9, 16, 145, 156, 160
   Pomes Penyeach, 156–58
   Ulysses, 116, 157, 158–59, 163
J. Walter Thompson Company, 11, 26, 27, 28, 30, 32, 222–23n29, 222n21

Kansas City Star, 114–15, 119, 227n49
Kenyon, Josephine Hemenway, 42
Keyes, Frances Parkinson, 1, 21, 22, 67–68, 75, 79, 81, 112, 117, 148, 153, 172, 232n8
   autobiographical writing by, 51–54
   Blair and, 144–46, 151, 152–56, 208
   "hamper of books" for, 145–46, 152–56
   "Letters of a Senator's Wife," 146
   The Old Gray Homestead, 146
   "Pages from My Scrapbook," 51–52
   political activity and, 154
   Republican Party and, 148
   "Satisfied Reflections of a Semi-Bostonian," 146
   "Seven Successful Women," 151

Kiernan, A. H., 185

Ladies' Home Journal, 6, 11, 25, 28, 92, 146–47
   advertising and editorial models developed by, 31
   advertising content in, 34–35
Lane, Rose Wilder, 116–17, 229n20
Larbaud, M. Valéry, 157
Latinx subjects, representation of, 63–5
Lawrence, D. H., 95
Lea, Fanny Heaslip, 1
League of Women Voters, 154
Leavitt, Sarah, 37
Leech, Margaret, 16
   Tin Wedding, 174
Lehmann, Rosamond, 19–20
   Dusty Answer, 19, 95, 208
Lennon, Charlotte, 69, 70, 72
Lewis, Edith, 32
Lewis, Sinclair, 16, 105, 109, 110–11, 134–137, 142
   Ann Vickers, 207, 208
   Arrowsmith, 126
   Babbitt, 107, 134, 136
   Elmer Gantry, 134–37
   Main Street, 134
   publisher of, 134–35
Lewis, Wyndham, 16
Lewisohn, Ludwig, 16
librarians, 177–78, 180–82, 187, 189, 190, 191. *See also* American Library Association
Library Journal, 177, 192, 193
Life, xii, 11, 112, 119
Lingeman, Richard, 134–35
literary criticism, 4–5. *See also* book reviews; critics
   position of women in, 156
literary critics. *See* critics
Literary Guild, 165
literary history, 166, 168
literary modernism, 5, 6–11, 110, 113, 120, 174, 201, 217n23, 217n24
   Anderson and, 117
   Blair and, 143–72
   Cather and, 118
   complexity of, 143
   concept of, 7–9

INDEX

critics and, 143–44
high modernism, 142, 166, 201
inaccessibility of, 143
middlebrow culture and, 10–23
"middlebrow modernism," 5, 6–9
misogyny and, 143
"modernist periodicals," 10
"modernist racket," 143–72, 201
position of women in, 156
"little magazines," 5, 10
Locke, William J., *Perella*, 61–62
Stone, Elinore Cowan, "Lonch for Two,"
    63–65, 84, 212
Loos, Anita, 15, 17
Gentleman Prefer Blondes, 174
Lost Generation, 16
lowbrow culture, 168, 169
Lucas-Dubreton, J., 106–8
Samuel Pepys, 106, 107
Lynd, Helen Merrill, 27, 206–7
Lynd, Robert S., 27, 206–7
Lyne, Russell, 6
Lytton, Bulwer, *My Novel*, 194

Mabie, Hamilton Wright, 5, 92, 216–17n11
Macaulay, Rose, 165
Machor, James L., 185
magazines, xi–xii. *See also specific magazines*
    "big magazines," 5, 10, 11, 18
"Big Six" women's magazines, 1, 5, 11, 25,
    26, 32, 56, 222n27 (*see also specific*
    magazines)
    cultural influence of, 121
    fiction content in, 120
    "little magazines," 5, 10
    magazine culture, 4–5
    national magazines, 18
    "small magazines," 5, 10, 18
    "smart magazines," 18, 32, 219n35
    women's magazines, 1–6, 11, 25, 26, 27, 32,
        56, 222n27 (*see also specific magazines*)
Mangum, Bryant, 234n3
Marchand, Roland, 35
market research, 25–6, 29–30
Marlowe, Christopher, 169, 170
Marsh, Dorothy B., 41
mass culture, 9
Mathiews, Franklyn, 175

Matt, Susan J., 195
McCall's, 25, 216–17n11, 222n27
McClure's magazine, 11, 120
McCracken, Scott, 8
McDowell, Kate, 183, 184, 187, 191
McGurl, Mark, 7
Melcher, Frederic, 175
Mencken, H. L., 17, 114, 174, 201
    "The Sahara of the Bozart," 111
menu planning, 40, 41–42
Meredith, Edwin T., 91, 147, 150
Miami Herald, 99
middlebrow culture, 6–9, 10–23, 108–9,
    168, 169, 206–7, 215n4, 219n35. *See also*
    middlebrow literature
    disdain of, 144, 145
middlebrow literature, 20, 118, 160, 212
    "middlebrow modernism," 5, 6–9
    progressive middlebrow ethos, 213
    studies of, 6–7
middlebrow readers, 131, 212
middlebrow reading mode, 18, 109, 210
middle-classness, 207
Millay, Edna St. Vincent, 137, 220n53
Miller, Caroline, *Lamb in His Bosom*, 209
misogyny, literary modernism and, 143, 145
The Missouri Woman magazine, 74, 146
Modern Library, 97
modernism. *See* literary modernism
modernist periodicals, 10
"modernist racket," 143–72, 201
modernist studies, 217n23
Moore, Anne Carroll, 175
Morrisson, Mark, 10
Morrow, Honoré Willsie, 227n49
    We Must March, 87–90

The Nation magazine, 168
national magazines, 18. *See also specific*
    magazines
Native Americans, 65–6, 130–2, 216n5. *See*
    also Indian affairs
    at boarding schools, 132
    representations of, 1, 65–6, 89–90, 216n5
    health care crises and, 132–33
needlework designs, 39–40
networking, 145–52, 154
New Criticism, 160

New Deal, 206, 236n25
new modernist studies, 217n23
New Orleans *Times-Picayune*, 115
newspapers, 5, 18. *See also specific newspapers*
New Statesman magazine, 6, 168
Newton, Edward, *The Greatest Book in the World*, 103–4, 107
New Yorker magazine, 6, 78, 82, 86, 112, 119
    "Tell Me a Book to Read" feature, 112
New York Times, 86, 88, 103–4, 105, 209, 211
New York Times Book Review, 82, 88, 113, 114, 119
Nicholson, Harold, 168
"normalcy," elevation of, 42
Norris, Kathleen, 56, 117
Norton, Mary Teresa, 79
nutrition advice, 41–42, 43–46

"objective method," 129
Odom, Howard W., 165
"old lady in Dubuque" paradigm, 111
Orlando, Florida, 169
Ostenso, Martha, 3
Ozarks, 138

parasocial relationships, 154
Parcell, Rachel, 81
Parchesky, Jennifer, 207
parenting content, 42
Parrish, Anne, 112
    The Perennial Bachelor, 83–87, 112–13
periodical studies, digitization and, 218n30
Perry, Bliss, 129
personal advice, 45–51
Peterkin, Julia, 17, 220n53, 220n54
    Black April, 211, 212, 237–38n48
    "The Diamond Ring," 17, 211, 212
Phillips, Dorothy Sanburn, "Her Job," 59–60
Photoplay magazine, 32
Pictorial Review magazine, 25, 222n27
Pope, Alexander, 170
Porter, Eleanor, 190
Porter, Gene Stratton, 56, 190
Pound, Ezra, 160
prescriptional advice, 45–46
Priestley, J. B., 6, 168
primitivism, 117
Progressive Era, 65, 177–78, 187, 191

progressive middlebrow ethos, 213
Proust, Marcel, 160
publishers, 170–71. *See also specific publishers*
publishing industry, regional representation in, 113–14
Pulitzer Prize, 209

The Quill, 30

Rabinowitz, Paula, 17
Radway, Janice, 6, 14, 94, 164, 227n55
Rainey, Lawrence, 7, 217n24
Raymer, Stella, "The Smell of the Stardust," 62–63
reader letters, 42–43, 49–50
    reader-discovered tips, 42–43
    reader-letter-driven features, 42–43
    reader queries, 43
readers, 4, 5, 9, 18, 19–21. *See also* reader letters; readership
    Blair's similarity with, 72–73, 77–78, 82
    class aspirations of, 43
    college-educated, xiv, 35, 211, 215n4, 220n48
    complaints of, 21
    empowerment of, 172
    expectations of, 11, 24–68
    ideal, 21
    identifying, 25
    judgment of, 40
    lay, 9
    make-believe, 139–40
    marginalization of "lay," 9
    parasocial relationships and, 154
    social expectations of, 43
    tastes of, 71–72
    trained through reviews, 128
Reader's Club, 98
Reader's Digest, xii
readership
    class and, 30–31
    market research and, 30
    models of, 200
    profiling of, 29–31
    race and, 30–31
    studies of, 27–31
    suburban, 30–31

INDEX

reading. *See also* reading modes
  as "anodyne," 155, 205, 206
  attitudes toward, 19
  contagion of, 173–97
  for escape, 155
  friendship and, 172
  "to learn," 130
  reading advice, 5, 40
  "reading formation," 225n3
  social success and, 67
  vicarious, 139–40
reading courses, 126, 128
reading modes, 130, 139–40, 141
  middlebrow, 18, 210
  modeling of, 83
  multiple, 71
recipe booklets, 41–42
regional representation, in publishing
  industry, 113–14
regional snobbery, Blair's dismissal of, 111
representative biographies, 51–55
Republican Party, 148
responsibility, ethos of, 24
rhetorical strategies, of "problems" and
  "responsibilities," 40–41
Richards, I. A., 113
Richmond (Indiana) Palladium and Sun, 106
Roosevelt, Franklin Delano, 37, 72, 74, 204,
  212–13, 236n25
Ross, Harold, 78, 111
Rubin, Joan Shelley, 6, 14, 66, 220n48
Ryan, Barbara, 49

Sabatini, Rafael, 15
Saporita, Nicole, 221n4
Saturday Evening Post, 6, 11, 32, 168, 173, 212
Saturday Review of Literature, 166, 211
  Reader's Guide column, 129
Scanlon, Jennifer, 34
scare copy, 32
Scherman, Harry, 164
Scholes, Robert, 10, 218n31
Schuyler, David, 201
scientific housekeeping, 34–35
Seguin, Robert, 110, 207
Seldes, Gilbert, 174
sentimentality, criticism of, 191

serialized novels, 56–57, 110, 120, 122–23
service departments, 25
Seyster-Montross, Lois, "A Peacock in the
  Dooryard," 58–59
Shakespeare, William, 168, 169, 170
Sharp, Margery, *The Flowering Thorn*, 209
Sheldon, Charles, "The Religious Hunger of
  Youth," 47–49
Sheppard-Towner Bill, 147
Sherman, Stuart Pratt, 136
shopping services, 40
Simmons, K. Merinda, 217n23
Sinclair, May, 15
Sinclair, Upton, 142
Sirk, Douglas, 237n39
"small magazines," 5, 10, 18
"smart magazines," 18, 32, 219n35
Smith, Erin, 47–49
Smith, Jessie Willcox, 1, 24, 31, 32, 215–16n2
social reforms, 206
social success, reading and, 67
Sopcak-Joseph, Amy, 222n15
spiritual advice, 47–51
Stallings, Laurence, 216–17n11
Stanford Silent Reading Test, 178
Starch, Daniel, 26
Stein, Gertrude, 16, 105, 143, 174
Stephen, Leslie, 162
stock market crash, 208
Stone, Elinore Cowan, "Lonch for Two,"
  63–65, 84, 212
Stout, Janis, 118
St. Paul Daily News, 105
Stratton-Porter, Gene, 117
Stuart, Henry Longan, 86–87
"subjective method," 128
subscribers, 222–23n29, 222n15, 222n21,
  222n27
  demographics of, 56, 222–23n29, 222n27
  loyalty of, 32
  marital status of, 56
subscription rates, 26–27, 222n15, 222n21
subscription strategies, 222n15
suburbia, 30–31
Suckow, Ruth, 220n54
Sullivan Melissa, 6
summaries, 21

248 INDEX

Swinnerton, Frank, 15
Swinnerton, James, 1, 216n5, 225n75
   Kiddies of the Canyon County, 65–66

Tarkington, Booth, 16, 164, 185
   The Plutocrat, 137
taste(s), 14, 40, 71, 143
   breadth and hybridity" of, 108
   children's literature and, 192, 193, 194
   concept of, 5
   individual vs. prescribed, 42
   performative aspect of, 82
   reader-driven, 20
tasting, concept of, 5
Tasting and Testing Books department, 144
   launch of, 151–52
Taylorist efficiency principles, 34
Tennyson, Alfred Lord, 170
Terrell, Mary Church, 210
testing programs, 25–26, 33
Texan Star, 183–4
Thacker, Andrew, 10, 218n32
Thackeray, William Makepeace, 91
Time magazine, xii, 11, 78, 211
Tolliver, Ellen, 92
Tom Swift, 190
Toombs, Eliz., 148–49, 232n8
transparency, critical, 21
"trashy" books, 176–77, 179–84, 189–93
travelogues, 51–52, 130, 131, 132
True Story, 32
Turner, Catherine, 9, 110
Tuttle, Grace Norman, 99
Twain, Mark, 188
   Huckleberry Finn, 185, 188–89, 190, 235n20,
      235n25
   Tom Sawyer, 182, 184–87, 188–89, 235n20
   Tom Sawyer Abroad, 190

Ullmann, William, 79
US Supreme Court, 45, 213

Vanderbilt, Cornelius Jr., 32, 233–34n2
Vanderbilt Theatre, 98
Van Doren, Dorothy, 96, 98
Vanity Fair magazine, 8

Van Vechten, Carl, 16
   Nigger Heaven, 117
Victorian literature, 170
Vogel, Mabel, 176–77, 180–81, 182, 189, 192,
   234n17
Vogue magazine, 8, 27, 145

Walker, Charles R., 140
Walpole, Hugh, 15, 156, 162
Washburne, Carleton, 176–77, 180–81, 182,
   189, 192
Washingtonian magazine, 79
Weber, Lenora Mattingly, 220n53
Wells, Carolyn, 190
Wells, H. G., 15
West, Rebecca, 21, 22, 144–45, 156–67, 172,
   233n47
   concept of "necessity," 161
   criticism by, 161
   review of *Orlando*, 166–67
   The Strange Necessity, 144, 156, 160, 166–67
Weston, George, *The Wondering Moon*,
   56–57
Wharton, Edith, 91–92, 142, 164
   The Age of Innocence, 91
   The Children, 228n74
   The House of Mirth, 91
*What Children Like to Read: Winnetka
   Graded Book List* (WGBL)., 176–77,
   177–82, 179
   how books were chosen for, 182–89
   trashy books and competing priorities,
   189–93
Wharton, Edith, 16, 91–2
   The House of Mirth, 92
White, William Allen, 136–37
Wilder, Laura Ingalls, 116
Wiley, Harvey Washington, 4, 43–46, 66
   "No Pure Food Action—Now," 44–45
   testimonials about, 45–46
Williams, Raymond, 7–8
Williams William Carlos, 158
Williams, Susan Millar, 211
Winfrey, Oprah, 72
Winnetka Graded Book List, 175–77, 193
Winnetka Public Schools, 181, 234n17

INDEX

Winnetka Study Method, 177–82
Wise, Julia, 175–77, 193–97
Witherspoon, Reese, 72
Woman's National Democratic Club, 74
women of color, inattention to, 30
Women's Home Companion, 25, 27, 28
women's magazines, 1–6, 25. *See also specific magazines*
  accessibility of, 27
  "Big Six," 1, 5, 11, 25, 26, 32, 56, 222n27
  cultural influence of, 121
  subscription strategies for, 222n15
Women's National Democratic Club, 78, 79
women's study clubs, 72, 104
women's suffrage, 74
Woolf, Virginia, 1, 6, 21–22, 142, 144–45, 156–67, 169–70
  attitude toward literary critics, 167–68, 170

  as book reviewer, 162, 168
  popular reception of, 145, 162–3
  "Middlebrow," 1, 6, 168, 215n1
  Mrs. Dalloway, 163
  Orlando, 144, 156, 163–64, 165–67, 168, 169, 172, 201
  A Room of One's Own, 158
  The Second Common Reader, 6
Wiley, Harvey Washington, 4, 42–7, 67, 131, 223n46
  Dr. Wiley's Question Box, 42–7
  Department of Agriculture Bureau of Chemistry, 43
  "No Pure Food Action—Now," 44–5
Wylie, Elinor, 98, 112
  The Venetian Glass Nephew, 97–99, 112

youth services librarianship, 177–78